GunDigest
SHOOTER'S GUIDE to
HANDGUNS

GRANT CUNNINGHAM

Published by

Gun Digest® Books, an imprint of F+W Media, Inc.
Krause Publications • 700 East State Street • Iola, WI 54990-0001
715-445-2214 • 888-457-2873
www.krausebooks.com

To order books or other products call toll-free 1-800-258-0929
or visit us online at www.gundigeststore.com

ISBN-13: 978-1-4402-3272-5
ISBN-10: 1-4402-3272-5

Cover Design by Al West
Designed by Mary Lou Marshall
Edited by Corrina Peterson

Printed in USA

CONTENTS

GrantCunningham is a world-renowned revolver gunsmith and certified Combat FocusShooting instructor, with experience teaching general handgun self-defense and revolver-specific courses. His articles and photographs have been published in *Concealed Carry Magazine,* on the Personal Defense Network website, and on his own popular website, GrantCunningham.com.

Many people and organizations contributed time, energy, and pictures to this book.

Thanks much to Todd Koonce at Koonce Custom Guns, who supplied some of the guns and ammo pictured, and even posed for a couple of the photos. He came through with things that I couldn't find anywhere else!

Jacq Shellito and Brenden Shellito were kind enough to pose for pictures on the range and allowed me to set up a few scenes in their home.

Carl Fitts graciously played a couple of parts in the live action pictures, and his son Grant Fitts (what a great first name!) played the kid trying to get the gun out of the closet.

My friend Georges Rahbani also supplied a couple of hard-to-find guns, and posed with them in a number of pictures.

Leroy Merz of Merz Antiques shared his pictures of collectible guns, and came through when others could or would not. Many others went above and beyond the call to locate or produce multiple pictures: engraver Weldon Lister, gunsmith Marc Morganti at Gemini Customs, gripmaker John VanZyck at VZ Grips, antique gun dealer Bob Adams at adamsguns.com, Dick Ruppert at Custom Digital Designs, bullet inventor Tom Burczynski, gunsmith Lou Biondo at Business End Customs, collector Bryan Lester, and Jim Amato.

Finally, my wife served as the model for many of the shots contained here without complaint. She also put up with my manic moods as deadline approached, which is a feat in itself. Thanks, Dear!

CHAPTER 1

SAFETY FIRST!

Before any shooting activity, be sure everyone understands how to safely handle and operate the guns you'll be using.

Safety should always be the very first thought in mind when handling a pistol or revolver. There is always an element of danger when handling any firearm, but the risk can be reduced if a few commonsense safety rules are always followed. Whether loaded or unloaded, following these rules is the best way to keep you and everyone around you safe.

1) Always keep the muzzle of the gun pointed in a safe direction.

What is a safe direction? One in which, should the gun fire unintentionally, no one - you or anyone else - will be hurt. From the instant the gun is picked up until it is put down, be aware of where it's pointing. Also be aware that the environment will dictate what the safe direction is: in a downstairs apartment, for instance, pointing the gun up (at the other apartments) is not safe; on the top floor, pointing it down is not safe. It's up to you to understand what the safe directions are, and to keep the gun pointed only in those directions.

2) Always keep your finger outside the triggerguard until you're ready to fire.

The only time a finger should enter the triggerguard is when it's time to fire. At any other time, the finger should be held in a position that prevents an inadvertent discharge. For handguns, the best place to keep the finger outside of the triggerguard is to extend it on the frame above the trigger. Autoloader or revolver, that position keeps the finger from getting inside the guard and onto the trigger, even if you are tripped or startled.

3) *Always remember that you are in control of a tool that, if used negligently or maliciously, can injure or kill you or someone else.*

This is the "big picture" - your understanding that a gun can be dangerous to you and others if you aren't consciously thinking about what you're doing. This rule reminds you to think about how the gun is transported, where the bullets will land, if there are any ricochet risks, and all of the many other things that can happen. You're responsible for every bullet that leaves the barrel of your gun, so make sure that when your gun is handled or fired it's done consciously and safely.

Earplugs are cheap, readily available, store easily, and work well.

PERSONAL SAFETY EQUIPMENT

Dressing appropriately and wearing proper safety equipment is an essential part of shooting safely. The bullet isn't the only thing that can cause injury, and making sure that you have proper personal protection equipment is vital to a safe and enjoyable shooting experience.

Hearing protection is mandatory for any shooting activity. When buying ear protection, look at the Noise Reduction Rating (NRR). The NRR is the amount, in decibels, of attenuation that the product provides; the larger the number, the better.

Foam earplugs are commonly available, cheap, take up almost no space, and provide adequate protection against handgun noise. They're also the perfect thing to keep in the car or range bag, to give to guests who don't have their own hearing protection.

Hearing muffs provide better protection than earplugs and have a much longer lifespan. Many people also find them more comfortable than having things stuck in their ears. Most muffs have foam earcups, but for the most comfortable fit around the ear - and the best sealing against noise - look for muffs with gel earcups. Gel earcups can substantially increase the noise protection offered by any set of muffs.

No matter what you're shooting, proper hearing protection is a must!

Protecting your vision is vitally important, and specialized shooting glasses like these from Rudy Project do just that.
Photo courtesy of Rudy Project USA

Some earmuffs come with very soft, form-fitting gel ear cups, which are more comfortable and do a better job of sealing against noise.

Electronic muffs allow you to hear what's going on around you, while still allowing you to shoot in comfort and safety. They're almost a necessity for taking any sort of shooting class, as they allow you to hear the instructor's commands clearly. Many people find them handy for hunting too, because their sensitivity can be turned up to hear game moving in the area. Electronic muffs usually have less noise reduction capability than conventional muffs.

Remember that indoor ranges require more noise reduction than outdoor ranges; many people double up - use foam plugs along with muffs - for maximum protection when shooting indoors.

Safety glasses are another important piece of personal protection. Flying bullet fragments are commonly encountered, and even ejected bits of gunpowder can be injurious to the eyes. It's important to have eye protection that is impact rated, as fragments can ricochet with enough power to shatter plain eyeglasses.

For those who wear prescription glasses, impact-resistant lenses are available. Ask your optician for polycarbonate lenses; they are only slightly more costly than plain acrylic, and are substantially safer.

For people shooting autoloaders (or around others who are shooting autoloaders), a baseball-type cap with a bill should be worn. It's common to have a piece of hot brass drop down onto the frame of safety glasses or drop into the area where the temples attach to the frames. Hot brass is capable of inflicting second-degree burns. A person holding a loaded handgun is apt to drop it or swing it in unsafe directions when the hot brass starts burning; the bill on the cap deflects the brass safely away from the face.

For this same reason shooters should refrain from wearing open or v-necked shirts while at the range. Ladies in particular are cautioned to wear shirts that come up to the neck to prevent hot brass from falling into open cleavage. (While your author has not personally experienced this, he is told by female colleagues that brass burns to the relatively tender skin in that area are especially painful and slow to heal.)

Many people like to shoot with gloves. They prevent blisters, cuts and abrasions from sharp metal edges on the handgun, and some models even have recoil-absorbing pads built in. When picking gloves, make sure that they fit very snugly to prevent fabric from being trapped between gun parts. Also be aware that gloves may alter the fit of the gun to the hand, making the gun harder to handle - especially for those with small hands.

SAFE TRANSPORT

When transporting firearms, it is important to know the laws that apply where you're traveling. In most cases, and in the absence of a concealed carry license, the law requires that handguns be transported unloaded in a locked container. That's a

A baseball-style cap is essential to protect the face from potentially serious brass burns when using an autoloader. If this piece of hot brass were caught by the shooter's glasses, or dropped inside the shirt, severe burns could result.

It's not responsible, or safe, to leave a gun in a glovebox or car console!

A quick-access lockbox, securely mounted to the vehicle's floor, is the best way to leave a handgun in a car.

good start, but what about actually protecting those guns from theft?

Leaving a loaded, unsecured gun in a vehicle, even if it's out of sight, is irresponsible. Car prowls are one of the most common forms of crime in the country, and a handgun is a great prize for any thief. A handgun should never be kept, even for a very short period of time, in a glove compartment, center console, or under the seat.

The safest place for a gun is either a) on your person, or b) in a locked, secure container. There are a number of small safes that are designed expressly for mounting in a vehicle and feature brackets or mounting flanges to allow that. They usually mount to the floor and some can even be located under a seat. This allows you (or any of your passengers) to remove your gun and store it when necessary. They're especially handy for trips which include entry into areas where guns are off limits.

Be aware that having a lockbox mounted within reach of the driver may violate laws that require the gun and its container to be out of reach. Research the laws in your area carefully, and if in doubt contact your state or local gun rights organization.

If you're simply transporting guns to and from the range, most state's laws allow for them to be placed in hard-sided, locked containers and stored out of the immediate reach of the driver. Always unload all guns before putting them in any sort of storage boxes! There are incidents every year in which people are shot by loaded guns in storage containers, largely because their soft interiors - so prized for preventing damage and scratches - touch the trigger when they're closed. If the trigger is in contact with something, it doesn't take much to move it enough to fire. Unload the gun, make doubly sure that it's unloaded, and only then put it into the case or box.

DRYFIRING SAFELY

Many people like dryfire practice, which is operating the action of the gun with no ammunition. Many believe that dryfiring has benefits for trigger control and general gun handling without the expense or distraction of

A box of copier paper, restacked so that the reams face the target side, makes a safe dryfire backstop.

Is It Safe To Dry-Fire My Gun?

There are a lot of opinions on this subject, ranging from "no!" to "no problem!" The answer lies somewhere in the middle.

Generally, most modern centerfire handguns can be safely dryfired occasionally without incident. However, it does no harm (and may prevent damage) to use snap caps - dummy rounds which are inserted into the chamber to soften the impact of the firing pin.

Any military surplus handgun of foreign manufacture should ALWAYS be dryfired with snap caps, as should any Colt revolver regardless of vintage. If you plan on regular and extensive dryfire practice, snap caps are cheap insurance for any gun.

Rimfire handguns must always use snap caps when dry firing. Without them, their firing pins can hit the edge of the chamber, eventually peening it so that new rounds cannot be inserted. (There is actually a gunsmith tool, known as a chamber iron, to fix that problem.) Over the years there have been a very few rimfires which claimed to not require this precaution, but it's best to default to using them on any rimfire - just to be sure.

This guy isn't practicing safely. Remove all distractions during dryfire practice: telephone, television - and do not drink before handling any firearm!

live ammunition. Dryfiring does carry with it the potential for serious accidents, and even seasoned gun handlers are not immune.

Consciously following these dryfire rules and procedures will greatly reduce the chance for a negligent discharge.

• Set up a specific area in which to dryfire; don't just sit on the couch and haphazardly snap the gun at the television. The area should have a bullet-safe backstop, such as a brick or cement wall or a bookshelf filled with books.

• Take a target and tape it to the backstop; on a bookcase, it would be the side so that a bullet would strike the books on their covers, not their bindings. A case of copier paper from the local office supply store, taped firmly shut, makes an ideal dry fire target that no handgun bullet is likely to penetrate.

• It's a good idea to remove the target immediately after the dryfire session, so that you don't reflexively point a loaded pistol at it and pull the trigger. (Think that's silly? There are lots of cases on record of people doing just that; deaths have occurred.)

• Double check that no ammunition or spare magazines are in the room. Don't allow any ammunition into the room at all.

• Turn off televisions, radios, and cell phones; don't allow any distractions that prevent your full concentration on what you're doing. This prohibition extends to children, spouses, and pets. Do not use alcohol before or during any dryfire practice session.

• Go outside the room and unload your gun (and magazine, if necessary). Leave all the ammunition and any spare magazines or speedloaders outside of the designated dry-fire area. Double-check that the gun is unloaded before going into the dryfire area.

• Go into the dryfire area and close the door. Double check the gun to make sure it's unloaded, then check it again!

• Keeping the gun pointed in a safe direction, engage in your dryfire routine. Remember: your dryfire target should be the safest direc-

tion. If it's not, re-think your practice strategy.

• When you're finished, return the gun to its storage area. If it is to be loaded, or you are carrying it, go outside the area to load. Repeat to yourself, "This gun is now loaded. If I pull the trigger, it will fire," several times as the gun is reloaded and stored or holstered. Make sure that your mind has transitioned from pulling the trigger to NOT pulling the trigger!

STORAGE

It's every gun owner's responsibility to make sure that his or her guns do not fall into the wrong hands. Whether it's the curious child who finds a gun his parents thought was completely hidden or the burglar who finds it and uses it to commit a more heinous crime, both can be deterred through proper storage.

Remember that there are only two safe places to store a gun: on your person, and in a locked, secured container. If the gun is carried for self protection, keeping it on you - in your custody and control - is the easiest way to prevent unauthorized access. Of course that's not possible all the time, nor is it the solution if you own more than one handgun. In those cases, some sort of secure storage, such

A quality safe, made of thick steel, is the most secure storage you can get. Photo by Pasquale Murena, courtesy of Cannon Safe

A fireproof safe, bolted to the floor, is the best way to store handguns - and other valuables.
Photo courtesy of Liberty Safe

as a safe, is the answer.

The ideal storage solution is a fireproof safe that's bolted to the floor. A safe that's not bolted down, no matter how heavy, is easy picking for thieves; you wouldn't believe how easy it is for two people to move a 600-pound safe into a waiting pickup. Bolt the safe down, preferably to a concrete floor. Make sure the safe is well constructed of thick welded plate, and that it has a combination lock. The common stamped steel storage lockers with keyed locks are almost child's play to penetrate, and should be considered no more than toddler deterrents.

Remember that such a safe has multiple advantages; it can be used to store jewelry, camera equipment, coin collections, and any-

thing else of value.

To keep items inside from rusting, install a dehumidifier rod or use desiccant packages to reduce the humidity. If buying a new fireproof safe, allow the dehumidifier or desiccant to work inside the empty, closed safe for a week before storing any corrosion-prone items; the materials used for the fireproofing material have an affinity for moisture and need time to dry out before use.

It should be self evident, but a safe that's left open is no protection. The safe should be closed and locked at all times, and the combination should not be written on anything in the room. (It's one thing to have it on a piece of paper in a wallet which is always carried, but another to be taped to a drawer in the same

Don't believe that a hidden gun, or one on a high shelf, will be safe from the kids. Children are very good at finding - and accessing - hidden treasure!

A fast-access safe with a keypad, such as this GunVault, is the best way to store a defensive handgun in a home with children. Bolted to the floor under a bed or in a closet, it allows fast emergency access to authorized users.
Photo by Pasquale Murena, courtesy of Cannon Safe

room as the safe itself. The former is secure, the latter is not.)

For defensive handguns which need to be kept handy, the best choice may be one of the small fast-access safes. These are sized to hold the gun and perhaps a couple of magazines or speedloaders. These low-profile safes easily fit under the bed or on the floor of a closet, and keep prying hands out while allowing the legitimate user to get to the gun in a hurry. They can also be bolted down, and it's highly recommended to do so - they're very easy to walk off with otherwise.

One caution: do not buy a safe with a biometric lock, such as those that recognize fingerprints. In personal testing they have proven to be extremely unreliable, particularly if the user's hands are wet, perspiring, or dirty. A better choice is a safe with a keypad that can be rapidly operated by the authorized person who knows the combination.

In the absence of some kind of safe, at least consider locking your handguns so that children can't use them. There are various kinds of devices that can be used to secure a gun, from those that cover the whole firearm to those that lock into the barrel to prevent a round from being chambered. They're not good solutions to a burglary, as they're easily removed with simple tools, but they will keep the children in the house from accidentally firing the gun.

One of the easiest methods to secure a revolver or semiauto is to simply open the cylinder or slide, and put a padlock through the frame. This prevents the gun from being loaded or even closed, dramatically limiting the opportunity for someone to "play" with the gun. It's cheap, fast, and very effective.\

The very worst strategy is to try to hide a gun. Children are remarkably adept at finding things that Mom and Dad don't want them to find, and burglars make their living by doing so.

No matter how well hidden you think it is, a gun that's not secured is an accident or crime waiting to happen. If they're not on you, lock 'em up!

A long-shackle padlock can be used to secure and disable both autoloaders and revolvers. (A length of heat-shrink tubing from the electrical aisle can be slipped over the shackle to prevent scratching the gun.)

Want to Know More?

LAWS AND REGULATIONS

www.handgunlaw.us - this website is the most up-to-date source of laws across the U.S.

www.nraila.org/gun-laws.aspx - this NRA site has a good overview of gun laws across the country, as well as resources for federal laws, interstate transport of guns, and guns on airlines

SHOOTING GLASSES

Oakley - widely available in many retail outlets, Oakley glasses have been favorites of shooters for years. www.oakley.com

Rudy Project - make a wide range of high quality glasses specifically for the shooting sports. Strong supporters of the shooting fraternity and sponsors several professional shooters. Will also custom make prescription shooting glasses. Rudy Project USA Inc., 1015 Calle Amanecer, San Clemente, CA 92673. (888) 860-7597 www.rudyprojectusa.com

Randolph - produces classic designs in impact resistant materials specifically for shooting and hunting. Randolph Engineering, 26 Thomas Patten Drive, Randolph, MA 02368. (800) 541-1405 www.randolphusa.com

Wiley - the Wiley X line of shooting glasses are favorites in the law enforcement and military fields, and with a good percentage of professional shooters as well. Wiley X Eyewear, 7800 Patterson Pass Road, Livermore, CA 94550. (800) 776-7842 www.wileyx.com

Hansen - makes custom prescription bifocals for sport shooters and hunters, featuring the bifocal portion at the top of the lens rather than the bottom. Hansen's Eagle Eye, P.O. Box 1175, Meadow Vista, CA, 95722-1175. : (866) 324-5374 www.hansenseagleeye.com

GUN SAFES AND LOCKS

Liberty - wide line of reasonably priced full-size gun safes and fire resistant safes, available at many dealers and sporting good chains. Liberty Safe and Security Products, Inc. 1199 West Utah Avenue, Payson, Utah 84651. (800) 247-5625 www.libertysafe.com

Browning - the Browning company, besides producing guns, also makes a line of safes that are available almost anywhere Browning guns are sold. Browning Inc., One Browning Place, Morgan, UT 84050. (800) 333-3288 www.browning.com

Cannon - range of gun safes, including in-wall and compact fire safes, available through dealers nationwide. Cannon Safe Inc. (800) 242-1055 www.cannonsafe.com

Fort Knox - makes gun safes and vault doors, including some of the largest gun safes available. Also makes a quick-access handgun safe and one designed to be mounted in a vehicle. Fort Knox Security Products, (800) 821-5216 www.ftknox.com

SportLock - manufactures a line of quick access handgun safes that meet California storage requirements. Sportlock LLC, www.sportlockllc.com

Gun Vault - widely recommended line of quick-access handgun safes that can be mounted in a home or vehicle. Also make a line of gun locks that go into the barrel or into the magazine well to render the gun inoperable. GunVault Inc. (800) 222-1055 www.gunvault.com

Sentry - line of affordable safes sold through major retailers nationwide. Also makes several quick-access safes appropriately sized for handguns. Sentry Group Inc., 900 Linden Ave, Rochester, NY 14625. (800) 828-1438 www.sentrysafe.com

V-Line - makes several quick-access handgun safes, including models that will mount under a shelf. Meets stringent

California storage requirements. V-Line Industries, 370 Easy Street, Simi Valley, CA 93065. (805) 520-4987 www.vlineind.com

AmSec - large line of standard gun safes, as well as quick-access handgun safes. American Security Products Co., 11925 Pacific Ave., Fontana CA 92337. (951) 685-9680 www.amsecusa.com

Franzen InterBore - locking device inserted into a gun's barrel to disable the firearm. Franzen Security Products, Inc., 40 Edison Avenue, Oakland, NJ 07436. (800) 405-2298 www.franzenint.com

TRANSPORT CASES

Americase - makers of heavy-duty aluminum gun cases; wide selection. Key locks built in. Americase, Inc., 1610 East Main St., Waxahachie, Texas 75165. (800) 972-2737 www.americase.com

MTM Case-Gard - plastic case manufacturer; pistol cases can be locked using a customer-supplied padlock. MTM Molded Products Co., 3370 Obco Court, Dayton, Ohio 45414. (937) 890-7461 www.mtmcase-gard.com

Pelican - known for extremely rugged glass-reinforced plastic cases, often called "indestructible". Several sizes for one to 36 handguns! CPD Industries, 4665 State Street, Montclair, CA 91763. (909) 613-1999 www.casesbypelican.com

SportLock - manufactures a line of secure, lockable handgun cases in a variety of sizes. Sportlock LLC, www.sportlockllc.com

B&W - German maker of lockable high-impact ABS cases, wide variety of sizes and colors. Available in the U.S. from a number of online sources. B&W International GmbH, www.b-w-international.com

SKB - well known, established case manufacturer. Produces lockable, tough glass-reinforced ABS handgun cases. SKB Corporation, Inc., 434 West Levers Place, Orange, CA 92867. (714) 637-1252 www.skbcases.com

HEARING PROTECTION

Peltor - well known, wide range of electronic and conventional hearing protection; make models especially for military and law enforcement use. Widely available at specialty retailers and online. 3M Occupational Health and Environmental Safety Products, 800-328-1667 www.peltorcomms.3m.com

Sordin - makes both earplugs and earmuffs; conventional and electronic hearing protection, often seen in military settings. Available at select dealers and online retailers. MSA-Sordin, (800) 672-2222 www.msasafety.com

Howard Leight - wide range of earplugs, as well as popular earmuffs in both standard and electronic styles. Sold nationwide and through many online outlets. Howard Leight/Honeywell Safety Products, 7828 Waterville Road, San Diego, CA 92154. (800) 430-5490 www.howardleight.com

Pro Ears - makes conventional and electronic hearing protection, including electronic earplugs. Popularly priced and widely available at retailers and online. Altus Brands, 484 W Welch Ct., Traverse City, MI 49686. 800-891-3660 www.proears.com

Want to Know More?

SHOOTING GLOVES

Gripswell - uses memory foam to protect the nerves that run through the center of the palm. GripSwell Gloves, P.O. Box 10215, Westminster, CA 92685. (714) 379-9413 www.gripswell.com

Blackhawk - well known producer of military and law enforcement gear offers a range of gloves. Blackhawk Products Group, 6160 Commander Parkway, Norfolk, VA 23502. (757) 436-3101 www.blackhawk.com

Filson - the iconic Northwest clothing manufacturer makes shooting gloves for both cold and warm weather. C.C. Filson Co., PO Box 34020, Seattle, WA 98124. (800) 624-0201 www.filson.com

Beretta - the Italian firearms manufacturer has a complete line of shooting gloves specially designed for the task. (800) BERETTA www.berettausa.com

Browning - in addition to their fine guns, Browning has a complete clothing line including shooting gloves for men and women. Browning Inc., One Browning Place, Morgan, UT 84050. (800) 333-3288 www. browning.com

Gehmann - the biggest selection of shooting gloves made from an old line German company. Renowned throughout the world and available in the U.S. from a number of online companies. www.gehmann.com

Pro-Aim - new gloves featuring modern design and materials, made expressly for shooters. L&R Engineering, (866) 977-6246 www.pro-aim.com

SNAP CAPS

A-Zoom - anodized aluminum snap caps known for long-term durability, available for over 120 different cartridges. Lyman Products Corp., 475 Smith Street, Middletown, CT 06457. (800) 225-9626 www.azoomsnapcaps.com

Triple K - makes plastic and aluminum snap caps available for most popular cartridges. Triple K Manufacturing Co., 2222 Commercial Street, San Diego, CA 92113. (619) 232-2066 www.triplek.com

SAFE DEHUMIDIFIERS

Remington - the famous gun manufacturer also sells dehumidifiers for gun storage. Remington Arms Company, LLC, P.O. Box 700, Madison, NC 27025 (800) 243-9700 www.remington.com

Eva-Dry - produces a line of silica-gel based dehumidifiers, in several sizes, for safes. Widely available at a variety of retailers and online. Eva-Dry Inc., 12157 W Linebaugh Ave., Westchase, FL 33626. (877) 382-3790 www.eva-dry.com

Goldenrod - electrical safe dehumidifiers that require no maintenance, sizes to fit most safes. Buenger Enterprises, Inc., P.O. Box 5286, Oxnard, California 93031. (800) 451-6797 www.goldenroddehumidifiers.com

CHAPTER 2

GREAT DESIGNERS, GREAT GUNS

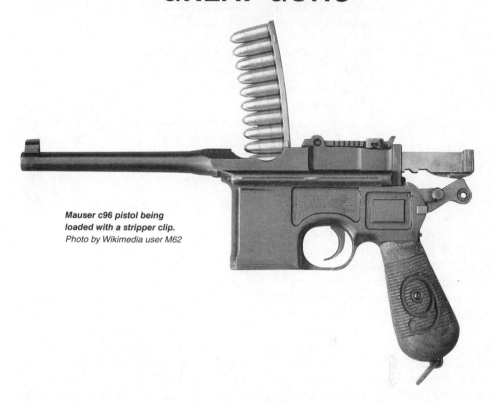

Mauser c96 pistol being loaded with a stripper clip.
Photo by Wikimedia user M62

There have been many talented handgun designers over the last couple of centuries, but some of them stand out for their enormous contributions to the field. Some blazed new ground in technical innovation, while others were astute businessmen who helped to make the handgun the popular possession that it is today. Any list of great designers is almost by definition incomplete, but here are those that this author feels any handgun-savvy enthusiast should know.

THE FEEDERLE BROTHERS AND THE MAUSER C96

If one had to pick the most recognizable handgun in the world, the Mauser c96 would be near the top of the list. The Feederle brothers - Fidel, Friedrich, and Josef - designed the iconic autoloading pistol for the Mauser Company in 1895, and it was put into production a year later. It was so popular that unlicensed copies were produced in China and Spain, and in a surprisingly wide range of calibers: 7.63x25 Mauser, 9mm Parabellum, 9mm Mauser Export (also known as the 9x25 Mauser), and even the American .45ACP!

The c96 was unusual in that the magazine was in front of the triggerguard, as opposed to being housed in the butt of the gun. This gave it a very distinctive silhouette, and the resulting small round grip gave rise to its nickname: the Broomhandle. (If you look closely, you'll notice that Han Solo's "blaster" in the original Star Wars movies is in fact a modified c96 prop gun!)

The 7.63x25 cartridge chambered in the original gun was no weakling, and had the distinction of being the hottest handgun round made until the introduction of the .357 Magnum in 1935.

FERDINAND RITTER VON MANNLICHER AND THE STEYR-MANNLICHER M1894

One of the world's most underrated yet trailblazing firearms designers, Ferdinand Ritter von Mannlicher is known for his rifle designs - but he was also a handgun designer, and produced the first commercial "blow forward" pistol design: the beautifully made Steyr-Mannlicher m1894.

In virtually all other autoloading pistols the mechanism is moved to the rear, being driven by the recoil of the firing cartridge. In the m1894, the same force that pushes the bullet down the barrel is used to shove the barrel forward, away from the standing breech. This ejects the spent casing, and as

M1894 pistol. Photo by Wesley Terrell

the barrel returns backward it strips a new round from the magazine.

It was an innovative solution to the problem of powering the mechanism but did not survive in the marketplace. Only a few other handguns have ever used a blow-forward mechanism, making it little more than a footnote in firearms history, but it nonetheless deserves to be recognized for the enormous talent which brought it forth.

HUGO BORCHARDT AND THE BORCHARDT C-93

Borchardt is credited with producing the first commercially successful autoloading pistol cartridge, the 7.65x25 Borchardt. That round would serve as the basis or in-

The distinctive Borchardt C-93.
Photo courtesy of Phoenix Investment Arms

spiration for a number of later cartridges, including the 9x19 - which today we call simply the "9mm".

The gun that chambered this new round was unique. Borchardt adapted the toggle lock used in the Maxim machine gun to his new pistol. The toggle lock, similar in operation to a human knee, kept the chamber closed until pressures reached a safe level. His adaptation, however, was incredibly ungainly. This finished pistol was huge and weighed in at over two and a half pounds - unloaded! It was very finely made and finished, but did not sell in great numbers. The concept and the cartridge were later refined by Georg Luger into the P-08 Luger pistol and 9mm Parabellum cartridge, a far more

John Browning's most famous design, the Model 1911 .45 caliber pistol. This example was made in 1917.
Photo courtesy of Leroy Merz, Merz Antiques

famous arm and a great combination in its own right. To be fair, though, Borchardt did it first!

(Borchardt also has the distinction of working for both Colt and Winchester, and at one point designed several new revolvers for Winchester. These were never introduced, and some people suspect that Winchester agreed to shelve those designs if Colt would cancel their plans for a new line of rifles. This has never been proven, but provides an interesting glimpse into the importance of new firearms designs at the time.)

JOHN MOSES BROWNING AND THE M1911

No list of great guns and their designers would be complete without John Browning. He developed a large number of firearms in his lifetime, many of which were wildly successful. In terms of handguns, his crowning achievement would have to be the Model of 1911 autoloading pistol.

The 1911 came about as the U.S. military was looking for a new sidearm. Over a period of years, Browning - working with the Colt Company - refined a new design. A tipping barrel inside of a reciprocating slide was his primary design innovation, and it made powerful handguns relatively easy to manufacture. Today the majority of autoloading pistols made use a variation of his original design.

The 1911 proved to be durable and reliable, and its .45ACP cartridge - another Browning invention - was exactly what the military wanted. It was adopted in 1911 (hence the name), and with only minor modifications served as the standard issue pistol for the United States until 1985.

Today the 1911 is produced in a dizzying array of models by a large number of manufacturers and continues to be a top seller. It ranks as a true classic in handguns and stands as a tribute to one of the greatest firearms designers.

DIEUDONNÉ SAIVE
AND THE P35 HI-POWER

Saive was a talented engineer who worked for the Belgian firm of Fabrique Nationale (FN). In 1921, France was looking for a new sidearm and approached FN. One of their requirements was a capacity of "at least" ten rounds, which was higher than most of the guns which were then in service. In response to the need for both high capacity and reasonable size, Saive developed a particularly compact double-stack magazine - so named because it held the rounds in two columns instead of the single column used in smaller magazines.

John Browning, a frequent contributor to FN, was asked to develop the firearm to accept the new magazine, but died just a few years into the development of the gun. This left Saive to take over and finish the project.

The resulting gun went into production, as the name suggests, in 1935 and is still being made.

At one point the P35 had the distinction of being the most widely issued military handgun in the world, having been used by more than fifty countries and still in use in many of them.

Debate exists about the extent of the contributions of both men, and many point to evidence which supports their contention that the bulk of the work was actually done by Saive, not Browning. While the debate may never be settled, the gun's defining feature, and the one which would give it its name, was Saive's double stack magazine.

Today the double stack magazine is common and can be found in autoloading pistols all over the world, accounting for a very large percentage of the pistol magazine designs on the market. Saive's work ushered in the era of the high capacity handgun and made compact firepower a reality.

The P35 Hi-Power is still being made today, and is a popular platform for customization.

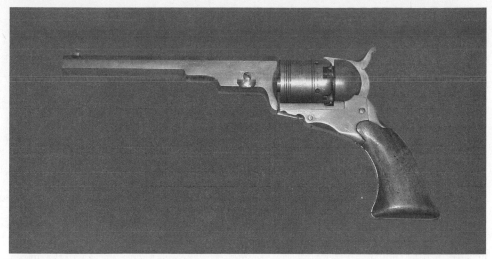

Colt's first practical revolver, the Paterson. Photo by Wikimedia user Hmaag

SAMUEL COLT AND THE REVOLVER

Samuel Colt was born in Hartford, CT, in 1814. He was interested in the fledgling field of repeating handguns but was unhappy with the designs then in service. His first foray into inventing was a positive indexing mechanism for the predominant repeater of the time - the so-called "pepperbox".

The pepperbox had a barrel for each round, making the guns rather unwieldy. Colt's idea was to have a single barrel and use his indexing method to rotate a separate cylinder containing the ammunition into alignment with the barrel. Colt got a patent on the basic functions of the revolving pistol in 1836.

His first revolver was a percussion arm called the Paterson Revolver, built by his Patent Arms Company of Paterson, NJ. It was not a success and the company soon folded, but Colt continued to refine his ideas and soon formed the Colt's Patent Fire-Arms Manufacturing Company in his hometown of Hartford, CT.

The Colt Company was quite prosperous and became well known for their "patented" revolvers. Colt's patent gave the company a virtual monopoly on the revolving handgun until it expired in 1857.

Ironically, Samuel Colt died before seeing the revolver that would become his company's most famous product. Colt died in 1862, only 47 years old, of complications from gout. Eleven years later, Colt engineers William Mason and Charles Richards designed the gun most associated with the name Colt: the Model 1873 Single Action Army. Their iconic design, often called the "Peacemaker" and credited with a large part in the settling of the West, is still being produced today.

ROLLIN WHITE: THE MAN WHO MADE SMITH & WESSON

Horace Smith and Daniel B. Wesson are undoubtedly great designers in their own right, having formed the Volcanic Repeating Arms Company in 1852 to produce their innovative repeaters. They left that company in 1856 to manufacture a new revolving pistol that took advantage of a seemingly simple patent from an ex-employee of Samuel Colt.

Rollin White had invented something called the "bored-through cylinder." It seems simple to us today because that is the normal sort of cylinder we're used to seeing. Back in his day, though, all revolver cylinders were

The Smith & Wesson Model 1, the first major success using White's patent.
Photo courtesy of Leroy Merz, Merz Antiques

closed in the back except for a small hole through which the percussion cap could ignite the powder charge. Those guns were all loaded through the front of the cylinder.

White's idea was to bore the cylinder straight through, allowing it to be loaded from the rear. This was necessary to be able to use the new rimfire cartridges that were starting to become popular. The rimfire cartridge, invented by Flobert in 1845, was by 1856 showing signs of becoming a hot product. Smith & Wesson, seeing the advantage White's patent could give them in the handgun market, licensed the patent and started the new "Smith & Wesson Revolver Company."

They quickly designed a new revolver using White's invention, which they called the Model 1, and a new rimfire cartridge of their own invention: the .22 Short. That cartridge would eventually spawn the most popular metallic cartridge of all time, the .22 Long Rifle.

The Model 1 and the .22 Short cartridge were incredibly popular, and soon White's patent was being used to produce a wide range of arms, in a number of larger calibers, for Smith & Wesson. White was mak-

ing money as his license gave him a royalty of twenty-five cents on every gun made, and in addition he was still free to use his patent to make his own guns - which he did in his new company, the Rollin White Arms Company.

He was not as successful as S&W, however, and sold most of the 4300 guns he produced to Smith & Wesson to help them keep up with the incredible demand his rear-loading cylinder had generated.

White could have simply sat in his living room and collected royalty checks, but an obscure provision of his license with Smith & Wesson proved his undoing. While he was paid a handsome royalty, it was his responsibility to defend the patent against infringement. So popular was this new technology that everyone, it seemed, was copying it.

White ended up spending the majority of his earnings defending his game-changing patent against all comers. He managed to get an appeal passed in Congress for an extension on his patent, but it was vetoed by President Grant. Despite making the modern revolver possible, White lived out his life in relative obscurity until his death in 1892.

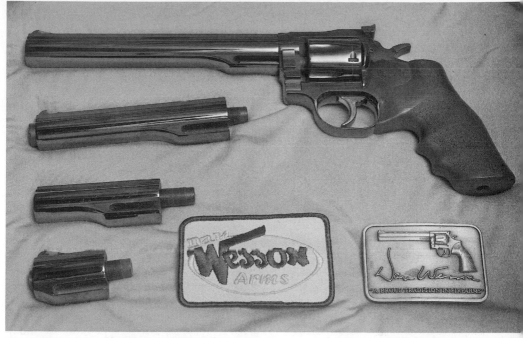

The Dan Wesson switch-barrel revolver designed by Karl Lewis.

KARL LEWIS, MASTER OF MODERN MANUFACTURING

High school dropout Karl Lewis was a police officer in the late 1940s when he caught the gun designing bug. He'd gotten some basic mechanical education at Great Lakes Naval Training Station, and had a job testing machine guns at Frigidaire, but was otherwise self taught.

It was in his spare time that he started developing a gun of his own: a switch-barrel revolver. His first prospect to produce the new product, Browning Arms, ultimately decided not to proceed with the project. They did, however, give him a design job at Browning where he invented a new rifle, the Browning BLR, among other things.

He still wanted to do handguns, however, so he went to work as an "Advanced Development Engineer" at Colt's Firearms Division. He didn't get to produce his groundbreaking design, but he did put a lot of his concepts to work by designing a gun that would spawn a whole new line at Colt: the Mark III revolver. It made heavy use of new production technologies such as metal sintering, which allowed the manufacturer to produce parts to close tolerances and with assembly-ready finishes. (While at Colt, he also found time to design what became the 40mm grenade launcher. That's quite a leap in caliber!)

Still, the idea of the switch-barrel revolver never left his mind. He'd made many prototypes over the years and finally found an amenable partner in Daniel B. Wesson, the great-grandson of the co-founder of the "family business," Smith & Wesson. Lewis contributed his interchangeable barrel system and his considerable design expertise, while Wesson put in the money and the metallurgical savvy.

The Dan Wesson revolvers, with their tensioned switch-barrel design, proved to be incredibly accurate and very durable.

They quickly made a name for themselves among the accuracy-obsessed people who shot handgun silhouette competition. Sadly the company fell on hard times, and Lewis moved on to other things - like designing an oxygen pack for Apollo astronauts and serving as the chief project engineer at New Britain Tool.

If considered in terms of the sheer breadth of his inventions, Lewis would probably win the top prize amongst gun designers, yet today remains largely (and oddly) unknown.

ROY MELCHER MAKES RUGER A POWERHOUSE

William Ruger, who with his financial partner Alexander McCormick Sturm, formed Sturm, Ruger & Company in 1949 to produce Ruger's design for an autoloading .22 pistol. The gun he had in mind would come to be called the "Standard," one of the best-selling handguns of all time. It was an inspired design, a classic in American arms, and started the company's fortunes growing.

Ruger was a talented designer his own right, but it would be a man that a 2011 Ruger press release called "one of the most prolific

Roy Melcher's legacy: the Ruger Security-Six and GP100.

Ghisoni's first revolver design, the wonderfully odd MTR-8. Photo by Bryan Lester

and talented designers the firearms industry has ever known" who really put the company on the map. That man was Roy Melcher.

Melcher joined Sturm, Ruger when he was just 24 years old. He soon made a big mark on the company, and the shooting public, by designing most of their wide handgun line: the Security-Six and its variants, the GP100, the Redhawk, and the gun that served as the basis of their extensive autoloading pistol line - the P85. If you own a Ruger centerfire handgun, you have Roy Melcher to thank!.

His talent wasn't limited to making great handguns, however, and he designed many of Ruger's famous rifles as well. Melcher would later work for Interarms and Beretta, but returned to his first home at Ruger shortly before his death in 2010. Millions of his guns are today in the hands of Ruger enthusiasts who know the man whose name is on the barrel, if not the one who actually brought it to life.

EMILIO GHISONI: THE LEAST SUCCESSFUL GENIUS IN THE BUSINESS

Emilio Ghisoni was a manufacturer of commercial food processing machines and a firearms enthusiast. He had some radical ideas about how handguns should be built, and due to his manufacturing and engineering background he had the skills to make his ideas become reality. Sadly, he didn't have the marketing and sales abilities he needed to make them a success.

His first design was a fairly conventional .22 autoloading competition pistol, which he produced and sold under the name "Mateba" (an acronym for Macchine Termo-Ballistiche, the full name of his company) but he quickly turned his attention to centerfire revolvers. One of his design goals was to reduce the muzzle rise that occurred when a handgun was fired rapidly, and he surmised that the way to do that was to bring the bore axis as low as possible.

His first attempt was the MTR-8. This odd revolver placed the cylinder in front of the triggerguard, which brought the barrel down as well. It was an oddly balanced arm, but reports indicate that it achieved its goal in reducing muzzle rise. Very few were ever sold.

Ghisoni then attacked the problem in another way, by bringing the cylinder back to a more conventional location but firing from the bottom chamber. This would become a trademark of sorts for Ghisoni, and his next three guns - the 2006M, the Unica autorevolver, and the Chiappa Rhino - would all have this design feature. Only the Rhino is currently in production, though not at all common.

Ghisoni's designs were radical and came with their own set of idiosyncrasies. The shooting public has never warmed to his unique guns, and Ghisoni died in 2008 without seeing his futuristic ideas reach mainstream acceptance.

ROBERT ADAMS AND THE DOUBLE ACTION REVOLVER

The single action revolver was the standard arm in 1851, when British gunsmith Robert Adams conceived a new idea: instead of cocking a hammer and releasing it with a trigger, he'd make a gun where the trigger did both jobs - what we now refer to as a "double action."

His first gun was the .436 Deane & Adams, so named because he came up with his idea while working for a gun manufacturer named George Deane. It was not only the first double action revolver, but also the first revolver with a solid frame. It was also the first double action only handgun, in that the hammer could not be manually cocked to fire.

By all accounts the guns were beautifully made and worked well, but they were expensive to make and to buy. The much cheaper Colt single actions sold better, and it wasn't until Frederick Beaumont modified Adams' design to permit both double- and single-action fire did the gun become popular.

Adams would go on to great success when his double action revolver became standard issue with the British Army in 1857 - decades before the U.S. issued an equivalent weapon. Today the double action revolver with a solid frame and single action capability is the most common type seen, thanks to Robert Adams.

HELMUT WELDLE AND THE POLYMER PISTOL

Not very much is known about Helmut Weldle, a star designer at the German arms powerhouse Heckler & Koch (HK). His designs, however, are another matter.

At HK he developed a number of unique guns, including the P7 - an iconic gas-impingement, squeeze-cocking pistol that was eventually adopted by a number of police forces (including a few here in the U.S.) It was his VP70, however, which introduced a type of construction that would later turn the gun world on its ear: polymer.

A decade before Glock, Weldle designed the VP70 to utilize high-strength plastics for the frame of the gun. While there had been plastic-stocked .22 rifles before, no one had used polymer for the structural parts of a handgun. The VP70 did. It was literally a decade ahead of its time.

The gun was unique in more ways than just the polymer frame, however. It was also double action only, striker fired, and had an optional shoulder stock that contained a burst-fire mechanism. (The latter was not available in the U.S., as it made the pistol into a short-barreled machine gun. All of the U.S. VP70s had the mounting slots filled in to preclude the attachment of any stock.)

The VP70 was quite large for a 9mm handgun and utilized a blowback design that required a stiff recoil spring and a heavy slide. It also boasted an 18-round magazine which fit into a surprisingly small, very ergonomically-shaped grip. The VP70 was produced between 1970 and 1989, and examples are fairly common on the used market.

If you like your modern plastic pistols, remember that it was Helmut Weldle who paved the way for Glock - and everyone else.

TRENDS IN HANDGUN DESIGN

In the last couple of decades there have been a number of trends in handgun design that affect both manufacturing and consumer demand. These trends have shaped the guns that will be with us for many years to come.

Two of these trends have come to dominate the world of handgun design: first is the increasing use of very lightweight materials, and second is the continuing downsizing of autoloading pistols.

At one time all handguns were made out of steel. In the mid-20th century lightweight aluminum frames became commonly available, but did not displace steel largely due to their

The HK VP70, the first modern polymer-framed pistol, was the brainchild of Helmut Weldle.
Photo courtesy of Robert Adams, AdamsGuns.com

The Steyr S9 on top, with its polymer construction, and the lightweight alloy frame of the Smith & Wesson Airweight below typify the move to lightweight handguns.

The trend in handguns is putting powerful self-defense cartridges into ever-smaller packages, like this palm-sized 9mm Rohrbaugh. Photo courtesy of John VanZyck/VZ Grips

Many people feel that luminescent sights make it easier to shoot in low-light conditions. Photo courtesy of Kimber Mfg.

Laser sights can make it easier to align the gun on target in less-than-perfect conditions. Photo courtesy of LaserMax Inc.

decreased durability. Aluminum guns wore more rapidly than their steel counterparts and were subject to frame stretching issues.

In recent years the use of lightweight polymers with imbedded steel bearing surfaces made lightweight autoloaders not just possible, but the norm. The use of high-strength aluminum alloys - sometimes including rare metals such as scandium - in revolvers made possible ultra-lightweight wheelguns that had excellent durability. More recently, polymers in conjunction with lightweight metals have made their entrance into revolver designs.

While handguns were getting lighter, they also were getting smaller. The appearance of increasingly small personal protection pistols is often credited to two surprisingly antagonistic occurrences: the Assault Weapons Ban (AWB) of 1994 and the boom in shall-issue concealed carry laws during the same period.

The federal AWB, among its other draconian provisions, made the purchase of magazines holding more than ten rounds illegal (except for police and military use). Until the AWB came into effect we were basking in the era of the Wondernine: high capacity 9mm handguns like the Glock, Browning HiPower, and S&W 59 series were very popular. After the ban, when even the largest handguns were limited to a ten-round capacity, there seemed little sense to continue to make big guns if they were going to be limited to the same capacity as a smaller, easier to handle and carry version. Manufacturers started thinking not in terms of high capacity, but about the smallest envelope that could contain one of the new post-ban magazines.

This fit perfectly with the new shall-issue carry legislation that states were increasingly enacting. All over the country it was becoming legal, with an easily obtained license, to carry a concealed handgun on one's person. Suddenly there was a demand for smaller, concealable firearms - which just happened to match what the manufacturers had been forced into making.

The happy result was a trend that is still going strong. Every year gun makers come out with new compact handguns that beat the size/power envelope of the previous year's offerings. New materials like the aforementioned polymers and alloys allow chambering ever more powerful rounds in ever smaller packages. What would have been a .380ACP pistol a few years ago is now a much more powerful 9mm.

Other major-sized cartridges are being chambered in smaller and smaller guns, ready for an eager market with concealed carry enthusiasts.

OTHER NOTABLE ADVANCEMENTS

Another trend which is not as far-reaching, but still worth noting, is the move toward making it easier to shoot in low light conditions. With the realization that a large percentage of armed encounters happen after sunset, accessory makers have stepped in to supply the need for better low light capability. Since these products have become popular, gun manufacturers have taken to incorporating them into factory offerings.

Luminescent sights, commonly called night sights or tritium sights, were the first products to make the jump from aftermarket to the manufacturer's floor. Today, a large number of factory guns are available with night sights, either stock or as a factory-installed option.

Laser sighting systems have enjoyed similar popularity, and today there are many guns available with lasers built in or added by the maker.

A flashlight attached to the gun is another way to make it easier to deal with dark conditions, and in the past it was necessary to do some alterations to a gun to mount a light. As the public began to demand more and more of those custom installations from their gunsmiths, manufacturers took notice. They started integrating a common mounting platform (the "rail") into their gun designs, and today most autoloading pistols come with a rail in front of the triggerguard onto which the owner can easily slide a powerful LED flashlight. Some of the flashlights even incorporate a laser for an all-in-one solution!

In the future, look for handguns to make it easier to get on target rapidly, to make eyesight issues irrelevant, and to enhance both close-range speed and long-range accuracy - all at the same time!

The Ruger LCR, with its hybrid polymer construction, is a major break from traditional revolver manufacturing. Photo courtesy Sturm, Ruger Co.

A flashlight attached to the gun is invaluable for self defense and police use in low light. Photo courtesy of Surefire, LLC

Want to Know More?

Greatest Handguns of the World by Massad Ayoob. ISBN 9781440228698. Krause Publications, (855) 864-2579 www.gundigestbooks.com

Gun Digest Book of Classic Combat Handguns by Dan Shideler. ISBN 9781440223846. Krause Publications, (855) 864-2579 www.gundigestbooks.com

Standard Catalog of Handguns by Jerry Lee. Large volume (750+ pages!) featuring background, pictures and values of handguns from around the world. ISBN 9781440230097. Krause Publications, (855) 864-2579 www.gundigestbooks.com

MatebaFan - the only website devoted to preserving the history and innovations of firearms designer Emilio Ghisoni. Many rare pictures and details of his life. www.matebafan.com

Merz Antiques - dealers in rare and antique firearms; one of the largest inventories available for sale. Also maintains a stunning firearm museum. Merz Antique Firearms, PO Box 494, Fergus Falls, MN 56538. (218) 739-3255 www.merzantique.com

Phoenix Arms - specializes in Lugers and other rare European firearms. Phoenix Investment Arms, 5506 Yadkin Road, Fayetteville NC, 28303. (910) 868-7620 www.phoenixinvestmentarms.com

Adams Guns - wide variety of unusual, rare, and collectible guns. Bob Adams, P.O. Box 23010, Albuquerque, NM 87192. (505) 255-6868 www.adamsguns.com

CHAPTER 3

WHAT KIND OF HANDGUN DO I NEED?

No matter what you like to shoot, there is a handgun for you. Whether you're interested in hunting, competition, or self defense, youcan find a handgun that exactly fits.

Handguns come in three basic styles: single shot, revolver, and autoloader. Each has strengths and weaknesses, and some are better suited to specific activities than others.

THE SINGLE SHOT

The single shot handgun is a staple of hunting and certain kinds of competitive shooting. The single shot has two major attributes: it's generally very strong and able to chamber cartridges that would destroy the typical revolver or autoloader, and it's usually extremely accurate. When you need to place powerful rounds accurately at long distance, the choice is often a single shot.

The powerful chamberings of the single shot handgun are ideal for handgun hunting.

Single shot handguns were common prior to the invention of the revolver. The classic flintlock, for instance, is (except for a few rare experimental designs) a single shot handgun. The Derringer, the type of gun which famously felled President Lincoln, is typical of a single shot.

Once the revolver was available and economically priced, the single shot rapidly lost favor. It wasn't until the middle of the 20th century, when handgun hunting and long range competition came into vogue, that the single shot made a well-deserved comeback.

Today's single shot handgun is a precision arm that's available in a wide variety of calibers, sighting systems, and barrel lengths - including cartridges that we usually only see in rifles!

The break action handgun, like this Thompson/Center, are simple, strong, accurate and reliable. *Photo courtesy of Thompson/Center Arms*

BREAK ACTION

The break action is so named because the two parts - the barrel and the frame - are hinged together and opened by "breaking" the gun. (This is very similar to how a double-barrel shotgun works.) Most break action handguns have interchangeable barrels, allowing the shooter to have multiple guns in one.

Break actions are inherently strong guns, and many of them are chambered in rifle cartridges. The Thompson-Center Encore, for instance, can be had in .30-06 and .45-70, among others.

While most break actions are large guns designed for hunting, small break action derringers are made by companies like Bond Arms and American Derringer. These are technically not single shots, as they contain two barrels, but no discussion of break actions would be complete without mentioning them. Available in a range of cartridges, the break action derringers are a popular self defense tool for some people.

ROLLING BLOCK

Although designed by an independent inventor, Leonard Geiger, the rolling block is almost synonymous with the Remington Company due to its adoption of his invention around 1863. Most people think of the rolling block as a rifle action, but Remington's first product utilizing Geiger's action was the Model 1865 pistol.

The rolling block is elegantly simple: the breech block is in the shape of a partial circle, and rotates on a pin. It's locked in by the similarly-shaped hammer, and can only be opened when the hammer is at full cock. When the hammer drops, it rotates into a depression machined in the breech block, preventing the block from rotating and keeping the cartridge safely contained.

The hammer and breech block are operated almost identically. To load, the hammer is cocked and the breech block thumbed back to open. A round is inserted, and the block is thumbed forward. On firing, the hammer locks the breech closed; once fired, the hammer is cocked again, the breech block is also thumbed open, and the spent cartridge can then be removed.

The rolling block is quite robust, mechanically simple, and very reliable. Today there are only a few rolling block pistols still made, mostly by the Italian reproduction arms companies.

BOLT ACTION

The bolt action pistol is generally regarded as the most accurate, most powerful type of handgun available (though owners of large break-actions like the Thomson-Center Encore might argue the point).

The bolt action pistol operates just like a single shot bolt action rifle. The first commercially successful bolt action pistol was the Remington XP-100, which appeared in 1963. For many years it was the only one of its type available, but in the 1980s and 1990s the growing sport of handgun silhouette (along with increasing interest in handgun hunting) prompted many other companies to make their own version: Weatherby (the CFP), Savage Arms (the Stryker), and Anschutz (the Exemplar), among others, entered the market. Like Remington, however, they discovered that the market was very small, and by 2010 all had been discontinued.

Today there is only one maker of bolt action pistols left, H-S Precision, who make the Pro-Series 2000 line of pistols. However, there are many used bolt action pistols on the market in a wide variety of calibers.

ROTATING BREECH

An unusual type of single shot pistol, called the Lone Eagle, was produced by Magnum Research. Long discontinued, it employed a rotating breech block similar to that used in some artillery pieces and was capable of handling powerful rifle calibers. No other handguns of this configuration are currently made.

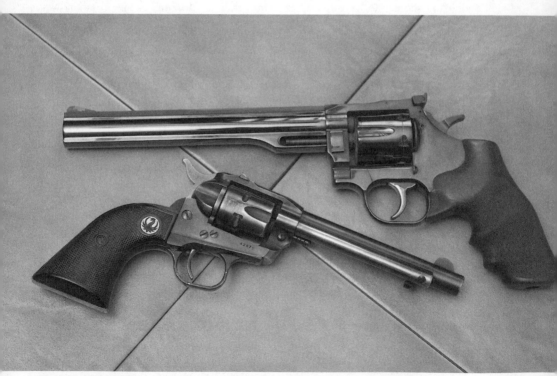

Revolvers come in single action (bottom) and double action. Both have their advantages in certain kinds of shooting.

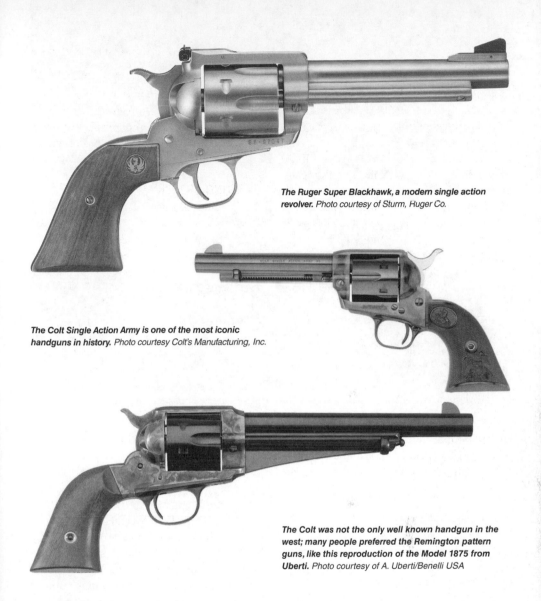

The Ruger Super Blackhawk, a modern single action revolver. Photo courtesy of Sturm, Ruger Co.

The Colt Single Action Army is one of the most iconic handguns in history. Photo courtesy Colt's Manufacturing, Inc.

The Colt was not the only well known handgun in the west; many people preferred the Remington pattern guns, like this reproduction of the Model 1875 from Uberti. Photo courtesy of A. Uberti/Benelli USA

THE REVOLVER

While the revolver predates the autoloader by decades, it's not at all outdated. The revolver is still made in a wide variety of sizes and calibers, and is still a viable tool for many kinds of shooting, from self defense to hunting.

There are two basic kinds of revolvers: single action and double action. Single-action revolvers are the simplest type: one simply thumbs the hammer back to cock it and pulls the trigger to fire. The term "single" action denotes that the trigger performs only a single task: releasing the sear.

Double actions are so named because the trigger both cocks and releases the hammer. In addition, most double actions can be cocked just like a single action, giving them the best of both worlds: rapid fire by

The double action revolver can be cocked just like a single action, making it an all-around performer.

simply pulling the trigger and precise shot placement by cocking the hammer and taking advantage of the short, light single action trigger.

SINGLE ACTIONS

The single action revolver is the earliest type of repeating handgun, having come into the form we know due to the work of Samuel Colt in 1836. The single action was tough, reliable, and simple to make. These attributes helped it dominate the revolver market in the U.S. well into the 1880s.

The most recognized single action revolver is probably the Colt Model 1873 "Peacemaker," also known as the Single Action Army, or SAA. Even if you've never held one, you've certainly seen them used in westerns on the big screen. This design has undergone only minor changes since it was introduced more than a century ago, and is still made today by Colt. In addition, there are many copies made in Italy as well as the U.S.

Modern single actions, like the Blackhawk from Ruger and the various Freedom Arms revolvers, are very strong and designed to chamber powerful Magnum cartridges. These modern guns are accurate and hard hitting even at a distance, and as a result see the most use in modern handgun hunting and long range competitive shooting.

The reproduction guns, such as the Single Action Army, are most commonly used in the very popular sport of Cowboy Action Shooting. Today it's easy to find high quality copies of the Colt, as well as various Remington and Smith & Wesson models, that fit right into the Old West theme.

DOUBLE ACTIONS

The double action revolver caught on in England long before it was common on these shores. This is slightly ironic, given that England and Europe are generally thought of as being the hotbed of autoloading pistol development.

The double action has changed very little in the last century. In fact, many of the re- volver designs on a dealer's shelf are quite similar to those produced in the opening de- cades of the twentieth century. That isn't to say that there hasn't been progress, however.

Today's revolver is smoother, easier to shoot, and chambers more powerful car- tridges than the guns of yesteryear. They're also lighter, often being made of lightweight

Striker-fired pistol (top) uses a spring-powered internal firing pin, as contrasted with the hammer-actuated firing pin of pistol below.

The trigger of the single action autoloader is crisp, light, and easy to shoot.

alloys and polymers. It's possible to buy a Magnum revolver that will fit in a pocket and be scarcely noticeable - in either size or weight. They might not be pleasant to fire because of the fierce recoil, however.

Many double action revolvers are used for personal and home defense, where their ease of shooting and fast reloading - compared to the single action - make them an ideal tool. Because double actions can usually be cocked to single action, they're also used for hunting and long range competitions. It's been said that the double action revolver is the most versatile handgun made, and there is some justification for that belief.

THE AUTOLOADER

According to industry data, well over half of all handguns sold in the U.S. are of the autoloading variety. The autoloading pistol, as its name implies, loads its own chamber after the previous round is fired. It is not fully automatic, as the trigger must be pulled for each round to be fired; they are accurately termed semi-automatic.

Autoloaders, or autos as they're sometimes erroneously called, are available in a wide variety of calibers and a number of different trigger systems. Autoloading pistols are fired by either a hammer, as one might see on a revolver, or by an internal striker as found on a bolt action rifle.

The single action auto, typified by guns like the Model 1911 and the Browning HiPower, is much like the single action revolver: the trigger simply releases sear, while the recoiling action of the slide cocks the hammer or striker. Single action autoloaders can have crisp, light triggers that aid in precision marksmanship. Because the gun is usually cocked and ready to fire, single action autoloaders almost always have some sort of safety mechanism that prevents the gun from firing if the trigger is accidentally depressed.

Another type of autoloader is the double/single action, sometimes referred to as "traditional double action" or abbreviated as "DA/SA." The first shot is made with the hammer down; the trigger pulls the hammer back and then releases it, much like the double action revolver.

Some guns, such as this SIG-Sauer, have a decocker on the frame. Middle of three controls is the decocker, activated by thumb of shooting hand.

Subsequent shots are made in single action, with a very short, light trigger throw.

When the round fires and the slide recoils, it cocks the hammer for the next shot, giving the shooter a lighter single action trigger. Subsequent shots are all done in single action mode. There are also striker-fired autoloaders which operate this way.

The double action auto usually has some sort of mechanism, called a "decocker," to allow the hammer or striker to return to the rest position without firing a round. When the gun is cocked, operating the decocker lowers the hammer or striker without allowing it to contact the round in the chamber. The decocker usually returns to its rest position under

Double action autoloaders need a method to "de-cock" the gun. This Smith & Wesson has decocker on the slide, which also functions as a safety.

spring pressure, but a variant is the combination decocker/safety: it decocks the gun but stays in the activated position, serving to prevent the trigger from functioning. It must be released to be able to fire the gun.

Most decockers are mounted on the slide, but the guns from SIG-Sauer are a notable exception. Their decockers are mounted on the side of the frame, just aft of the trigger.

The double action is the most complicated of all autoloaders to use, first because of the differing trigger pulls (the first being long and heavy, and the remaining being short and light), plus the added controls to decock (and possibly on-safe) the gun.

An increasingly popular variant of the double action is called "double action only," usually abbreviated to DAO. The trigger cocks the hammer or striker, releases it, and when the gun recoils the hammer or striker returns to the rest position. The trigger pull is the same all the time: long and heavy, especially compared to a single action gun.

Some people call DAO autos "self loading revolvers," because the two have very similar trigger operation.

Most autoloaders are designed with some variation on these three mechanisms, even if not readily apparent. The Glock pistols, for instance, feel to the shooter like they're single action because they have relatively light, short-travel triggers. Technically, though, they're really double action only, because their striker is never fully cocked - it is only pretensioned, and pulling the trigger brings the striker back to the fully cocked position just before it is released.

Autoloaders carry their ammunition in magazines which are inserted into the grip of the gun. Historically this was not the case - there were pistols which loaded with a stripper clip, and those whose magazines were not in the butt - but today all follow the magazine in the grip convention. This makes reloading the autopistol fast and easy.

The Glock pistols feel much like single actions, but aren't fully cocked until trigger is pulled.

The Glock pistols feel much like single actions, but aren't fully cocked until trigger is pulled.

This .25 Auto pistol is typical of small blowback-operated handguns chambering less powerful rounds.

BLOWBACK, LOCKED BREACH, RECOIL AND GAS OPERATED AUTOS

All autoloaders need a method to keep the brass casing from ejecting before pressures have dropped to a safe level. Having the breech open while still under high pressure could result in serious injury to the shooter.

The simplest method is called "blowback." The breech is held closed by a very strong recoil spring, which slows the movement of the slide just enough for the pressures to drop. This is suited primarily to small, relatively low pressure cartridges and is commonly found on pocket pistols and .22 caliber handguns.

There have been blowback operated guns in calibers like 9mm and .45ACP, but they are not common. The power of their cartridges necessitates extremely strong recoil springs which make their slides difficult to operate. The recoil impulse of a blowback auto is generally more pronounced than that of other mechanisms, making them more difficult to control in rapid shooting. The simplicity of the blowback operation, however, means that the guns are much less expensive to manufacture, which accounts for the low price tags attached to many of them.

The most common form of autoloader operation is the locked breech. There are many different mechanisms to do this, but the concept is simple: the breech is locked in the closed position until the slide has traveled backward a set distance. At that point the pressures have been reduced, and the breech is then allowed to unlock and the empty case is ejected. Because the breech is physically locked and doesn't rely on heavy spring pressure, the slides are usually much easier to operate.

Recoil operated locked breech guns get their motive power from the recoil of the cartridge. The barrel and slide are locked together and the recoil impulse of the round shoves them both backward. After traveling a certain distance, the barrel stops, unlocks from the slide, and allows the slide to continue rearward. As it does it pulls the empty case out of the chamber and throws (ejects) it from the gun. When it hits its rearward travel and starts forward again it strips a new round from the magazine, pushes it into the chamber, and the slide and barrel lock themselves together and travel into their forward rest, or "battery," position - ready for the next shot.

Gas operated autoloaders are much less common. Their breech stays in the lock position as the bullet travels down the barrel; when the bullet reaches a certain point it passes a small hole (or port) which directs a portion of the propellant gas back to the bolt, where it is used to push the slide into an unlocked position. As the slide moves back it behaves much like the recoil operated mechanism, ejecting the old round and, on the return trip, picking up a new round and going back into the battery position.

There have been many variations on these systems over the years. One is the gas delay system, most famously used on the HK P7 pistol (among others.) The gun is essentially a blowback pistol, but in addition to spring pressure it uses some of the gases to hold the breech close. When the round fires, some of the gas is immediately ported into a small chamber containing a piston which is firmly attached to the slide. The pressure in the chamber delays the piston from being forced back into the chamber, thus delaying the opening of the breech.

The goal of all these mechanisms is the same: to make the gun safe to use. In that

The gas-operated autoloader is relatively uncommon, usually chambers very powerful cartridges - like this Desert Eagle. *Photo courtesy of Magnum Research*

When this HK P7 is fired, the piston - the ribbed rod attached to the slide - is pushed forward by high gas pressure, counteracting the rearward thrust on the slide and delaying its opening until the pressure has dropped.

Magazines or Clips?

Just about any online gun forum will sooner or later have a heated discussion about magazines (or "mags") and clips. Many people use the two interchangeably, referring to a pistol's ammunition carrier as a clip. Technically this isn't correct: a clip is an open device which holds each round of ammunition by its groove, rim, or base, while a magazine is an enclosed device in which the rounds are simply contained by spring pressure. All autoloading pistols available today use magazines, not clips.

Clips hold rounds via their rims and are open; magazines hold the rounds in an enclosed box.

sense they all work, but as with any mechanical device they all have their advantages and disadvantages.

AUTOLOADING PISTOL
SEQUENCE OF OPERATION

The autopistol is loaded by inserting a magazine into the grip. The slide (or bolt, in some .22LR pistols) is pulled to the rear and released. As the slide goes forward, it contacts the top round in the magazine and pushes it forward; as the round is pushed, it slides up and into the chamber. The slide then closes on the round.

A single action or traditional double action gun will now be cocked and ready to fire. A DAO-style auto will have the hammer (or striker) in the rest position, ready to by cocked by the trigger. If the gun isn't to be fired immediately, the safety must be engaged or the hammer/striker must be decocked.

To fire, the safety (if any) is released and the trigger pulled. On a single action auto, this releases the hammer or striker to fly forward and ignite the round in the gun. On a double action or DAO gun, the trigger moves the hammer or striker against the mainspring's tension to the fully cocked position, then releases it to fire.

The firing pin/striker hits the primer, which ignites and sets off the powder charge. The gunpowder burns extremely rapidly and liberates a large amount of very hot gas. This gas very quickly builds to high pressure and forces the bullet out of the case and into the barrel. The gases continue to expand, driving the bullet forward and out of the barrel.

The gun's slide (or bolt) is driven backwards by one of the mechanisms discussed previously. As it starts to move back the barrel unlocks from the slide, usually by dropping down, allowing the slide to continue backward.

As the slide moves to the rear, it pulls (extracts) the empty case from the chamber and ejects it from the gun. As the slide travels back it pushes the hammer (if the gun has one) down and back, cocking it. When the slide hits its rearward travel it stops and then starts forward, pushing the top round in the magazine ahead of it.

As the slide comes back into battery position, it pushes the round fully into the chamber and, if a locked breech design, locks the barrel and slide together. Striker fired guns are usually pre-tensioned at this point as the striker catches on the trigger's sear. The gun is now ready to fire.

DOUBLE ACTION REVOLVER SEQUENCE OF OPERATION

Once the cylinder has been loaded and closed, the pulling of the trigger does several things simultaneously. First, it unlocks the cylinder so that it is free to rotate to a loaded chamber. Once the cylinder is unlocked, a part usually referred to as a "hand" is pushed out of the frame and into contact with the lobes on the extractor star. The hand causes the cylinder to rotate. As all this is happening, the hammer is being cocked against the pressure of the mainspring.

As the trigger continues back, the cylinder continues to rotate until the fresh round is in the position where it aligns with the barrel. Just as it gets there, a small piece of metal (called a bolt or catch) pops into one of the locking notches on the outside of the cylinder, locking the cylinder into proper alignment with the barrel. The trigger usually continues a very small distance and fi-

What Keeps the Autoloading Pistol from Going "Full Auto"?

A handgun that fires more than one round when the trigger is pulled is called fully automatic, or "full auto." To keep that from happening, autoloading mechanisms have what's generally called a disconnector - a device that keeps the trigger from continuously releasing the sear as it reloads itself. The disconnector is operational as soon as the shot is fired, and while the mechanisms vary they all do the same job: they keep the trigger from tripping the sear as it resets. Usually they're tied into the slide movement: as soon as the slide starts moving to the rear, the disconnector un-mates the trigger and the sear and keeps them that way until the slide has returned to battery and the trigger has been released.

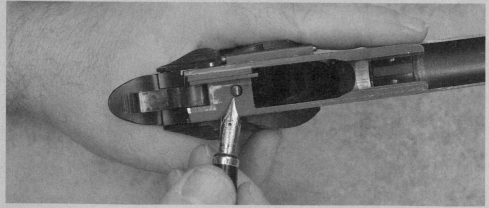

Pen points to disconnector, which keeps the gun from firing until the slide has closed completely and the trigger has been allowed to reset.

nally allows the hammer to drop, igniting the round.

When the shooter releases the trigger after firing, it travels forward and resets the hand, cylinder bolt, hammer, and any internal safeties - ready for the next cycle.

(The Smith & Wesson Bodyguard uses a different method of rotating the cylinder, but the sequence is the same.)

THE PERENNIAL QUESTION: REVOLVER OR AUTOLOADER?

Both have their vocal adherents, and both have advantages and disadvantages.

The most commonly cited attribute of the revolver is its inherent reliability. While any mechanical device can malfunction, revolvers have historically had a much longer interval between malfunctions than the autoloader. The revolver also has a simpler manual of arms; there are fewer controls and the gun is more easily reloaded and checked than is the autoloader. The revolver handles ultra-powerful rounds that an autoloader simply can't, making it far more suitable for hunting and long range competition.

The autoloader typically holds more ammunition than does the revolver, and it's generally easier to shoot than a double-action revolver.

One advantage of the autoloading pistol is capacity - loaded Glock on left carries the same number of rounds as all these revolvers put together.

The autoloader's slim magazine is easier to carry than a bulky revolver speedloader, and is slightly faster to reload.

Given equal practice most people can reload the autoloader faster than any other handgun, and the autoloader is easier to shoot quickly due to the typically shorter trigger travel. Its ammunition supply is carried in flat, easily-exchanged magazines and the gun itself is flatter - making it, in some opinions, easier to conceal.

How to decide between the two? Start with the expected use. There are some areas where the revolver is going to be the choice: handgun hunting and long-range competitions are areas where autoloaders struggle to keep up. For self defense, a majority of people prefer an autoloader, but there is a strong contingent of people who make the revolver their choice in protection. In competitive shooting matches some are revolver neutral, where others clearly favor the auto.

The dedication of the shooter is a big determinant as well. The double action revolver is harder to shoot well than the autoloader and demands a greater practice commitment on the part of the shooter. The autoloader, in contrast, is often easier to shoot but has

A revolver's grips can be easily exchanged for smaller or larger sizes to better fit the shooter's hand.

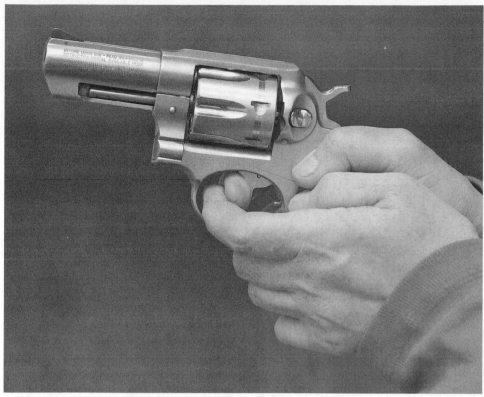

While the revolver is simpler to operate than an autoloader, it requires hand strength to fire - sometimes both hands!

a more difficult manual of arms; it requires more knowledge and care in handling and doing administrative tasks like loading, unloading, and cleaning.

Sometimes physical needs come into play. The autoloaders will generally have a fatter grip than the revolver, making it harder to handle by shooters with shorter fingers or smaller hands. The revolver can be more easily modified for smaller or larger hand sizes simply by changing the grips. Some autoloaders have interchangeable grip parts, but overall still don't have the adjustability of the revolver.

The autoloader's slide can be harder to manipulate for those with muscular issues, while the revolver's cylinder is easy to open and close. Similarly, the revolver's heavy double action trigger requires more finger strength than does the typical autoloader. For someone whose hands are a little on the weak side, the revolver presents a greater challenge than the auto.

One deciding factor is that the auto's slide manipulation is more a matter of technique than strength, but there is no corresponding solution for the person who can't pull the revolver's long and heavy trigger. (In the chapter on shooting techniques, we'll go over the procedure that allows almost anyone to operate almost any autoloader slide, regardless of upper body strength.) In most such cases the autoloader is the better choice.

Of course, for the person who is still having trouble deciding, there is an alternative: buy both!

GETTING THE RIGHT FIT

Shooting a handgun well is greatly helped by proper hand fit. So important is hand fit that some types of competition handguns have grips that are actually molded to the owner's hand. While it's not necessary to go to that extreme for most purposes, making sure that the gun is sized correctly for the hand using it will make it much easier to get good, consistent hits.

To determine whether a given gun and hand are compatible, first make sure that the gun is unloaded; if there is someone else present, have them double-check and verify that it is unloaded. For an autoloader, lock the slide in the open position; for a revolver, leave the cylinder open; for a single shot handgun, leave the bolt or break action open.

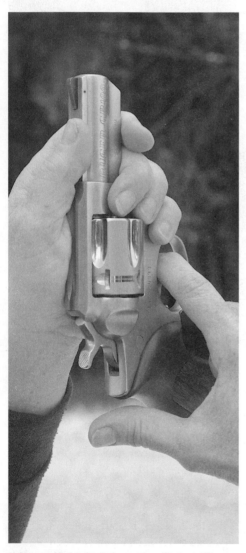

Using a verified unloaded gun, place finger on trigger as noted in text.

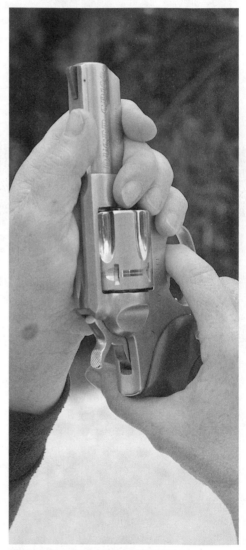

Work backwards, wrapping hand around grip.

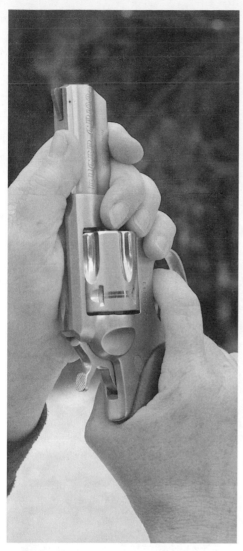

Finish by grasping the gun firmly as you would if actually shooting.

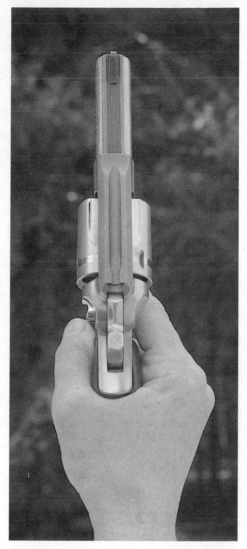

If the barrel lines up with the forearm, the gun fits the shooter correctly.

Start by placing the finger in the proper position on the trigger. For a single action trigger, the pad of the finger should be centered on the trigger face; for a double action trigger (or any trigger with a pull weight in excess of six pounds or so), it's best to put the crease of the first joint on the face of the trigger for best leverage.

With the trigger finger in place, wrap the rest of the hand around the grip and see which direction the barrel is pointing relative to the bones of the arm. If it's pointing away from the centerline of the forearm, the gun is too large for the hand; if pointing toward the centerline, the gun is too small.

A gun that is too large for the shooter's hand channels painful recoil to the bones and joints of the thumb, rather than into the palm.

by the hand and the forearm, but against the thumb. The further out on the thumb the recoil is directed, the more painful it will be and the less control the shooter will have over recoil.

Second, the trigger finger will not be able to press the trigger straight to the rear; it will almost always be pushed sideways, causing the muzzle of the gun to drift and the shots to hit to the side of the desired point of aim. This is referred to as "steering the gun," and it's a common cause of poor shooting. While the experienced shooter can compensate for the effect by watching the sights and adjusting where the gun is pointed as the trigger finger moves, the results are never optimal. It's best to have a gun which fits correctly from the start.

Revolvers and most single shot handguns can have smaller grips installed on the gun, and that often results in dramatic changes to the sizing of the gun. Some autoloaders have replaceable grips, though their sizing is not as flexible as with the revolvers and single shots. Some of the newest autoloading pistols have backstraps that are user-replaceable, and they can be a superb solution to fit issues both large and small.

A too-small gun is much easier to deal with than one which is too large. With care it can usually be shot well as-is, and it may be possible to take up the extra space with larger grips. It's the opposite situation - when the gun is too big for the hand - which causes problems.

A too-large gun presents two issues. First, the recoil of the gun will be directed not toward the palm, where it is easily absorbed

Want to Know More?

BREAK-ACTION PISTOLS

Comanche Pistols - Eagle Imports, 1750 Brielle Ave. Unit B-1, Wanamassa, NJ 07712. (732) 493-0302 www.comanchepistols.com

Thompson/Center - Thompson/Center Arms, Inc. 2100 Roosevelt Ave., Springfield, MA 01104. (866) 730-1614 www.tcarms.com

Bond derringers - Bond Arms Inc., P.O. Box 1296, Granbury, Texas 76048. (817) 573-4445 www.bondarms.com

Freedom Arms - Freedom Arms Inc., 314 Highway 239, Freedom, WY 83120. (307) 883-2468 www.freedomarms.com

Wichita Arms - Wichita Arms, Inc., 923 E Gilbert, Wichita, KS 67211. (316) 265-0661 www.wichitaarms.com

RPM - RPM XL, 15481 North Twin Lakes Drive, Tucson, AZ 85739. (520) 825-1233 www.rpmxl1.com

BOLT-ACTION SINGLE SHOT PISTOLS

H-S Precision - www.hsprecision.com

ROLLING BLOCK SINGLE SHOT PISTOLS

Uberti - Stoeger Industries, 901 Eighth Street, Pocomoke, MD 21851. (301) 283-6981 www.uberti.com

REVOLVERS - SINGLE ACTION

Colt - Colt's Manufacturing Company LLC, P.O. Box 1868, Hartford, CT 06144. (800) 962-COLT www.coltsmfg.com

Chiappa - Chiappa Firearms, 6785 W 3rd St, Dayton, OH. www.chiappafirearms.com

Beretta - Beretta USA, (800) BER-ETTA www.berettausa.com

EAA/Bounty Hunter - EAA Corp., P.O. Box 560746, Rockledge, FL 32956-0746. (321) 639-4842 www.eaacorp.com

USFA - United States Fire Arms Mfg. Co., Inc., P.O. Box 1901, Hartford, CT 06144-1901. (860) 296-7441 www.usfirearms.com

Uberti - Stoeger Industries, 901 Eighth Street, Pocomoke, MD 21851. (301) 283-6981 www.uberti.com

EMF (imports several makes) - EMF Company, Inc., 1900 East Warner Ave. Ste. 1-D, Santa Ana, CA 92705. (800) 430-1310 www.emf-company.com

Magnum Research - Magnum Research, Inc., 12602 33rd Avenue SW, Pillager, MN 56473. (508) 635-4273 www.magnumresearch.com

Ruger - Sturm, Ruger Co., 411 Sunapee Street, Newport, NH 03773. (603) 865-2442 www.ruger.com

REVOLVERS - DOUBLE ACTION

Smith & Wesson - Smith & Wesson Holding Company, 2100 Roosevelt Avenue, Springfield, MA 01104. (800) 331-0852 www.smith-wesson.com

Chiappa - Chiappa Firearms, 6785 W 3rd St, Dayton, OH. www.chiappafirearms.com

Taurus - Taurus International MFG, Inc. USA, 16175 NW 49 Avenue, Miami, FL 33014. (305) 624-1115 www.taurususa.com

Want to Know More?

REVOLVERS - DOUBLE ACTION

Rossi - Braztech International, L.C., Inc., 16175 NW 49 Ave., Miami, FL 33014. (305) 474-0401 www.rossiusa.com

Sarsilmaz - www.sarsilmaz.com.tr/en

Charter Arms - Charter Arms, 281 Canal Street, Shelton, CT 06484. (203) 922-1652 www.charterfirearms.com

EAA/Windicator - EAA Corp., P.O. Box 560746, Rockledge, FL 32956-0746. (321) 639-4842 www.eaacorp.com

EMF (imports several makes) - EMF Company, Inc., 1900 East Warner Ave. Ste. 1-D, Santa Ana, CA 92705. (800) 430-1310 www.emf-company.com

Ruger - Sturm, Ruger Co., 411 Sunapee Street, Newport, NH 03773. (603) 865-2442 www.ruger.com

AUTOLOADING PISTOLS

Smith & Wesson - Smith & Wesson Holding Company, 2100 Roosevelt Avenue, Springfield, MA 01104. (800) 331-0852 www.smith-wesson.com

Beretta - Beretta USA, (800) BER-ETTA www.berettausa.com

Springfield - Springfield Armory, 420 W. Main St., Geneseo, IL 61254. (800) 680-6866 www.springfield-armory.com

Caracal - Caracal USA, 7661 Commerce Lane, Trussville, AL 35173. (205) 655-7050 www.caracal-usa.com

Cabot - Penn United Technologies, 799 N. Pike Road, Cabot, PA 16023. (855) THE-1911 www.cabotgun.com

Wilson Combat - Wilson Combat Inc. 2234 CR 719, Berryville, AR 72616. (800) 955-4856 www.wilsoncombat.com

Les Baer - Les Baer Custom, 1804 Iowa Drive, LeClaire, Iowa 52753. (563)289-2126 www.lesbaer.com

Kimber - Kimber Mfg. Inc., 555 Taxter Road Suite 235, Elmsford, NY 10523. (888) 243-4522 www.kimberamerica.com

Kahr - Kahr Arms Inc., 130 Goddard Memorial Drive, Worcester, MA 01603. (508) 795-3919 www.kahr.com

Kel-Tec - Kel-Tec CNC Industries, Inc., PO Box 236009, Cocoa, Fl 32923. (321) 631-0068 www.keltecweapons.com

Seecamp - L.W. Seecamp Co., Inc., 280 Rock Lane, Milford CT 06460. (203) 877-7926 www.seecamp.com

Taurus - Taurus International Mfg. Inc. USA, 16175 NW 49 Avenue, Miami, FL 33014. (305) 624-1115 www.taurususa.com

Para Ordnance - Para USA, Inc., 10620 Southern Loop Blvd., Pineville, NC 28134. (704) 930-7600 www.para-usa.com

HK - Heckler & Koch, 5675 Transport Boulevard, Columbus, GA 31907. (706) 568-1906 www.hk-usa.com

Browning - Browning Inc., One Browning Place, Morgan, UT 84050. (800) 333-3288 www.browning.com

FN Herstal - FNH USA, 7918 Jones Branch Drive Suite 400, McLean, VA 22101. (703) 288-3500 www.fnherstal.com

Magnum Research - Magnum Research, Inc., 12602 33rd Avenue SW, Pillager, MN 56473. (508) 635-4273 www.magnumresearch.com

Walther - Walther USA, 2100 Roosevelt Avenue, Springfield, MA 01104. (800) 372-6454 www.smith-wesson.com/walther

Witness/Tangfolio - EAA Corp., P.O. Box 560746, Rockledge, FL 32956-0746. (321) 639-4842 www.eaacorp.com

FMK, Accu-Tek, Accel, EMF - EMF Company, Inc., 1900 East Warner Ave. Ste. 1-D, Santa Ana, CA 92705. (800) 430-1310 www.emf-company.com

Ruger - Sturm, Ruger Co., 411 Sunapee Street, Newport, NH 03773. (603) 865-2442 www.ruger.com

GRIP MAKERS

Altamont - OEM grip supplier for some S&W handguns. P.O. Box 309, Thomasboro, IL 61878. (800) 626-5774 www.altamontco.com

Hogue - one of the largest gripmakers, with wood & rubber grips for a huge variety of handguns. P.O. Box 1138, Paso Robles, CA 93447-1138. (800) GET-GRIP www.getgrip.com

Pachmayr - rubber, nylon grips for many revolvers & autoloaders. Lyman Products Corp., 475 Smith Street, Middletown, CT 06457. (800) 225-9626 www.pachmayr.com

Nill Grips - old-line German maker of high quality grips for revolvers and autos. Many different surface textures; makes grips for a number of gun companies. Has a U.S. warehouse, online ordering. Karl Nill GmbH, www.nill-shop.com

Don Collins - custom gripmaker for revolvers and autoloaders. Works in wood, ivory, and Corian. Collinscraft, 7761 Lakewood Dr., Unionville, IN 47468. www.collinscraftgrips.com

Craig Spegel - specializes in concealment grips for select autos and revolvers. Has a large range of common and rare woods available. P.O. Box 387, Nehalem, OR 97131. (503) 368-5653 www.craigspegel.com

Eagle Grips - makes wood & plastic grips for many hard-to-fit handguns; one of the few to offer a selection of Ruger grips. 460 Randy Road, Carol Stream, IL 60188. (800) 323-6144 www.eaglegrips.com

Herretts - true custom-fit grips at reasonable prices. Many options. Herrett Stocks, Inc., P.O. Box 741, Twin Falls, ID 83303. (208)-733-1498 www.herrettstocks.com

Blu Magnum - High end custom grips, primarily for S&W revolvers. 2605 East Willamette Ave., Colorado Springs, CO 80909. (719) 632-2780 www.blu-magnum.com

LB Custom Grips - The only craftsman who makes grips for Dan Wesson revolvers - exclusively. www.lbcustomgrips.com

Gemini Customs - top quality custom grips for select revolvers and autoloaders. 717 Botkins Lane, Frankfort, KY 40601. (502) 226-1230 www.geminicustoms.com

Esmerelda - grips in rare woods from an acclaimed maker, for select autoloaders and revolvers. Unusual checkering patterns are one of her specialities. Online sales only. www.esmeralda.cc

Boone Grips - one of the few sources for ivory grips from elephant, mastodon, mammoth, and narwhal; offers stag, bone, and simulated ivory too. For autos and revolvers. Boone Trading Company, PO Box 669, Brinnon, WA 98320. (800) 423-1945 www.boonetrading.com

Want to Know More?

GRIP MAKERS

Jim Badger - highly polished finger-groove grips in various laminated woods, for revolvers and autoloaders. Badger Custom Grips, 1138 White Horse Rd., Suite A, Greenville, SC 29605. (864) 283-5700 www.badgercustomgrips.com

Ahrends - CNC-machined wood grips for S&W revolvers and Colt autos. Ahrends Grips, PO Box 203, Clarion, IA 50525. (515) 532-3449 www.ahrendsgripsusa.com

Handmade Grips Online - this company, based in Turkey, produces spectacular engraved and inlaid grips for autos and revolvers. They are particularly well versed in making custom grips for European guns, a service which can be hard to find in the U.S. www.handmadegrips.com

NCO Grips - makes grips for an extremely wide (over 1,000) variety of handguns in ivory, bone, stag, Corian, exotic woods, and faux mother-of-pear. Also does reproduction grips for antique guns, many exclusives. If you have a rare handgun, they can probably supply grips! N.C. Ordnance, PO Box 3254, Wilson, NC 27895. (252) 237-2440 www.gungrip.com

Rio Grande - unique full-color grips; they can even make grips from customer-supplied photos, perfect for personalizing a gun. Rio Grande Custom Grips (303) 330-2812 www.riograndecustomgrips.com

VZ Grips - very unique modern grips for pistols and some revolvers, made from micarta and G-10 laminates in various colors. VZ Grips, 2867 Industrial Plaza Drive, Tallahassee, FL 32301. (850) 422-1911 www.vzgrips.com

Wicked Grips - true custom high end grips for 1911 and other select pistols. Rare woods, burls, and precious metal inlays available. www.wickedgrips.com

Omega Grips - one of the few makers that specializes in grips for the CZ line of pistols. Exotic woods and laminates available. Omega Custom Grips, www.czgrips.us

CLC Custom - fancy and exotic wood grips for Ruger single action guns, including stabilized woods. CLC Custom Grips, (951) 928-4210 www.clccustomgrips.com

Two Feathers - custom grips in a wide variety of materials for many revolvers and pistols. Also does carving and inlay embellishments. "From cowboy to crazy!" Tommy Two Feathers, (910) 893-6695 www.tommy-2feathers.com

Outlaw Grips - collector grade custom grips in fancy and exotic woods for single action revolvers and 1911 pistols. Joe Perkins, 2318 W. Rapallo Way, Tucson, AZ 85741. (520) 888-6799 www.outlawgrips.com

OPERATING MANUALS

Steve's Pages - online treasure trove of gun manuals. Virtually every manufacturer is represented, and there are manuals for vintage guns you can't find anywhere else. www.stevespages.com

CHAPTER 4

CALIBERS AND CARTRIDGES - PICKING THE RIGHT ONE FOR THE JOB

Handguns have been chambered in a huge variety of calibers and cartridges, and no matter what shooting activity you might want to try, there is no doubt a round that will be perfect.

Cartridges come in two main types: rimfire and centerfire.

RIMFIRE CARTRIDGES

Rimfires are the earliest type of self-contained metallic cartridges. They contain their priming material in the hollow rim of the casing, which is where they get their name. During manufacture the wet priming mixture is inserted into the rim area and allowed to dry before the powder and bullet are added. When fired, the firing pin on the gun hits the edge of the rim and slightly crushes it. The priming mixture, being pressure sensitive, ignites and sets off the powder which is

The firing pin crushes a small portion of the rim, causing the pressure sensitive priming mixture to detonate, which then causes the powder in the case to ignite. Note fired casing on bottom compared to unfired round at top.

in contact with it. Because the case itself is damaged, and because the priming material is not easily replaced, rimfire cartridges are not practical to reload. Luckily rimfires are very economical to shoot, as their cartridges and priming system are inexpensive to construct relative to the centerfire. In the late 19th century, when the rimfire was in its heyday, there were a wide variety of calibers available - up to and including the .58 caliber Miller rimfire rifle round. The .41 Short rimfire was for a time a popular self defense round, though its anemic ballistics would be considered woefully inadequate today.

The .41 rimfire shows us the limitation of the rimfire cartridge in general: strength. To better the performance of the .41 caliber projectile it would need to be launched at a higher velocity. That requires higher pressure inside the cartridge, which in turn requires a stronger (thicker) casing. The rimfire case, however, has to be thin enough to allow a firing pin to crush its rim. The rim is the weak point, and because it needs to be weak to work this limits the pressures the case can contain. The rimfire is thus self-limiting.

Today rimfire cartridges are limited to small calibers: .22 and under. That doesn't mean they're not useful, however. The various rimfires are extremely popular competition and small game rounds and are made in huge quantities. The .22 Long Rifle, for instance, is the most popular cartridge in the world (and one of our oldest, having been introduced in 1887.) Experts estimate that somewhere between two and four BILLION are sold every year!

Current rimfire cartridges (those for which guns are still being manufactured) include:

- .22 Short and .22 Long Rifle (including low-velocity powderless varieties such as the CB cap)

- .22 Winchester Magnum Rimfire (aka .22 WMR)
- .17 Hornady Magnum Rimfire (aka .17 HMR)
- .17 Hornady Mach 2 (aka .17 HM2)

Obsolete rimfire cartridges (for which guns are no longer made, but ammunition is still being produced) include:
- .22 Long
- .22 Winchester Rimfire (aka .22 WRF)
- 5mm Remington Rimfire Magnum

CENTERFIRE CARTRIDGES

Centerfire cartridges are so named because their priming mixture is contained in a small metal cup which is pressed into the center of the case head. When the primer is struck by the firing pin, the priming material is crushed between the cup and a small anvil which is part of the primer. The resulting flame is directed through a hole under the primer and sets off the powder charge.

Since the deformation occurs to a separate piece - the primer cup - it can be removed and a fresh primer inserted. This makes the centerfire cartridge reloadable, in contrast to the non-reloadable rimfire.

WHAT'S WITH BERDAN AND BOXER?

There are two centerfire priming systems in use today: Boxer and Berdan. The Boxer system uses a primer with a self-contained anvil, while the Berdan system has the anvil formed into the case head. The Boxer system is used primarily in the United States, while the Berdan system is the choice in Europe and Great Britain. The systems are externally identical, and can be fired interchangeably. Only when you look inside the cartridge can you spot the difference: the Boxer cartridge has one flash hole, while the Berdan has two.

While both systems are technically reloadable, the lack of primers and reloading tools in this country make reloading the Berdan case impractical. The Boxer priming system is easily reloaded, and there are a wide variety of tools and supplies to do that.

Ironically, it was an Englishman - Edward Boxer - who invented the priming system

Fired centerfire and rimfire cases show the location of the priming mixture.

used in the U.S., while the Berdan system - used in England and all over Europe - was invented by an American, Hiram Berdan.

A SHORT PRIMER ON BALLISTICS

Ballistics describes how bullets behave upon firing and is divided into three broad areas: internal ballistics, external ballistics, and terminal ballistics.

Internal ballistics is concerned with the propulsion of the bullet: what the bullet does from the moment of ignition until it clears the barrel of the gun. Internal ballistics is particularly important to gun designers (whose creations must withstand the pressures that the cartridge can generate) and people who reload their own ammunition (so that it doesn't exceed the pressures the gun was designed to handle.)

Bullets are propelled by the combustion gases of the powder charge. This requires tremendous pressure - some cartridges produce nearly instantaneous pressures of 37,500 psi! This pressure varies considerably depending on a number of variables: the volume of the cartridge, how much powder is used, the burning rate of the powder, even the shape of the powder granules.

The bullet's maximum velocity is reached as it clears the muzzle. Things like the bullet size relative to the bore, how much friction is generated in the rifling, and how long the barrel is all affect the velocity of the projectile.

It's a complicated field of study that can also be dangerous if either the designer or the user is not careful.

External ballistics covers the bullet's flight from the muzzle until it contacts the target. Because the bullet is non-powered once it leaves the barrel, gravity and air resistance affect its flight. External ballistics looks at things like muzzle velocity, flight time and trajectory.

There are two terms in external ballistics that are important to understand. The

Internal ballistics deals with everything that happens right up to the point that the bullet leaves the muzzle.
Photo of .40 S&W Gold Dot bullet in flight by Tom Burczynski, Experimental Research

Round-nose bullet has a better ballistic coefficient than flat-nosed bullet, has less drag when traveling through air.

first is the ballistic coefficient of the bullet, which simply means how "slippery" the bullet is in the air. It describes, in mathematical terms, how well a projectile overcomes air resistance. The bullet's weight, diameter, and shape dramatically affect its ballistic coefficient; the higher the number, the better it slices through the air.

Ballistic coefficients, and in fact exterior ballistics in general, aren't of much concern to most handgunners. However, any handgunning which includes long range shooting (as in hunting or long range handgun competition) requires at least a basic understanding of the topic to pick or develop the best loads for the job.

Terminal ballistics deals with what the bullet does from the instant it contacts the target until it comes to rest. Penetration, wound channel, and fragmentation are all part of terminal ballistics.

Terminal ballistics is important in any handgun activity where something other than targets are being used. Hunters and those

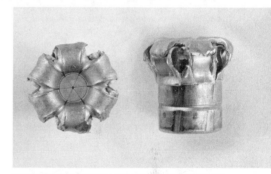

Terminal ballistics is concerned with what the bullet does when it hits a target. This 9mm Hornady bullet was fired into ballistic gelatin to study its terminal characteristics. Photo courtesy of Hornady Manufacturing

interested in self defense find terminal ballistics to be of great interest and importance - the former to making humane kills on game and the latter to stopping violent criminal activity as quickly as possible.

There are some key points to remember about terminal ballistics. First, a very streamlined bullet (like a round nose) behaves in a target the same way that it behaves in air. In

Hollowpoint bullets are designed to expand outward, making a larger wound channel and reducing penetration

other words, it slips through the target without leaving much of a wake (wound channel.) It will tend to penetrate further through the target than a less streamlined slug, because it doesn't have to use its kinetic energy to fight as much friction.

A flat-faced bullet generally won't cleave the air quite as cleanly, which also means it won't go through the flesh of a target quite as cleanly as the round nosed projectile; its wound track will be larger. That larger face also causes the bullet to use up a lot of its own energy simply pushing itself through, which (all other things being equal) translates to a slightly lower amount of penetration.

A bullet which expands on hitting the target, such as a hollowpoint or softpoint, dramatically increases its frontal surface area, greatly increasing drag and lowering the amount of penetration. It also makes a much larger wound track, making it a faster and surer "stopper."

Those who shoot steel reactive targets also care about terminal ballistics, though they may not be aware of it. A bullet that needs to topple a heavy steel target cannot use up its energy in fragmenting itself. A hollowpoint bullet, for instance, will disintegrate upon hitting a steel surface because the energy of that bullet is used to destroy itself rather than to overcome the inertia of the target. A solid bullet, on the other hand, generally stays in one piece and the energy it carries is used to move the target mass. The solid bullet, however, can present a ricochet risk, which points out the need for understanding and using terminal ballistics to best advantage.

VELOCITY AND ENERGY

Velocity refers to the speed of the bullet, and in the U.S. is measured in feet per second (fps). The usual measurement point is as the bullet leaves the muzzle (or as close as possible given the limitations of the equipment). The speed is measured by a device called a chronograph, which uses optical sensors that "see" the bullet as it passes. By calculating the time it takes the bullet to cross two such sensors placed a known distance apart, it's possible to determine the speed of the bullet to a very precise degree.

Many hunters and defensive shooting researchers feel that the faster the bullet travels,

The chronograph is an electronic speed gun for bullets. The bullet travels through the sensor triangles. The CPU calculates its speed and displays the result on the LCD display for the shooter.

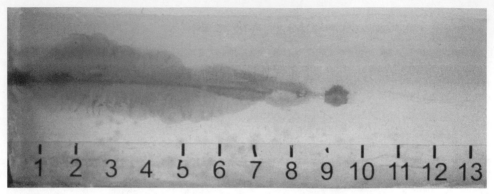

Gelatin block shows the temporary cavity made by a bullet as it passes through.
Photo courtesy of Hornady Manufacturing

the more surely it will drop an animal or incapacitate an attacker. This is generally based on the concept of the temporary cavity, or the balloon-like area that a bullet generates as it enters a fluid-rich environment such as living tissue. This is different than the "permanent cavity," which is the actual hole the bullet makes as it parts that tissue.

The importance of the temporary cavity is hotly debated. One school of thought holds that most handgun cartridges don't really develop enough of a cavity in actual flesh to really make a difference, while the other side argues that analysis of damage to organs which the bullet passed but didn't actually contact proves that the temporary cavity definitely does contribute to the bullet's performance.

One part of bullet performance is directly tied to velocity, and that is the deformation or expansion of the bullet itself. Hollowpoints and softpoints require a certain amount of velocity to expand properly; below that, the bullet is traveling too slowly to carry the amount of energy it needs to deform itself. How much velocity is necessary depends on the design of the bullet, as it's possible to make a bullet which deforms at relatively low velocities. However, that bullet may be so fragile as to expand far too quickly when it is driven

beyond the speed for which it was designed. For this reason most expanding bullets are made to be fired inside of a specific range of velocities to achieve proper results.

Supersonic and subsonic are general classifications to indicate the expected speed from a particular kind of ammunition. A supersonic bullet is one that travels in excess of the speed of sound, which is 1,126 fps in dry air at sea level. In general, bullets traveling faster than that are considered supersonic; those that travel less than that are called subsonic. Most of the time these classifications are used to easily choose rounds that will be fired through a suppressor. In that case, supersonic bullets will have the noise of the combustion reduced but the loud "crack" as the bullet breaks the sound barrier will still be audible. Subsonic bullets don't produce a sonic crack and are thus much easier to suppress.

Energy refers to the kinetic energy contained in the bullet, and is a function of both the mass (weight) of the bullet and the velocity. In the U.S., energy is expressed in footpounds.

If the weight and speed of the bullet are known, the energy can be easily calculated with the formula: ((Velocity x Velocity) x Bullet weight) / 450,400

Using this formula, a .32ACP bullet of 71 grains traveling at 900fps produces 127.68 ft-lbs of energy. By way of comparison, a .45ACP bullet of 230 grains traveling at 890fps produces 404 ft lbs, while a .500 S&W firing a 325 grain slug at 1,800 fps generates a whopping 2,338 ft-lbs of energy. (Compare that to our current M-16 military rifle, which only manages to put out 1,255 ft-lbs!)

Many people hold the energy of the bullet is directly related to the amount of damage it is capable of inflicting in a target. There have even been formulae based on bullet energy that attempted to mathematically predict the performance of ammunition in a live target, but their usefulness and predictive abilities have been hotly debated. Some states factor bullet energy into their minimum requirements for legal hunting calibers, and some competitive shooting events do a variation of this as well.

How many miles per hour does a bullet travel? It's easy to figure out how fast a bullet is traveling relative to a car by using the simple formula: 1fps = 0.682mph. Let's take a 135 grain .40 S&W bullet with a muzzle velocity of 1200 fps as an example: 1200 x 0.682 = 818.4 mph, or more than 50mph faster than the current land speed record!

CURRENT HANDGUN CARTRIDGES

This list is not all inclusive. There are many cartridges still being commercially loaded for which guns are not being made, and many more cartridges - some production, some wildcat - being chambered in custom or limited run firearms. The old .38-40 Winchester, for instance, is being loaded by a number of ammunition companies and is available in a few reproduction revolvers. It is not a mainstream cartridge, by any means.

A list of every single cartridge would entail a book unto itself, so this list is limited to those handgun cartridges for which factory guns are still being made. It's still a long list

.17 HMR

The .17 Hornady Magnum Rimfire was introduced in by the Hornady company in 2002. It's basically a .22 Magnum cartridge necked down to accept a .17 caliber bullet. It is a very high velocity cartridge primarily suited for small game hunting. There have been a few short barrel (less than 4") revolvers chambered for the HMR, but it really needs a longer barrel to take advantage of its performance characteristics. Smith & Wesson and Taurus chamber revolvers in this round.

The .17HMR is an ultra-high-speed rimfire round best suited to long barrel revolvers.

The .22 Long Rifle is the world's most popular cartridge, and is available in a wide variety of bullet types; this is but a small fraction of the selection made!

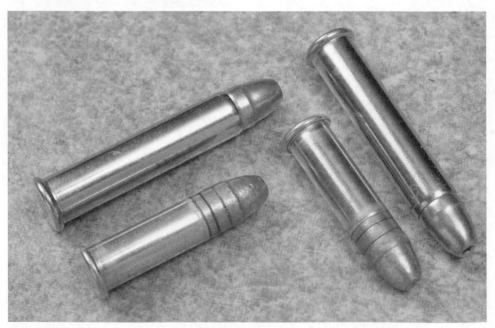

The .22 Winchester Magnum Rimfire is substantially larger than the .22 Long Rifle, and generates significantly higher velocity and energy. It's also the basis for the .17HMR round.

.22LR

The .22 Long Rifle is the single most popular cartridge in the world, and there is a wide variety of handguns from nearly all manufacturers chambered for it. There are single shots, revolvers, and autoloaders made for this ubiquitous cartridge, and many more are available on the used market. There are also barrels chambered for some of the break-action single shot handguns. The .22LR is an ideal cartridge for plinking, small game hunting, and target competition. A handgun in .22LR remains one of the best ways to introduce someone to the world of handgun shooting, as the negligible recoil and muzzle blast aren't intimidating to the new shooter.

.22 WMR

The .22 Winchester Magnum Rimfire is a more powerful round than the .22 Long Rifle, and extends the range and terminal effectiveness of the rimfire to a substantial degree. There are many guns chambered for the WMR, including revolvers, autoloaders, and single shots, from a variety of manufacturers. Ruger and Charter Arms produce revolvers which chamber both the WMR and the LR for maximum versatility.

5.7X28mm

This round was developed by Fabrique Nationale to be chambered in a personal defense weapon (PDW), a sort of compact submachine gun. It was later chambered in the FN Five-Seven autoloading pistol. The 5.7x28mm is a very high velocity bottle-necked centerfire cartridge (one of the few of that type ever made) that is sometimes touted as a self defense round for people who are recoil sensitive. It is not widely available despite having a very devoted following.

.25ACP

The diminutive .25 Automatic Colt Pistol (ACP) round was developed by John Browning for his FN Model 1906 "vest pocket"

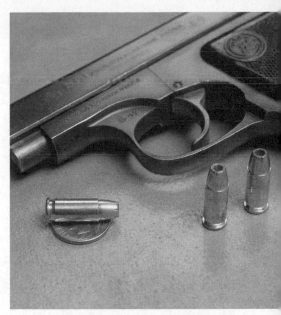

The .25 ACP, barely bigger than the dime on which it sits, has long been chambered in small pocket guns like this classic CZ45.

pistol. This round (and the gun which chambered it) became very popular as a so-called "ladies" gun. The .25ACP has often been compared to the .22LR in terms of effectiveness, though generally considered more reliable due to its centerfire design. It is often derided as a weak and ineffectual round yet remains popular. Taurus and Beretta still offer a good selection of pistols in .25ACP, as do "value" makers like Phoenix Arms. Companies producing reproductions of the original Baby Browning pistol come and go seemingly constantly.

.32ACP

The .32ACP is yet another round from the fertile mind of John Browning. Originally designed for his FN Model 1900 pistol, where it was called the 7.65mm Browning, it was later adopted by Colt and given its more common name. Intended as a self defense cartridge, the .32ACP has been chambered in a wide

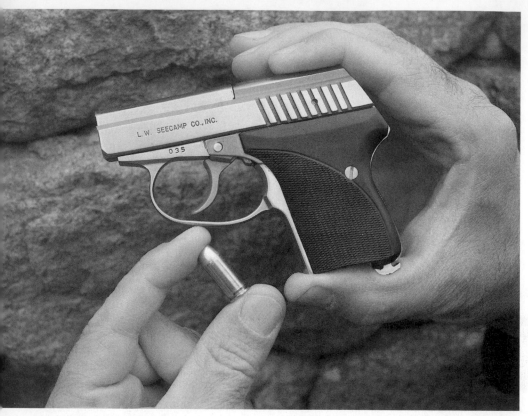

One of the more popular of the small pistol rounds, the .32 ACP has been chambered in a large number of guns like this classic Seecamp pocket pistol.

variety of handguns over the years and still accounts for a good number of pocket pistol sales. It is substantially more effective than the .25ACP in the self defense role, though most self defense authorities do not recommend it because of its diminutive size. Today it's chambered, at a variety of price points, in guns produced by Kel-Tec, Walther, Seecamp, and others.

.32 H&R MAGNUM

The .32 H&R Magnum was developed by Harrington & Richardson, in partnership with Federal Cartridge, in 1984. It's based on the much older .32 S&W Long, but lengthened for more powder capacity. While sometimes touted as a defensive cartridge, it seems to have attained greater respect in small game hunting. It was once available from a number of gun manufacturers, but today only Charter Arms still chambers it in their snubnose revolvers. It has been largely replaced by the .327 Federal.

.327 FEDERAL MAGNUM

This cartridge was a joint venture between Sturm, Ruger and Federal Cartridge. It is based on a stretched .32H&R Magnum case and was intended to provide the power of a .357 Magnum in a smaller package. It has been sold primarily as a self defense cartridge, and most of the guns so chambered have been of the short barreled, concealable variety. Ruger makes guns in this caliber, as do Smith & Wesson.

.380ACP

Yet another in the long line of cartridges designed by John Browning, the .380ACP is also called the 9mm Browning, 9mm Corto, and 9mm Kurz, reflecting its widespread use around the world. It is typically chambered in small, concealable autopistols from a wide variety of manufacturers and is extremely popular in the concealed carry market. Though considered by many to be slightly underpowered for personal defense, modern ammunition has significantly improved its performance in that role. All major ammunition manufacturers offer this caliber and many new guns have appeared in the last few years.

9X18 MAKAROV

This cartridge was developed in the Soviet Union as the round for their issued sidearm, the Makarov PM pistol. It saw wide adoption in the USSR as well as the various Eastern Bloc countries. In the late 20th century, large quantities of surplus pistols from various countries were imported to the U.S. and established this previously unknown round on our shores. While not available in large numbers, new guns from the Czech and Hungarian makers often come to the U.S. at bargain prices. Several domestic companies load this round and many more brands are imported.

The .380ACP, designed by John Browning, was intended for use in small pocket guns that could take advantage of its compactness. The .380 round shown fits into the tiny Colt Government Model .380 pistol on the bottom; note size difference with a Government Model .45!

The 9x19 round, also called simply the 9mm, is one of the most popular calibers in the world. Part of the reason is the large number of rounds many 9mm guns carry: the magazine of this Glock 19 holds 15 rounds.

9X19mm
(9mm PARABELLUM/9mm LUGER)

There have been a large number of 9mm caliber cartridges made around the world, but when someone says "nine millimeter" in the United States they almost always mean the 9x19. This is the most popular military caliber in the world (it became the issue sidearm in this country in 1985), and one of the top selling self defense calibers in this country. Virtually every maker of autoloading pistols offers guns in this caliber, and ammunition companies large and small produce a wide variety of ammo with various bullet weights and styles. Very few handgun cartridges are as ubiquitous as the 9mm Luger.

.38 SUPER

The .38 Super is also known as the .38 Super Automatic or sometimes "Super .38." It is a high pressure variant of the John Browning-designed .38ACP, and is usually marked with a "+P" to help differentiate it from that older round. The .38 Super was introduced around 1930, supposedly with enough power to shoot through car doors and the bullet-resistant vests being worn by gangsters. Though never wildly popular in this country, it did generate a small cult-like following. In the 1970s the Super enjoyed a major comeback as a competition cartridge for the then-new sport of Practical Pistol shooting, where its power and magazine capacity was a competitive advantage over the .45ACP. Today it remains a popular competition round, though no longer as dominant as it once was. Several manufacturers produce full-sized 1911-pattern autopistols chambering the Super, and most ammunition companies manufacture it as well.

.38 SPECIAL

It's been said that the .38 S&W Special is the most popular centerfire handgun round ever produced, and it's easy to see why. The .38 Special, formally known as the .38 Smith & Wesson Special, was introduced way back in 1898 as an answer to complaints about the .38 Long Colt's performance. It was originally loaded with black powder, but by the turn of the century was loaded with the increasingly popular smokeless powder. The Special turned out to be a very accurate cartridge for target shooting and a noticeably better defensive cartridge than the then-common .32 caliber guns issued in most police departments. Those attributes combined to make the .38 Special the dominant cartridge for both police and private use through the latter part of the 20th century. Though no police departments today issue revolvers chambered in .38 Special, many authorize it as an off-duty or backup caliber and it remains a top-selling target and self defense round. Almost every ammunition maker offers multiple Special loadings, and every revolver manufacturer offers guns in the caliber.

The .38 Special round is a perennial favorite of shooters in many disciplines, from target shooting to self defense. Virtually no cartridge is available in a greater variety of bullet weights and types than the .38 Special.

.357 MAGNUM

In the early 1930s the need was felt for a powerful handgun cartridge that could stop cars and pierce gangsters' bulletproof vests. Colt's .38 Super Automatic was just barely up to the job, and police voiced their desire for something better. Smith & Wesson teamed with ballistic experimenters Elmer Keith and Phillip Sharpe and came up with a lengthened .38 Special case loaded to very high velocities. The result was the .357 S&W Magnum, and it became the most powerful handgun round then in existence. The Magnum proved as accurate as its parent cartridge as well as possessing enough power to drop even large game. It quickly gained an almost mythical reputation as a self-defense and police service cartridge. Over the years Magnum re-

Is the .357 Really a .38?

The .357 Magnum is nothing more than a lengthened .38 Special case loaded to higher pressures, using the same bullets. Why, then, the difference in caliber designation? The .38 Special uses a .357" diameter bullet, but was called a .38 because of the diameter of the loaded case - approximately .38" in diameter. When the Magnum was introduced, it was felt that calling it a .38 would cause too much confusion; instead it was named for the bullet diameter. Oddly enough, no such confusion was caused by the .44 Special and .44 Magnum, which enjoy the same sort of relationship. Cartridge nomenclature can never be accused of being consistent!

The .357 Magnum is a lengthened .38 Special case with a larger powder charge. Specials can be fired in Magnum-chambered guns, offering the greatest flexibility.

volvers proved themselves not only capable but also versatile, as they also chambered the .38 Special rounds. For many people, one gun could do it all! Today the .357 is loaded by nearly everyone, and almost every revolver maker has at least one - sometimes many - Magnums in their lineup.

.357 SIG

The .357 Magnum developed an almost mythical reputation for stopping power in police service and self defense, and many enthusiasts openly wished for a cartridge offering similar performance for use in an autoloading pistol. in 1994 German gun maker SIG-Sauer teamed up with Federal Cartridge to produce the .357 SIG cartridge, which they felt duplicated the Magnum's performance. Essentially a .40 S&W cartridge necked down to accept the .357 diameter bullet, the round was originally offered in SIG-Sauer handguns. Positive reports from field use indicated that the new round performed very well in its assigned role, and popularity rose. Though still not quite a mainstream round, the .357 SIG has been adopted by many police agencies and has a strong following in the private sector self defense field as well. Many ammunition makers offer the .357 SIG, and gun makers like Glock, HK, and Smith & Wesson, among others, produce guns in this caliber.

10mm AUTO

The exact origin of the 10mm Auto is a bit murky. It may have started with a wildcat developed by Whit Collins in the 1970s, but beyond that there were several well-known personalities involved complete with conflicting stories about who did what first. What is clear is that the round was developed to be a powerful personal defense and service cartridge, and was first chambered in the ill-fated Dornaus & Dixon "Bren Ten."

Originally produced by Swedish ammunition manufacturer Norma AB, the 10mm Auto was given a big boost when the FBI adopted it in 1983 for their issue sidearm. Problems with the specially ordered Smith & Wesson auto pistols and complaints about excessive recoil eventually caused the FBI to drop the 10mm, but in the private sector it developed an almost cultish following.

The 10mm has been chambered in both autopistols and revolvers, and particularly in the latter developed an excellent reputation as a hunting cartridge. Today only a few gun companies produce 10mm pistols, the most notable being Glock. All of the major manufacturers (and a few minor ones) produce 10mm ammunition, though the offerings tend to be limited.

The .40 S&W, left, can be thought of as a shortened version of the 10mm Auto round on the right. The .40 S&W is more popular, but the 10mm is substantially more powerful. They are not interchangeable.

.40 SMITH & WESSON

The .40 Smith & Wesson was developed jointly by Winchester and Smith & Wesson. The FBI, in an effort to make their 10mm guns easier to handle, had settled on a loading which produced less power than the normal 10mm round. It soon dawned on someone that since the downloaded 10mm used less powder, it didn't need such a large case. Eventually this realization resulted in shortening the 10mm case, which essentially results in the .40 S&W. Once Smith & Wesson legitimized the new cartridge it rapidly gained a huge following in police use. It uses the same diameter bullets as the 10mm, but at a reduced velocity which makes it easier to control. Being shorter than the "Big Ten," it is also able to be chambered in smaller guns that are easier to handle. These traits caused fans of the 10mm to derisively refer to the round as the ".40 Short & Weak," but its performance has proved it to be anything but.

Today it is the most common caliber for police use in this country, as well as holding large shares of both the concealed carry and competition shooting market. Every pistol manufacturer makes handguns chambered in the .40 S&W, from full sized duty pistols to compact concealed carry arms. Virtually all ammunition companies produce the ammo, offering a wide variety of bullet types.

.41 MAGNUM

The .41 Remington Magnum is to the revolver what the 10mm is to autoloader aficionados: a very powerful, capable mid-caliber round that never seemed to really catch on. The .41 was originally to be a police service cartridge of modest velocity, but when development was finished what appeared was a fire-breathing monster. The .41 Magnum sends a 210 grain bullet out the barrel at over 1,500 fps and a 170 grain slug at a blistering 1,800 fps. The guns chambering it are, by necessity, large and heavy. The round also generates significant recoil. As a result

the .41 was never really embraced by law enforcement.

As a hunting round, however, it proved to be extremely capable and that is where its niche lies. Handgun hunters praise its performance and controllable recoil compared to the larger Magnums available. Today, .41 Magnum ammunition can be found in the catalogs of most of the manufacturers, and Smith & Wesson, Ruger, and Taurus all make revolvers chambering this high performance round.

.44 SPECIAL

The .44 S&W Special was developed in 1907 for a then-new Smith & Wesson revolver model. It was made by lengthening the .44 Russian, which was then a common black powder round. The .44 Special quickly gained a reputation for superb accuracy and was for many years used as a target/competition cartridge. It fell out of favor when its progeny, the .44 Magnum, was introduced. Today it lives on primarily in with revolver enthusiasts, and its popularity waxes and wanes perhaps more than any other cartridge. The majority of ammo companies produce the .44 Special, and there is a limited selection of revolvers - both double and single action - produced by the major manufacturers.

.44 MAGNUM

The .44 Special was so popular at one time that many enthusiasts experimented with "hot-rodding" the round. One of these was noted gunwriter Elmer Keith, whose high performance loadings of the Special caught the attention of S&W and Remington. They agreed to commercialize Keith's idea, only with a lengthened case to prevent its being chambered in guns not up to handling the greatly increased pressures. Despite being co-developed by S&W, the .44 Remington Magnum was first offered to the shooting public in the Ruger Blackhawk single action.

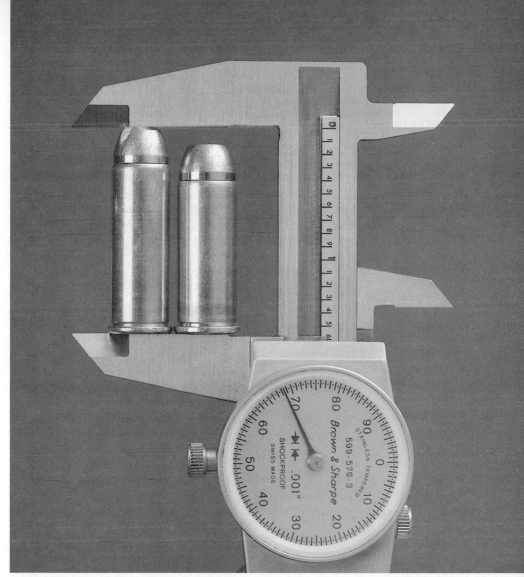

Like the .38/.357, the .44 Magnum is a lengthened .44 Special. Also like their smaller cousins, Specials can be fired in guns chambered for the Magnum, but not the other way around.

It was quickly adopted by other manufacturers. Its mainstream success is arguably due to its prominent role in the 1971 film "Dirty Harry", where the S&W Model 29 in which it was chambered was said to be "the most powerful handgun in the world."

The .44 Magnum and .44 Special share the same relationship that the .357 Magnum and .38 Special do: because they're simply lengthened cases, the Specials can be chambered and safely shot in a Magnum gun. The .44 Magnum is a superbly accurate hunting and silhouette competition round, though at the expense of significant recoil. Ammunition is widely available and guns are made by all of the major revolver manufacturers. It's also chambered in the Magnum Research Desert Eagle autoloading pistol.

.45ACP

The .45ACP, or simply ".45 Auto," has been called John Browning's crowning achievement. Developed for the Colt Model 1905 autoloading pistol, it came about as a response to the Army's request for a .45 caliber service cartridge. The Model 1905 would be considerably redesigned before its adoption as the Model 1911 pistol, but the Army apparently liked the cartridge from the beginning. It, along with the 1911, became almost a symbol of the American military until the adoption of the 9mm service cartridge in 1985. The .45ACP proved itself to be a capable military round and was soon adopted by the private sector as well. Today it is one of the top selling cartridges of all time, and can frequently be found in law enforcement, concealed carry, and competition settings. There are a wide number of autoloading pistols and revolvers chambered for the round - the latter using "moon clips" to hold the rimless rounds in their chambers - and it would be quite difficult to find an ammunition maker who didn't offer the .45 ACP. If any cartridge could claim the title of "classic," it would be this one.

.45 GAP

The .45 Glock Auto Pistol was developed by CCI/Speer Ammunition in response to a request from Glock for a shorter .45 caliber round that would duplicate the performance of the .45ACP. The design goal was to get the large caliber into a more compact firearm. It has been adopted by a few police agencies, and was for a short time chambered by at least two other gun manufacturers, but adoption in the private sector has been slow. Today only Glock makes pistols which chamber

The classic American handgun round: the .45ACP, designed for the Model 1911 in the background.

The .500 S&W Magnum is a heavy, high performance round for large revolvers. Photo courtesy of Hornady Manufacturing

their namesake round, and the ammunition selection is quite limited.

45 COLT

When people talk about handguns in the "wild" west, the cartridge that most commonly comes to mind is the .45 Colt, chambered in the most famous handgun of the time, the Colt Model 1873 Single Action Army. The round is often referred to as the .45 Long Colt, to differentiate it from the .45 Short Colt of the same period.

The .45 Colt was developed in 1871 and adopted by the U.S. Army in 1872. It has been in continuous production ever since. The .45 Colt has a reputation for great accuracy and power, and modern guns have allowed experimenters to greatly increase the power generated by the round. It is commonly used for hunting and vintage competitions like Cowboy Action Shooting. A wide variety of single action revolvers both domestic and imported are chambered for the round, and both Smith & Wesson and Ruger produce double action revolvers in .45 Colt.

.454 CASULL

The .454 Casull was developed in the late 1950s by Dick Casull and Jack Fulmer, but it was decades before it was chambered in a commercial firearm. The .454 is essentially a lengthened .45 Colt case, though strengthened considerably to contain the enormous pressures generated. It shares the same kind of relationship with the .45 Colt that the .357 Magnum does with the .38 Special: .45 Colt can be chambered and fired in a Casull, but not the other way around.

The .454 Casull is a very powerful handgun round, capable of taking large and dangerous game at extended distances. It develops much more energy than even the heaviest .44 Magnum rounds, and the recoil it produces is not for the uninitiated! It's produced in single shot pistols and both single and double action revolvers by a number of companies. The major ammunition companies make Casull ammo, as do a number of the smaller and specialized ammunition manufacturers.

The .454 Casull (right) is a large, powerful round suitable for big game hunting. Note size difference with .357 Magnum softpoint hunting round on left.

.460 S&W

Introduced by Smith & Wesson in 2005, this cartridge - despite the naming difference - is a stretched .454 Casull (which is in itself a stretched .45 Colt.) The .460 S&W can therefore be described as the grandchild of the venerable Colt round.

The .460 develops substantially more energy than the mighty .454 Casull, which itself is no weakling. With a 360 grain bullet, the Casull has roughly 1800 ft/lbs of energy. That same bullet from a .460 produces over 2800 ft/lbs of energy, which is in the territory of many rifle rounds. Recoil is best described as "awesome." It is chambered in revolvers by Smith & Wesson and Magnum Research, along with some single shot pistols; ammunition is available from the major ammo companies and some of the boutique ammunition loaders.

.480 RUGER

The .480 Ruger was developed in a joint effort between Sturm, Ruger and Hornady. The caliber is actually .475". The .480 was developed as a high-performance hunting cartridge for their Super Redhawk double action revolver. The goal was to strike a better balance between power and recoil than other "super magnums." It has an advantage over the .45-caliber class in that it can use much heavier bullets for greater penetration. It's currently available in revolvers from Ruger, Magnum Research, and Freedom Arms, and in barrels for single-shot handguns like the Thompson-Center.

.500 S&W MAGNUM

When "Dirty Harry" came out in 1971, Smith & Wesson achieved some notoriety (and not a small amount of financial gain) for producing "the most powerful handgun in the world." It wasn't, really, but the public didn't know that. After losing the title - justifiably - to newer cartridges like the .454 Casull, Smith & Wesson set out to recapture their title. The result was the mighty .500 S&W Magnum.

Developed jointly with Cor-Bon Ammunition, the .500 was correctly named: the bullet is exactly a half-inch in diameter. The size necessitated a new extra-large revolver frame to house it, which S&W calls the "X frame." The cartridge is able to generate over 3,000 ft/lb of energy with some bullets, and the recoil is difficult to control for all but experienced handgunners. Aside from the S&W revolvers, the round is also chambered in single shot pistols. Ammunition is available from Cor-Bon, Hornady, Winchester, and several of the smaller manufacturers.

.50 AE

The .50 Action Express was developed in 1988 by former ATF agent Evan Whildin, while working for the Action Arms Company. It was the second cartridge of his design - the other being the almost forgotten .41AE - and became a modest commercial success. It has found a small following in metallic silhouette competition as well as large game hunting.

The cartridge is designed to allow a half-inch bullet to be able to be fired in an autoloading pistol. The cartridge is of a rebated-rim design, meaning that the rim is of a smaller diameter than the rest of the case. The first gun to chamber the round was the Desert Eagle gas-operated autoloader from Magnum Research. It's also chambered in revolvers from Magnum Research, as well as Freedom Arms. Ammunition is available from Speer/CCI and Hornady, as well as imports from Israeli Military Industries (IMI.)

WHAT DOES "+P" MEAN?

In the U.S., ammunition standards are set by the Sporting Arms and Ammunition Manufacturers' Institute (SAAMI). Among other things, they establish the dimensions and pressure limits for all standard (commercial) cartridges.

The standard pressure levels SAAMI sets are sometimes very modest to maintain compatibility with all the guns which have ever chambered a particular cartridge. In the case of a cartridge like the .38 Special, which has been around a very long time, there may be some guns which would be damaged by a higher pressure round. There are a large number of more modern guns which chamber that round, however, and they're capable of handling higher pressures. Those higher pressures, even if still relatively modest, can often deliver much improved performance, but SAAMI's role as a standards agency demands that they set guidelines which work for every gun.

How to reconcile the difference between what the standard is and what the cartridge is capable of doing? SAAMI established the "+P" designation to show that a particular cartridge is loaded to a higher pressure, in effect creating a new cartridge. There are +P standards for a number of cartridges to allow ammunition manufacturers to produce loads which still meet standards, but deliver higher performance.

Not every cartridge has a +P standard, however. Some manufacturers - most notably the smaller "boutique" ammo loaders who are not SAAMI members - sell ammo with the +P marking for which there are no guidelines. Buyer beware!

SAAMI has a website where anyone can download the technical specs for every cartridge in their database. They also have a list of SAAMI members. Before using an unknown brand of ammunition, it's always a good idea to check to see if they're members of SAAMI. If not, proceed with caution.

WILL +P AMMO HURT MY GUN?

Remember that +P ammunition is loaded to higher pressures than standard rounds, resulting in higher velocity and recoil. This in-

The "+P" designates a round that is loaded to higher pressures than a standard round, should be used only in guns specified as safe by the manufacturer.

Many older guns cannot tolerate the use of +P ammunition. If in doubt, contact the manufacturer or a knowledgeable gunsmith.

What is a "Wildcat"?

A wildcat is a non-factory cartridge made to fit a specific purpose. Some shooting enthusiasts find that factory offerings don't possess all the characteristics they wish to have, and design their own cartridge which (hopefully) answers their needs. Sometimes it's a modification of an existing cartridge, while other times it may be something completely new.

In some cases, certain wildcats have become so popular that ammunition manufacturers adopted them to be factory produced. A good example in the handgun world is the powerful .454 Casull, which started as a wildcat and was made a mainstream commercial round in 1998. It's based on an existing cartridge, the .45 Colt, with a lengthened case for more powder capacity.

creased pressure and recoil increases the stress to which the chambers, cylinder or slide, and frame are subjected. This results in increased wear over standard pressure ammunition.

Because of this increased wear some manufacturers recommend against using "+P" rounds in guns chambered for a standard pressure cartridge (like the .38 Special.) Those that do approve higher pressure ammunition often require shorter inspection intervals to check for any problems.

Your handgun probably won't immediately break if you shoot "+P" ammo, but wear will be increased - sometimes noticeably. If you want to use "+P" rounds in a gun which has no specific rating, it is imperative that it be within factory specifications in every respect. If there is any deficiency, the increased wear from "+P" use can result in repairs being needed.

Be aware that the use of +P ammunition in a gun not rated for it will void any warrantee! Also remember that you will experience increased wear with every round of "+P" ammunition. It's often not a question of whether the gun can handle it, it's more a question of how much expensive maintenance it will require afterward. You don't have to be afraid of +P ammunition, just understand that each +P round you put through your non-rated handgun will result in more wear than a standard pressure load. It is up to you to maintain the gun appropriately.

Want to Know More?

Sporting Arms and Ammunition Manufacturers' Institute (SAAMI) - the standards organization for the shooting world. SAAMI, 11 Mile Hill Road, Newtown, CT 06470-2359. www.saami.org

Cartridges of the World by Frank C. Barnes - the singular reference to ammunition from all over the globe, including obsolete and historic cartridges. Should be on every serious shooter's bookshelf. ISBN 9780896899360. Krause Publications, (855) 864-2579 www.gundigeststore.com

The Cartridge Comparison Guide by Andrew Chamberlain - enables the reader to directly compare the ballistics of any rounds, rifle or handgun. Huge amount of information packed into this book, invaluable for hunters. ISBN 9780979033520. Krause Publications, (855) 864-2579 www. gundigeststore.com

Ammo & Ballistics by Robert Forker - ballistics (trajectory) tables for virtually every cartridge, from almost every manufacturer, available today. Absolute must for any long range shooting. ISBN 9781571573452. Krause Publications, (855) 864-2579 www. gundigeststore.com

Ballistics By The Inch - also known as "BBTI', this website chronicles experiments in ballistics, specifically on how the length of a barrel affects velocity. Very good and reliable information. www.ballisticsbytheinch. com

The Box O' Truth - readable, accessible information on terminal ballistics. While originally focused solely on penetration, their work has important information on bullet expansion as well. Reliable reference for the layperson, lots of myth-busting (and some occasional fun.) www.theboxotruth.com

Applied Ballistics by Bryan Litz - one of the best technical books on ballistics currently published. While focused on long range rifle competition, the technical information is applicable to all shooting. ISBN 0615452566. www.appliedballisticsllc.com

Understanding Firearm Ballistics by Robert A. Rinker - good introduction to the subject of ballistics. Suited for the person just getting started in understanding ballistics; clear and readable. Mulberry House Publishing, ISBN 0964559854.

CHAPTER 5

CHOOSING AMMUNITION

Handguns exist to fire ammunition. Without ammo, a handgun is little more than a decorative object; with proper ammunition, it becomes a useful tool for hunting, self defense, target shooting, and plinking.

Not all ammunition is the same, however. Handgun ammo comes in an almost bewildering variety of bullet shapes, weights, and purposes. Choosing the right one for the job is essential to getting good results.

BULLET WEIGHTS

Bullet weights in the U.S. are denoted in grains and abbreviated "gr". At 437.5 grains per ounce, that means a typical .45ACP slug weighs in at over half an ounce!

For any given caliber there will generally be a range of bullet weights available, allowing the shooter to pick the one that gives the results needed. The more popular the cartridge, the more choices the shooter will have - with revolver cartridges almost always having the greatest variety from which to choose.

Two bullets of the same caliber, but different weight. The heavier bullet has to be longer to accommodate the extra metal.

For any specific caliber, as bullets get heavier they also get longer. (Makes sense - if the diameter can't change, the length has to!) It's possible to have bullets that are so long they present fit or function issues in the gun, particularly with semiautomatic pistols. Autoloading pistols are the most sensitive to bullet weight changes. The dimensional limitations of the gun's magazine and the necessity to slide up a ramp and into a chamber limit how long the bullets can be. Their recoil systems require a certain amount of force to work correctly; too little and the gun won't cycle, too much and feeding problems can result. As a result, the range of bullet weights that will work in an autoloader tends to be narrow.

Autoloading pistols are sensitive to bullet weight, length, and shape. Ammunition for use in an auto must be thoroughly tested in the gun for reliability; these differently shaped rounds may not all feed reliably in this gun.

Revolvers aren't sensitive to bullet weights at all, and so can operate with even the shortest, lightest bullets. Heavier bullets work well too, as long as the overall length doesn't extend beyond the cylinder. As a result there is a wider variety of bullet weights in revolver cartridges than in autoloaders.

The single shot pistol has even fewer limitations than the revolver, as there is no cylinder in which the rounds need to fit. Single shot pistols can use very light to extremely heavy bullets, very long or very short, making them the most ammunition-versatile handguns.

BULLET TYPES AND SHAPES

Over the decades bullets have been designed to do a range of specific jobs, and as a result we have many different types to choose from.

The first choice is usually between lead and jacketed bullets. Lead bullets are just that: plain lead, no covering or coating. Lead bullets are the oldest and most basic type of projectile; they're cheap, widely available in a variety of weights and types, and often can be the most accurate because they can be precisely made to fit a specific gun's bore size.

Lead bullets are usually cast, though some are swaged (pressed) from very soft lead. Lead bullets generally have grooves in their surface which hold a solid wax-like lubricant to reduce friction when the bullet is fired. Lead bullets are usually found in the most affordable ammunition, because they are the least expensive bullet to make. In the larger calibers, solid lead bullets in heavy weights are often used by serious handgun hunters. While often handloaded, they can also be found in the products offered by specialized ammunition makers.

Revolvers are less sensitive to ammunition changes than are autoloaders. All of these different rounds will function in the revolver shown; the same is not true of autoloaders.

Lead bullets have the potential to be extremely accurate. Their sizes and weights are very consistent, as opposed to a jacketed bullet which can have variance in both the core and the jacket. (Variances affect the weight and concentricity of the bullets, which affects the deviation of any given round.) It's for this reason that high-precision handgun target loads, regardless of caliber, are frequently made with a plain lead bullet.

There are some downsides to lead. First is that they're, well, lead - a toxic heavy metal. When a lead bullet is fired the burning powder vaporizes a small amount of the metal on the base of the bullet. This vapor escapes into the atmosphere when the bullet leaves the barrel, and the result is a minute amount of exposure every time the gun is fired, particularly in an enclosed space like an indoor range. For this reason most indoor ranges today forbid the use of lead bullets, and many of them also restrict the firing of jacketed bullets that have an exposed lead base.

When a lead bullet is fired and squeezed through the barrel's rifling, a small amount of the metal is scraped off and adheres to the bore. As more and more lead bullets are shot, the amount of metal in the bore increases. After a large number of rounds are fired the bore's ability to stabilize and guide the bullet can be affected.

Called "leading," the metallic deposits can also cause an increase chamber pressures as it becomes more difficult to push the bullet down the barrel. For this reason some handgun manufacturers warn against the use of lead bullets in their guns - particularly those which use polygonal rifling in their barrels.

A bore that's been leaded is also difficult

Lead bullets are economical, easy to shoot, and can be astoundingly accurate.

to clean. We'll deal with cleaning in another chapter, but suffice it to say that a leaded barrel requires a lot of elbow grease.

All lead bullets will foul the bore to some degree. While it's possible to dramatically reduce the amount of leading by picking the correct hardness grade and carefully sizing the bullets to the bore, the shooter who doesn't handload can't do so. For these reasons lead ammunition today isn't terribly popular, except among handloaders and serious enthusiasts.

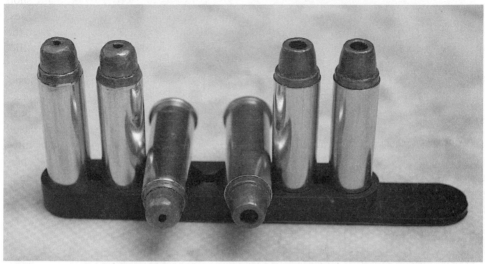

Lead hollowpoint bullets are very soft. If carried in a pocket, like those on the left have been, the nose can close up and fail to expand as designed. Compare to the undamaged examples of the same bullets on the right.

What is Polygonal Rifling?

Most barrels use conventional rifling, which consists of spiral grooves cut into the surface of the bore. The resulting lands press on the side of the bullet when it is forced, by the pressure of the combustion gases, into the bore. As the bullet is pushed down the bore, the lands are able to exert rotational force on the bullet, causing it to spin. It's an old system and by far the most common worldwide.

Polygonal rifling works differently. Imagine peering down a tube whose cross-section looks like a stop sign. Now twist that tube; the result is similar to the polygonal bore. The benefit of this style of rifling is that it has less friction than spiral grooves, in theory permitting higher velocities and longer barrel life. The gas seal between the bullet and bore is said to be better, and maintenance is easier - no sharp corners between land and groove to clean out.

On the downside, polygonal barrels are generally thought to be less accurate than grooved barrels, and most makers of guns using polygonal rifling caution against using lead bullets; the rifling is said to collect leading faster than conventional rifling, which theoretically can lead to dangerously increased pressures.

The polymer-coated bullet on left leaves fewer deposits in barrel than plain lead variety, is cleaner and safer to handle.

The Federal Nyclad is the only factory ammunition available with a coated lead bullet. It's designed as a low-recoil self-defense round.

An often overlooked problem with lead projectiles is that the bullets are soft and easily deformed. Spare ammunition, particularly hollowpoints, carried in a pocket can easily be dented and misshapen. Care must be taken to protect the exposed lead noses. Some lead bullets are available with polymer coatings that reduce or eliminate the bore contact which causes leading. They also keep the combustion gases from vaporizing the bullet's base, reducing airborne lead. They're only slightly more costly than plain lead projectiles, but for some reason have not become as popular as the uncoated variety.

Part of the reason may be a perceived lack of accuracy from the coated bullets. Because the coating can vary in thickness around the bullet the stability of the projectile may be affected, reducing accuracy. The coated bullets are also subject to the same wear and deformation issues that affect their plain brethren.

Coated bullets aren't generally found in commercial ammunition, though Federal Cartridge makes a nylon-coated round called "NyClad." Designed specifically to prevent barrel leading at higher velocities, the NyClad was intended as a self-defense round to be used in the small five-shot revolvers from companies like Smith & Wesson and Charter Arms. They are still available but somewhat difficult to find.

Lead bullets can also be plated with a very thin covering of metal, usually copper, in order to achieve an economical bullet which doesn't lead barrels. The plated bullets have the same advantages and disadvantages as the polymer coated variety, though in practice are a little more resistant to wear.

Plated bullets look like jacketed bullets, but the metal plating covers the entire bullet and is much thinner than a jacket.

The author has extensive experience with both coated and plated bullets, and finds that concerns about accuracy are well-founded. No matter the brand, it seems more difficult to get accurate loads from coated or plated bullets than from the plain lead or jacketed varieties.

Jacketed bullets consist of a lead core surrounded by a thick copper or brass shell, which is the "jacket." This hard shell makes them extremely durable and has the advantage of not leaving lead in the bore. They are also more expensive than plain lead. That thick, tough jacket also makes for a bullet that doesn't deform as readily when impacting a target. This can enhance penetration on things like tough-skinned animals, but it can also be so tough that the bullet doesn't mushroom or expand unless properly designed. The tough jacket also requires a larger powder charge to move down the bore at a specific velocity than does a plain lead bullet, resulting in increased recoil and muzzle blast.

A jacketed bullet has a lead core surrounded by a tougher copper jacket. This jacketed bullet, a Hornady FlexLock, is a hollowpoint with a special insert to aid in consistent expansion. *Photo courtesy of Hornady Mfg.*

BULLET SHAPES FOR EVERY USE

Round nose bullets, sometimes referred to as "ball" ammunition, are the staple of all shooting. They're cheap and widely available in plain lead, jacketed, and plated varieties, and come in a range of bullet weights. Most often used as plinking, competition and training rounds, their streamlined noses are autoloader-friendly and make revolver speed reloads easier. That same streamlining makes them less than desirable as self defense or pure target shooting rounds, as they do not expand or cut clean holes as they traverse the target. You'll see them abbreviated as "RN" (round nose) or "LRN" (lead round nose). The jacketed varieties are usually referred to as "FMJ" (full metal jacket), though technically the term could apply to any solid bullet shape carrying a jacket. A variant of the round nose is the flat nose bullet, which can be either round or more of a flattened cone shape. Their use, availability and cost are similar to the round nose and are generally considered to be interchangeable. The wadcutter is a simple cylinder of lead that's flat on the leading side. The flat surface cuts a clean, full-caliber circle in a target which makes scoring easy. Those clean holes make the wadcutter the standard target competition load. Wadcutters are often seated so that their face is flush with the case mouth, which makes reloading the

The round nose bullet is a common bullet style, available in jacketed, plated, and plain lead.

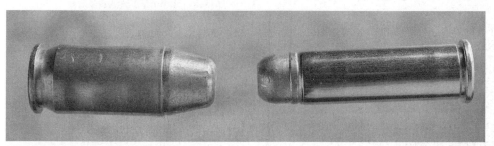

he flatnosed bullet may be in the form of a flattened round (right) or a truncated cone.

revolver slower and more difficult. That flat face also makes them unusable in autoloaders. Wadcutters are almost always loaded to very mild velocities, and are generally light to medium weight for their caliber. There are two wadcutter varieties: where the trailing side has a cavity they're called hollow base wadcutters (HBWC), and if both ends are flat they're called double ended wadcutters (DEWC.) Semi-wadcutters are a cross be-

tween a regular wadcutter and a round-nose, the semi wadcutter ('SWC" or "LSWC," the "L" standing for "lead") consists of a tapered, flat-pointed nose of less than full diameter that appears to sit on top of a wadcutter. The taper makes them easier to drop into a revolver chamber or feed through an autoloaders, while the full diameter shoulder cuts a clean hole in the target (though not of the "paper punch" appearance of a

The flat-faced wadcutter on left is a revolver round noted for its accuracy and mild recoil. Note the difference between that and the semi-wadcutter on the right.

The semi-wadcutter is a good compromise between a round nose and a flat wadcutter, and will often feed in autoloaders where flat wadcutter will not.

regular wadcutter.) The SWC is available in heavier weights than regular wadcutter. Semi wadcutters are also available in a hollowpoint configuration, abbreviated labeled "SWCHP" or "LSWCHP." Semi-wadcutters are a staple of bullseye shooting where autoloaders are used, such as at the Camp Perry championships. A softpoint bullet is a type of jacketed bullet (technically, they're semi-jacketed, as the jacket ends partway up the bullet nose.) For hunting applications it's desirable for a bullet to expand, or increase in diameter, when it contacts the target. This produces a larger wound channel and dispatches the animal more humanely. The jacket on a bullet is very resistant to this kind of deformation, in comparison to the soft lead core which makes up the rest of the bullet, making it difficult to get a jacketed bullet to expand. By jacketing only the back two-thirds of the slug and leaving the soft lead nose exposed you get the advantages of a jacketed bullet with some of the performance of a soft lead bullet: it doesn't lead the bore, stays together even in very tough tissue, and still expands reliably. Softpoints are usually available only in the heavier weight classes, are usually used in revolvers and single shot pistols, and are most often abbreviated "SP" or "JSP."

Hollowpoints are bullets whose nose is dished, or hollow. On contact with the target the hollowpoint's thin walls are pushed outward by the hydraulic pressure of tissue and fluid, which dramatically increases the bullet's diameter. The cavity that the bullet causes in the target is greatly enlarged and promotes rapid incapacitation. For this reason they are the preferred choice for law enforcement and self defense use, where rapid incapacitation of an attacker is greatly desired. Because their design, construction and testing are more involved than any other bullet, hollowpoints usually carry a premium price. Hollowpoints are available in plain

Marking rounds are specialized cartridges for police, military, and self defense training. Used properly, they leave a bright mark when they hit their target but will not cause injury. Photo courtesy of GD-OTS/Simunition

lead, plated and jacketed varieties and usually carry the designator "HP" somewhere in their shorthand.

Frangible bullets are designed to disintegrate, or at least break up into smaller pieces, on impact with the target. Sometimes called "pre-fragmented," their main use is to increase shooter safety when using hard targets such as steel plates. Some makers have sold frangible ammunition as self defense rounds, touting their minimized penetration effects, though they have not been generally accepted by the self defense or law enforcement communities.

Marking cartridges are specialty rounds made of plastic and filled with paint or dye. When they hit a target the capsule bursts and releases the paint onto the target. They're made as aids in law enforcement and self defense training, where two or more participants role-play attackers and defenders and actually shoot at each other. These rounds are very low powered and produce little recoil, but are still dangerous and require proper safety gear and procedures to minimize risk. Such rounds are often generically referred to as "simunitions," but the term is actually a trademark for the marking rounds produced

by GD-OTS, a Canadian firm. Similar products are produced by Speer. They're generally made in only the most popular calibers.

AMMUNITION FOR SPECIFIC USES

Picking ammunition for specific handgunning activities often involves a lot of personal preference, and there are no doubt people who can quibble with any (or all) of the choices below. However, even with a wide range of opinion as to what works best, some choices are more common (and logical) than others. Here are the general trends among shooters in each of these disciplines, based on the author's experiences and observations.

PLINKING

For plinking the primary criteria is cost. An afternoon plinking session with friends (and perhaps a few responsible kids) can burn up a lot of ammunition, making economy a real concern. Plinking doesn't demand ultimate accuracy, just reliable functioning. Solid round nose bullets are the perfect choice, either lead (usually abbreviated LRN), plated (RN) or jacketed (FMJ). Round nose flat points (RNFP) and flattened

Plinking is recreational shooting at its purest, is not demanding of bullet shape or weight - anything works!

or truncated cones (TC) are interchangeable for this use.

COMPETITION SHOOTING

Bullseye competitors using revolvers almost invariably choose wadcutter loads (WC, DEWC, or HBWC designations) for the clean holes they cut in the targets. Autoloader shooters will usually employ semi-wadcutters (SWC) to get close to the same performance, and some revolver shooters do as well. PPC competitors and Bianchi Cup shooters will often make the same choice, for the same reasons. Bullet weight and recoil concerns will generally be secondary to accuracy. If they heavier bullet is more accurate, that's what the shooter will use in these precision events.

Competitors in Steel Challenge types of matches will often use a light hollowpoint (HP or JHP) round, which reduces recoil and more reliably disintegrates when it hits the steel plates. This greatly reduces any chance of ricochet, and the hollowpoints also reduce wear and tear on the expensive hardened steel - a fact much appreciated by match sponsors. Autoloaders will generally be set up specially to run on these light loads, using weaker recoil springs to compensate for the lower recoil impulses. Speed is everything, and the faster the gun recoils and gets back on target the better the score.

Cowboy action shooters are limited by match rules to solid lead ammunition, usually made of very soft lead (to better disintegrate on the steel targets) and loaded to very low velocities (to reduce recoil to the greatest degree possible). The term "cowboy load" has come to denote this special type of soft, solid, low recoil ammunition.

The various action shooting events, such as USPSA/IPSC and IDPA, see a large variety of bullets used. The targets are not scored with the hair-splitting precision of the bullseye types of competition, so having really sharp full-caliber holes is not the most important concern. Instead, since these matches have a prominent time component and jams waste time, shooters usually make their choice on the basis of reliability in their gun - with accuracy considered second. In any given match it is common to see people using a variety of different bullets: round nose (and their relative, the truncated cone), semi-wadcutter and even hollowpoints are all commonly seen. Semi-wadcutters are common with revolver shooters, while truncated cones and flattened round nose bullets seem to be favorites of the autoloader shooters. Some shooters will use hollowpoint rounds, as long as they prove to be reliable and accurate in their guns. Bullet weights are generally selected to minimize recoil, but since there is a power requirement that

Handgun Silhouette competition needs tough, heavy bullets to knock down the large steel targets. 180 grain bullet on right does that much better than the lighter 125 grain bullet commonly found in the .357 Magnum.

The softpoint bullet combines a half-jacket and an exposed solid lead tip to promote mushrooming on impact along with deep penetration. Often chosen for hunting medium to large game.

each competitor must meet, light loads are not allowed.

Silhouette shooters have an interesting problem: they need to be as accurate as possible at long distances, but still deliver a lot of energy to topple heavy steel targets. This requires a bullet with a streamlined shape for the best trajectory, tough construction to hold together while the target is being moved, and heavy weight to deliver the most energy at the longest distances. Revolver users will usually pick a round nose or truncated cone bullet, which are relatively streamlined, in heavy-for-caliber weights: in .357 Magnum, for instance, 180 grain and 200 grain bullets are the most used. At the longest distances, 158 grain slugs - the heaviest normally found on a dealer's shelf - don't have enough power to reliably knock over the targets.The single shot handguns using pistol calibers will use the same choices, while those firing rifle calibers or the specialized high-power handgun cartridges will usually pick a very streamlined bullet. These long, tapered bullets will give the flattest trajectory at long ranges, making those tough shots just a little

easier. The bullets will generally be on the heavy side and of robust construction to really knock the steel animals down.

HUNTING

Ammunition for hunting is chosen primarily for the ability to incapacitate animals quickly, regardless of the size of the quarry, but also taking into consideration the goal of the hunt.

Those doing varmint hunting or pest control usually pick a rapidly expanding bullet, which results in very large wounds and the fastest, cleanest kills. These rounds will usually destroy a lot of flesh and organs in the process, which make them the most humane choice because the animal is dispatched as quickly as possible. Despite delivering the most humane kills, they aren't really suitable for animals where the meat or hide is being recovered. Most such rounds tend to be very light for the highest velocity, which enhances the wounding potential.

For rimfires, these bullets are the high velocity hollowpoints or - in the case of the .17 HMR - bullets with a polymer tip specially designed to initiate rapid expansion when they hit a target. Centerfire handgun cartridges will be equipped with hollowpoints, the lighter the better, while the specialized single shot handgun rounds will often be loaded with polymer tip or softpoint bullets which reliably expand at long distances.

Smaller animals hunted for meat or pelts are often taken with solid bullets, often of the flat-tipped variety, for a good combination of humane incapacitation and small wounds that save meat and fur. Some hunters of meat animals, particularly with the .22 Long Rifle, swear by subsonic hollowpoints that expand to make a larger wound, but not so violently that they destroy a lot of valuable meat. Some pelt hunters recommend the .17 HMR loaded with the most fragile bullets, which make extremely small entry wounds but fragment violently inside the animal, resulting in very fast kills without a secondary (exit) hole.

The hollowpoint is designed to expand rapidly when it contacts the target, and speeds incapacitation. Generally considered the best choice for self defense.

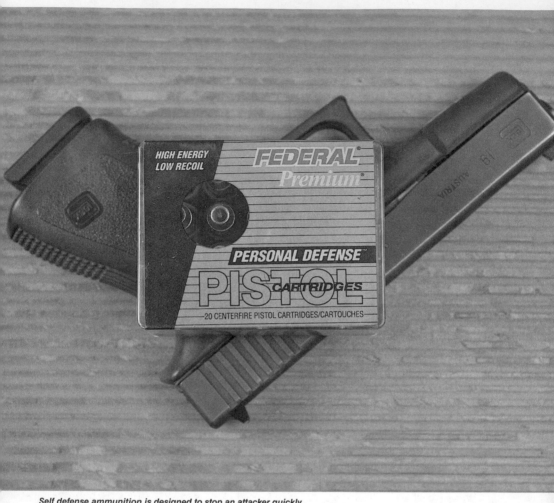

Self defense ammunition is designed to stop an attacker quickly.

Large game is usually taken with bullets that produce deep, penetrating wounds to maximize damage to vital organs. Fast-expanding bullets have a tendency to produce wounds which are too shallow to do this, so the watchword for big game hunting with a handgun is "controlled expansion." Depending on the quarry and the cartridge, bullet weights will generally run to the heavy side, usually with a softpoint or bonded hunting hollowpoint. (The heavier the bullet in any given caliber, the deeper the penetration will usually be.)

Hunting hollowpoints are designed for relatively slow expansion and resistance to fragmentation; fragmenting bullets tend to produce shallow wounds and destroy meat, neither of which is conducive to a successful hunt.

The largest and most dangerous game - from North American bears to the large African species - is usually taken with the most powerful cartridges firing solid, hard lead bullets for maximum penetration through thick hide and heavy bone.

SELF DEFENSE

The purpose of a self-defense handgun is to cause an attacker to stop what he/she is doing. This is very different from a hunting scenario, where killing is the primary goal. A wound can be lethal yet still not stop the attacker; a .22 Long Rifle wound to the abdomen may prove fatal a week later, but if it doesn't stop the attack, then it has failed at its task. There are many people alive today who were wounded in shootouts with police but were still able to kill an officer, regardless of the wounds they received. A self defense bullet needs to penetrate far enough so that it can reach vital organs at any angle, yet not so far that it comes out the other side and endangers innocent bystanders. It also needs to produce a solid wound track; bullets with very streamlined shapes, like the solid round nose, tend to slip through flesh without doing much damage. Bullets that make a large wound track that doesn't easily close on itself are generally the most effective.

To do all those things, self defense experts almost invariably recommend a good hollowpoint bullet that penetrates and expands reliably - but doesn't penetrate too far. Most modern hollowpoint designs are quite good at this.

How to find a "modern" hollowpoint? Without having to learn the history of hollowpoint bullet design, the easiest method is to look for one that the manufacturer calls "bonded." Bonded hollowpoints are simply those where the jacket and core are locked together, preventing the jacket from separating inside the target. These are usually designed specifically for each caliber to expand reliably at handgun velocities, maximizing their ability to stop a threat.

In general, bullet weights should be in the middle of those available for the caliber. For instance, 9mm defensive hollowpoints are available from 115 grains up to 147 grains.

The 124-127 grain slugs are in the middle and make great choices.

The exceptions are for the smaller calibers, where heavier bullets should be chosen to maximize the otherwise shallow penetration, and the Magnum calibers where lighter bullets are picked to prevent the over-penetration those rounds are known for.

Many people pick higher velocity +P ammunition for personal defense, and in fact the majority of uses for +P ammo are in self defense. The +P ammunition usually results in better incapacitation, but at the risk of increased recoil and decreased shooter control. Since a single round is not likely to be effective at immediately stopping a threat, it is likely that a defender will need to fire multiple rounds to stop the threat. If the shooter is unable to do that because of the increased muzzle flip and recoil of the +P rounds, then it's better to go back to a standard pressure load; the increase in controllability and faster follow-up shots is generally thought to offset any perceived loss of effectiveness.

Despite many years and many attempts, there is no way to predict if any given bullet will be effective against a human adversary. The best course of action is to pick a good gun and good ammunition, then get professional training in how to best employ them.

Want to Know More?

BOOKS ON AMMUNITION

Cartridges of the World by Frank C. Barnes. ISBN 9780896899360. Krause Publications, (855) 864-2579 www.gundigeststore.com

The ABCs of Reloading 9th Edition, by C. Rodney James. ISBN 9781440213960. Krause Publications, (855) 864-2579 www.gundigeststore.com

Reloading for Handgunner by Patrick Sweeney. ISBN 9781440217708. Krause Publications, (855) 864-2579 www.gundigeststore.com

AMMUNITION MAKERS

Winchester - besides their famous guns, Winchester also produces some of the most respected hunting, law enforcement, and self defense ammo available. Olin Corporation, 190 Carondelet Suite 1530, Clayton, MO 63105. www.winchester.com

Remington - if it seems that Remington makes everything, that's not far from the truth. Their line of ammunition is large and well established, and covers every handgun use. Remington Arms Company, LLC, P.O. Box 700, Madison, NC 27025; (800) 243-9700 www.remington.com

Federal - one of the largest "old line" ammunition companies in the U.S., Federal has an extensive line of target, defense, and hunting rounds. Federal Cartridge Company, 900 Ehlen Drive, Anoka, MN 55303-7503. (800) 831-0850 www.federalpremium.com

CCI/Speer - CCI is a major player in the shooting world. Their CCI line is primarily rimfire and shotshell, while Speer Ammunition produces centerfire ammo that takes advantage of the premium bullets produced by their namesake bullet division. The CCI/Speer Gold Dot line of defensive ammunition is considered by many to be a standard. CCI/Speer, 2299 Snake River Avenue, Lewiston, ID 83501. (866) 286-7436 www.cci-ammunition.com www.speer-ammo.com

CorBon - one of the first makers of premium self-defense ammunition. Their large line now includes practice and hunting ammo in a very wide variety of calibers in addition to several types of defensive and law enforcement ammunition. Dakota Ammo, Inc., 1311 Industry Rd., Sturgis, SD 57785. (800) 626-7266 www.corbon.com

Wolf - popular line of value-priced ammunition, they also have a premium line of pistol ammo. P.O. Box 757, Placentia, CA 92871. (888) 757-9653 www.wolfammo.com

Black Hills - respected high precision ammunition manufacturer, popular with competitive shooters. Makes self defense, hunting, target loads for many handgun calibers. PO Box 3090, Rapid City, SD 57709. (605) 348-5150 www.black-hills.com

Fiocchi - Italian manufacturer of a very wide range of handgun ammunition, from blanks to self defense to hunting rounds. Has ammunition for rare calibers not readily available from U.S. manufacturers. 6930 N. Fremont Road, Ozark, MO 65721. (417) 725-4118 www.fiocchiusa.com

Hornady - ammunition for self defense, law enforcement, hunting, and cowboy shooting. Very innovative and well regarded bullet designs. 3625 West Old Potash Hwy., Grand Island, NE 68803. (800)338-3220 www.hornady.com

Double Tap - high performance heavy hunting and self defense ammunition, especially in the Magnum calibers. 646 S. Main St. #333, Cedar City, UT 84720. (866) 357-10MM www.doubletapammo.com

Old Western Scrounger - specializes in hard-to-find ammunition in rare calibers, both new and vintage. The only source for many odd cartridges. 219 Lawn Street, Martinsburg, WV 25405. (304) 262-1651 www.ows-ammo.com

Grizzly Performance Ammunition - makes handgun hunting ammunition, specializes in the larger Magnum calibers. P.O. Box 1466, Rainier, OR 97048. (503) 556-3006 ww.grizzlycartridge.com

Ultramax - many different calibers and bullet types, including specialty law enforcement and cowboy ammo. Ultramax Ammunition, 2112 Elk Vale Road, Rapid City, SD 57701. (800) 345-5852 www.ultramaxammunition. com

BULLET MAKERS

Swift - though best known for rifle bullets, they also produce a line of heavy hunting hollowpoints for handguns. PO Box 27, Quinter, KS 67752. (785) 754-3959 www.swiftbullets.com

Sierra - well established maker of hunting and high-precision competition bullets. 1400 West Henry Street, Sedalia, MO 65301. (660) 827-6300 www.sierrabullets.com

Speer - renowned for hollowpoint designs for self defense and hunting. Speer Bullets, 2299 Snake River Avenue, Lewiston, ID 83501. (866) 286-7436 www.speer-bullets.com

Hornady - wide selection of jacketed bullets, from round nose to high performance hollowpoints. 3625 West Old Potash Hwy., Grand Island, NE 68803. (800)338-3220 www. hornady.com

Berry's - makers of plated bullets, the only company that makes a plated and encapsulated wadcutter style. 401 North 3050 East, St. George, Utah 84790. (800) 269-7373 www.berrysmfg.com

Rainier Ballistics - produces a wide line of totally encapsulated plated bullets. 4500 15th Street East, Tacoma, WA 98424. (800) 638-8722 www.rainierballistics.com

Powerbond Bullets - plated bullets in a variety of styles. P.O. Box 123, McCammon, ID, 83250. (208) 880-4124 www.powerbond-bullets.com

Precision Bullets - polymer coated bullets that resist leading. 33112 CR2142, Kemp, TX 75143. (903) 498-8451 www.precisionbullets. com

Montana Gold - complete line of jacketed bullets, including hollowpoint styles. P.O. Box 9050, Kalispell, MT 59904 (406) 755-2717 www.montanagoldbullet.com

Penn Bullets - long established east coast producer of lead bullets. P. O. Box 756, Indianola, PA 15051. (412) 767- 4670 www. pennbullets.com

Meister Bullets - long-time producer of quality cast lead bullets and ammunition. P.O. Box 1835, Ozark, MO 65721. (417) 708-5279 www.meisterbullets.com

Desperado Bullets - specially made soft lead bullets for cowboy action shooters, designed to work safely at the lower pressures and velocities in that sport. PO Box 165, Dayton, WA 99328 866-428-5538 www. cowboybullets.com

Oregon Trail Bullets - makers of highly accurate cast lead bullets. PO Box 529, Baker City, OR 97814. (800) 811-0548 www.lasercast.com

Leadhead Bullets - cast lead bullets used by major ammunition manufacurers. 349 NW 100th Street, St. John, KS 67576. (620) 549-6475 www.proshootpro.com

Beartooth Bullets - cast lead bullets, specializes in heavy hunting styles. PO Box 491, Dover, ID 83825. (208) 437-1865 www. beartoothbullets.com

Winchester - many of the bullets used in Winchester's premium ammo are available as reloading components. Olin Corporation, 190 Carondelet Suite 1530, Clayton, MO 63105. www.winchester.com

Remington - like Winchester, sells their quality bullets to reloaders. Remington Arms Company, LLC, P.O. Box 700, Madison, NC 27025 (800) 243-9700 www.remington.com

TRAINING/MARKING CARTRIDGES

Simunition - General Dynamics Ordnance and Tactical Systems Canada Inc., www. simunition.com

Speer Force-On-Force - ATK Armament Systems, 2299 Snake River Avenue, Lewiston, ID 83501. (800) 831-0850 www. forceonforce.com

CHAPTER 6

HANDGUN SHOOTING TECHNIQUES

Since a handgun is capable of being fired by only one hand, it's imperative that the grip be strong enough to control the recoil generated.

It's not unusual for shooting enthusiasts - and even sometimes shooting instructors - to disagree on handgun shooting technique. There are many different activities in which handgunners might participate, and not all of them call for the same shooting technique.

Of course the person doing the shooting may find that one way works better than another for a specific activity, and sometimes physical needs may dictate the technique used. Sometimes a technique might need to be modified to fit the individual; the help of an experienced and educated instructor can be helpful in those cases.

Here are the most common techniques and variations, with some notes about the activity in which they are most commonly used.

GRIP (AKA "GRASP')

The handgun, particularly in the heavy Magnum cartridges, is capable of generating recoil forces that tax the muscles and joints of even the strongest shooters. It's necessary that the shooter's grasp be strong enough to hold the gun on target, resist movement from the trigger press, and control the recoil that it generates. A weak, tentative grasp will not do any of those things, and makes it very difficult to achieve accurate hits.

Getting the hand as high as possible, so that the web of the thumb is in firm contact with the frame tang of the autoloading pistol, greatly increases recoil control.

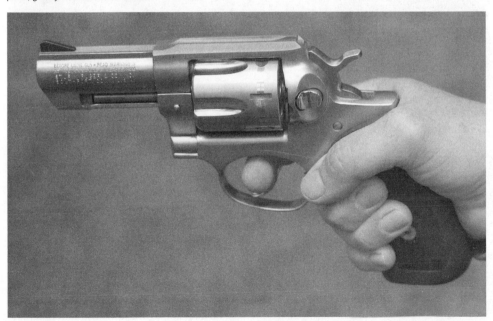

The revolver doesn't have a frame tang, so getting a high grip means to the top of the frame shoulder, but not so high as to interfere with the hammer.

The single action revolver should be gripped as high as is comfortable.

The trigger finger is indexed on frame above trigger, should be kept there unless actually firing.

On an autoloader, the middle finger of the firing hand should be in contact with the bottom of the trigger guard.

The shooting hand should be placed as high on the back of the grip as possible; a high grip helps to maximize control and recoil recovery. The lower the hand is placed, the more pronounced the muzzle flip from recoil will be.

On an autoloading pistol, the grip should be high enough that the web between the thumb and forefinger contacts the underside of the grip tang. On a double action revolver, the hand should be high enough that the web is even with the top of the frame shoulder.

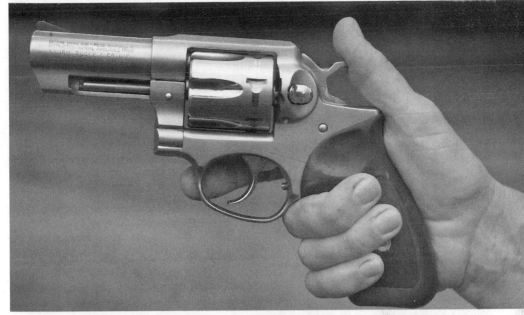

If the space between the revolver triggerguard and grip is filled, as on this Ruger GP100, the middle finger of shooting hand should be in contact. If not, the grip should be as high on the back as is comfortable without regard to middle finger placement.

On a single action revolver there is usually no frame shoulder. The hand should be placed as high as is comfortable, without interfering with the operation of the hammer.

The fingers of the shooting hand are wrapped around the grip (with the trigger finger extended on the frame above the trigger until ready to fire).

On an autoloader, the top of the middle finger should be in contact with the bottom of the triggerguard.

On a revolver, the top finger should be as high up as is comfortable in the space behind the triggerguard. (This isn't always possible, especially on guns where the grips don't fill that space).

The shooting hand thumb can be curled down in a "hammer fist" grip, or pointed toward the muzzle. Having the thumb forward works best with an autoloader, because it forces the web of the hand into firm contact with the frame tang and helps control muzzle flip.

On autoloader, thumb pointing forward places maximum flesh under the tang, increasing control.

With a revolver, curl both thumbs down - pad on fingernail.

The heel of the support hand is placed into the gap on opposite side of the grip.

The forefinger of the support hand should be in contact with the bottom of the triggerguard.

On a revolver there is no tang to provide that mechanical advantage. Curling the thumb down gives a solid constriction between the thumb and middle finger, keeping the gun from moving downward, inside of the hand, during recoil.

There are those who shoot the revolver with thumbs forward, like they would with an autoloader. This puts the front thumb close to the cylinder gap, which can result in injury.

The fingers of the support hand are laid over the top of the shooting hand fingers.

On an autoloader, the thumbs of the hands are layered alongside the frame of the pistol.

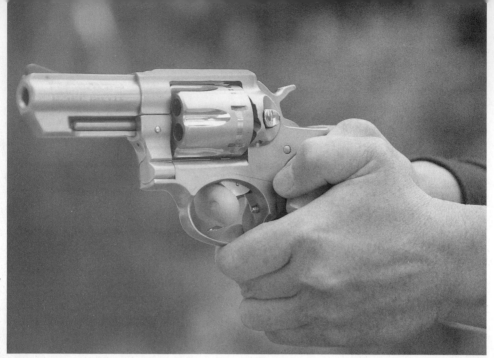

Best thumb position for revolvers is "pad on fingernail," which keeps the thumbs out of the blast from the barrel gap.

Regardless of the thumb position, the grip will leave a gap on the opposite side of the gun. If shooting with two hands, the heel of the support hand is laid into that gap.

The forefinger of the support hand should be in contact with the underside of the triggerguard.

The fingers are wrapped around the grip, on top of the shooting hand's fingers.

With the thumbs forward grip, the support hand thumb is simply pointed forward and the shooting hand thumb is layered on top.

Sometimes the curled thumbs get in the way of the trigger finger; one solution is to move the thumb up onto the first knuckle of the shooting thumb.

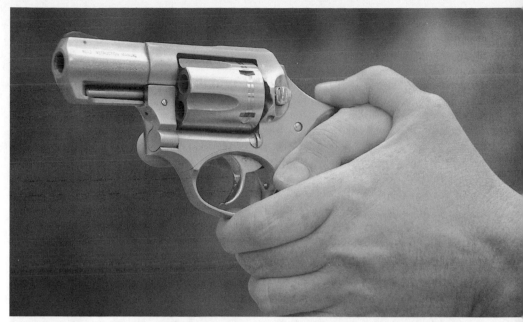

Wrapping the support hand thumb around the grip is a last-resort technique to deal with extremely long fingers on a small gun. This is not a generally recommended practice, as doing so on an autoloading pistol will result in serious lacerations from the slide.

For revolvers, the proximity of the barrel gap makes a forward thumbs position uncomfortable, or even unsafe. The best course is to place the pad of the support hand thumb on top of the fingernail of the shooting hand thumb.

ALTERNATIVE REVOLVER THUMB POSITIONS

Sometimes the thumbs get in the way of trigger manipulation when shooting a revolver. There are a couple of variations that may help make the necessary clearance. First, the support thumb can move up and rest on the shooting thumb's knuckle. This sometimes results in slightly diminished recoil control and is indicated only when the shooter's hands are too big to do the "thumb on thumbnail" placement.

The other option is to wrap the support hand thumb around the back of the gun. This is a possible solution for those whose fingers are much longer than average. However, it should only be adopted if the shooter will never use an autoloader!

Placing the support hand thumb across the back when using an autoloader places it in a position where the slide can hit it during recoil. The slide is driven back with considerable force, and it's quite possible to be severely injured when that happens. There are many instances of the slide cutting through the thumb clear down to the bone! Autoloading pistols should never be held in this manner.

GRIP PRESSURE

There are many theories about how much pressure the shooter should exert in the grip. Many defensive shooting instructors recommend gripping the gun with an equal amount of pressure in both hands, and as much as the shooter can comfortably generate. This is often called a "crush" grip, and is intended to provide maximum control over the gun in rapid fire with powerful defensive ammunition.

The way to determine this level of pressure is to grasp the gun properly, extend the arms as if shooting, and increase the grip pressure until the hands shake from the exertion. Then relax the pressure just enough so that the shaking stops. Pay attention to how that feels, then recreate it whenever you're actually shooting. After a few repetitions, it will become second nature.

Many competition and target shooters recommend a somewhat looser grip, often stating that it should be like a firm handshake. The goal is to allow the trigger finger to operate as freely as possible and to minimize gun movement and fatigue during extended shooting competitions. Again, this should be a matter of experimentation for the shooter, but always with the intended use in mind.

SHOOTING STANCES

The stance is simply the position the body takes while shooting. There are a huge number of possible combinations of head, arms, hands, torso, legs, and feet, and lots of debate about all of them, so we'll concentrate on the most commonly taught.

STANDING STANCES

The Isosceles is so named because the shooter's arms, if viewed from above or below, make an isosceles triangle with the body. This squares the body to the target,

The isosceles stance is so named because the arms form a readily identifiable triangle. Note that both arms are extended equally, placing the gun in the center of the shooter's eyesight.

Classic Isosceles shooting stance.

Locked elbows give maximum control in stressful conditions, and are well suited to shooters with less muscle mass.

Competition version of Isosceles uses elbows as shock absorbers, is not as aggressive as the classic version.

which is consistent with observed reactions to lethal attacks, and is an advantage to police officers and soldiers whose body armor is most effective when directly facing a threat. Most defensive shooting instructors today teach some form of the Isosceles stance for those reasons.

Like most shooting techniques, there are variations of the Isosceles stance. The classic or "natural" Isosceles starts with the feet and body squared off to the target, with the feet roughly shoulder width apart. The knees are very slightly flexed to allow the torso to lean forward from the waist, and for the hips to push slightly back. This brings the most weight behind the gun and lowers the body's center of gravity for the best resistance to recoil forces.

Once the proper grasp has been achieved, the arms are simply thrust straight out, each extending the same amount. This brings the gun to the centerline of the body, allowing the head to center itself behind the gun. This is important to those whose eyes are cross-dominant, where the primary (shooting) hand and the primary (favored) eye don't match. With the Isosceles, eye dominance is not an issue; the shooter doesn't even need

Some recommend placing the strong side foot well back to further enhance recoil control.

to know that he/she has a dominance mis-match. The head is brought down to align with the sights, further adding to the strong forward weight bias.

The elbows are locked to help channel the force of recoil through the skeletal frame and into the mass of the torso. This makes the Isosceles a good choice for shooters without a lot of muscle mass, as it allows the whole body to aid in controlling recoil during rapid fire.

A variant, called the competitive or re-laxed Isosceles, allows the elbows to be slightly bent, using the arm muscles as sort of shock absorbers to help control recoil. The relaxed Isosceles is generally best used by those shooters with good muscle tone in their arms.

Note foot position of buttressed Isosceles compared to the classic version.

The Weaver stance has elbows bent, body bladed to target.

In contrast to the classic Isosceles, the competitive Isosceles variant brings the gun up to the sightline rather than the rather than the head down to the gun. The upper body is not leaned forward as aggressively. The knees are slightly bent, enhancing recoil control. Like the classic version, the feet are squared to the target to allow rapid movement in any direction, necessary in the action shooting games, as well as defensive encounters.

Another variant of the classic Isosceles is championed by some defensive shooting instructors. The foot position is changed so that the strong side foot is slid back and the knee locked, with the feet at the corners of an imaginary square box.

Proponents of this position feel that it helps to control strong recoil forces. Critics charge that it is not as flexible, that it doesn't allow for fluid movement during a fight, and that it doesn't fit in with the body's natural threat reactions. For these reasons it is not as commonly taught as it once was.

There are many fans of what's come to be called the Weaver stance, named for the man who is most associated with it: Jack Weaver. While it has fallen out of favor as a defensive shooting technique, there are people who find that their best accuracy is achieved through some variant of the Weaver - and there are many variants. Even Jack Weaver didn't do it the same way every time, so it's hard to say which variant is the most authentic, but here is the most mainstream version.

The Weaver stance's most distinguishing characteristic is the bending of the arms at the elbow. Rather than being straight (or fairly so) in the Isosceles, the arms are bent noticeably to allow for a greater shock absorber effect.

The support elbow is brought down, pointing roughly at the shooter's support side foot. This makes the support arm a little shorter than the shooting arm, requiring the shooter to blade him/herself toward the target. The feet are adjusted to allow this to happen, which places the strong side foot distinctly behind the support side foot.

The support hand pulls the gun back into the shooting hand, which must push forward to compensate. The result is strong isometric tension which helps with recoil control. The knees are very slightly bent, and the body stays relatively upright. The Weaver stance brings the gun much closer to the shooter's eyes than the Isosceles, which may be a problem for those with close-focus issues.

The Weaver is best suited to those with good muscle mass in their arms and torso, as it relies on strong muscle tension to achieve full control over the gun. It is also less appropriate for those armed professionals who wear body armor, as it exposes the weaker side panels and arm holes to enemy fire. The Weaver is also not well suited to those with weak wrists.

The push-pull tension tends to make for a very stable platform, at least until the tensioned muscles become fatigued or start trembling. Many people find that they achieve their most solid shooting platform, if not the best recoil control, with the Weaver stance. It makes for a good hunting and target shooting stance.

There is one variation of the Weaver stance that has become known on its own.

Weaver stance support elbow points at the ground.

Chapman stance has shooting arm locked straight like the Isosceles stance, but support hand bent and push-pull tensioned like the Weaver stance.

Most famously used by champion shooter Ray Chapman, from whom it gets its name, the Chapman stance combines the straight shooting arm of the Isosceles with the bent support arm and push-pull tensioning of the Weaver. The body leans forward just a little more than in the Weaver, and the feet and torso are a little more square to the target.

The Chapman stance gives some of the recoil control of the Isosceles and some of the stable platform of the Weaver. Those who don't have the muscle mass or the strong wrists necessary to make a Weaver work find that the Chapman gives them some of the

same advantages in a stance that they can use. Many shooters consider it the best combination of attributes for general handgun shooting, and point out that it is the same stance that is usually used with the rifle and shotgun.

With both the Weaver and Chapman, shooters with cross-dominance will need to make adjustments to their head position to compensate - including, if necessary, closing the non-dominant eye.

Most handgun shooting is done from a standing position, but there are times when it's desirable (or necessary) to shoot from another position. Sometimes it's to get bet-

Double high kneeling is fast and easy to do, but doesn't really give much of a stability advantage.

Dropping lower allows better use of low cover or supports.

ter stability, while other times it's to remain safely behind cover or to be able to shoot around an obstacle.

Stability is an often misunderstood concept in shooting a handgun. Even when using both hands to grasp the pistol or revolver, there is still only one point of contact with the body: the hand. It's not possible to add a point of contact to a handgun without turning it into a rifle, so the next best course is to add a point of contact as close to the gun as possible. This usually means resting the hands or arms on something that isn't moving as much as they are.

Dropping to one knee is very fast; height of position is varied by bending forward at the waist.

Braced kneeling gives noticeable stability increase, and is no slower than unbraced positions.

KNEELING

The kneeling position is primarily useful for shooting over cover, as it lowers the profile of the shooter considerably. In a self defense scenario it's useful for staying protected behind cover while returning fire, while in a hunting situation it's valuable for crouching in concealment so the quarry doesn't spot the hunter.

There are a number of different kneeling positions. The double kneel is fast to assume and can be used for both high and low cover, but offers little stability increase over a standing position.

A more mobile option is to simply drop to one knee, leaving the other in a raised position. Like the double kneel it offers little stability enhancement, but is faster to get in and out of.

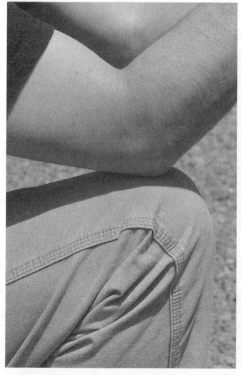

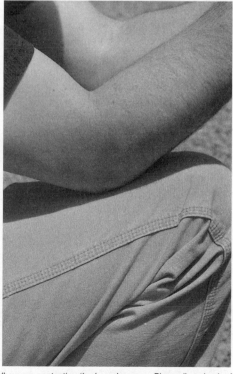

Picture at far left shows incorrect elbow placement - bones of elbow are contacting the bony kneecap. Place elbow back of kneecap, or kneecap behind elbow.

Classic sitting position is stable. Like braced kneeling, the contact between elbows and knees should not be bone-to-bone.

Sitting with one knee up as in the braced kneeling position is stable, comfortable. Note contact position.

Leaning back against a solid object greatly increases stability of sitting position, and extends duration of comfort.

The classic braced kneeling is the only style that does result in a definite increase in stability, because it adds a contact point to the arms. Bracing the elbow on the knee significantly reduces wobble in the hands and increases accuracy, particularly at longer distances. It's not as flexible in terms of the cover that can be used as the other kneeling methods, because it's limited to one height.

If the braced position is chosen, it's important that the elbow and kneecap not come into direct (bone-to-bone) contact. Place the knee on the fleshy backside of the elbow, or place the elbow behind the kneecap where there is some padding.

SITTING

The big advantage of the sitting position is that it can deliver significant gains in stability, as well as being able to use very low cover. It's also the slowest to get in or out of, but it does have the advantage of being very comfortable for longer periods of time.

Classic prone position raises body on elbows and enables shooter to see over low cover, but can be tiring to hold f or long periods.

Many shooters find that simply bringing one knee up greatly increases comfort in the prone position.

Placing one knee in the up position and curling the other leg under is similar to the braced kneeling, but with slightly better side-to-side stability. Bringing both knees up and bracing both elbows is better still, but generally can't be held for long periods of time.

The best enhancement to a sitting position is to use a solid object - a tree or vehicle - as a backrest. This allows the knees to be brought up higher, and the point of contact with the arms much closer to the hands. This reduces gun wobble to the greatest degrees, and is comfortable for extended shooting sessions or long waits for game to appear.

PRONE

The prone position isn't used much in handgun shooting, though it may have

What is the Difference Between Cover and Concealment?

Many people use the terms cover and concealment interchangeably, but they're not the same! Cover is anything which will stop (or dramatically slow) a bullet, keeping the person behind it safe from injury. Concealment is anything which hides the person behind it, but it may not provide cover.

A clear Lexan sheet will stop bullets, but still allows a clear view of anyone using it - it is cover, but not concealment. A blue plastic tarp hanging from a tree will generally hide anything on the other side, but a bullet won't even notice it's there; it is concealment, but not cover. A brick wall is both - it stops (most) bullets and hides the person crouching behind it.

In rollover prone, shown here with left-handed shooter, support side knee is brought up and body rolls over to the strong side; cheek contacts bicep.

some utility in certain kinds of hunting situations and is sometimes touted as useful in police training.

A standard prone position has both elbows on the ground, raising the gun far enough off the ground for the sights to be acquired. It also gives clearance over low obstacles that otherwise might get in the way of making the shot.

Some shooters bring a knee up toward the chest, which makes the position a little more comfortable.

Rollover prone is the most stable position. The support side knee is brought up far enough to cause the body to roll over a bit to the shooting side. The cheek can now be rested on the shooting arm's bicep, which allows the sights to be seen even with

The Creedmore position. A leather leg protector is strongly recommended when using this position with a revolver!

the pistol's butt rested on the ground. The rollover prone is also the most comfortable for long periods of time, but the low position may allow obstacles on the ground to interfere with the shot.

The rollover prone is most commonly seen in competition shooting, particularly the accuracy-intensive games like NRA Action Pistol.

CREEDMORE

A position used primarily in long range handgun competitions, the Creedmore is used to stabilize handguns with long, heavy barrels and may have some utility to the handgun hunter. The shooter lays on his or her back with the support hand propping up the head. The shooter's legs are bent and the feet are flat on the ground, with the gun's barrel resting on the side of the leg. (Caution: the barrel must be long enough to clear the leg, and a protective pad is necessary for revolvers to keep hot gases from the barrel/cylinder gap from burning the leg!)

Variations on the Creedmore have the legs tilted as far as possible to the support side, or with both knees dropped toward the ground, to give a flatter area on which the barrel can rest. The shooter can also use a back rest, such as a tree or stump, to provide a less fatiguing method of keeping the head up.

RELOADING TECHNIQUES

Sooner or later the handgun is going to run dry and need to be reloaded. Just as in shooting stances, there are many variations on reloading techniques - so if you see a technique that's not the same as you see here, give it a try - it may work better for you.

The following techniques presume a right-handed shooter. Left-hand variants will be shown at the end of this section.

Photo 1

Photo 2

AUTOLOADING PISTOL
BASIC AUTOLOADER RELOAD

The most important reloading method to master is when the pistol is at slide lock, out of ammunition. In defensive shooting circles this is called an emergency or critical incident reload; in competitive shooting it's gen-erally referred to as a speed reload. There are many variations in procedure for this kind of a reload, so we'll start with one most suited to - and efficient for - defensive purposes.

When the autoloader is empty the slide should lock back. (Photo 1) Some - very few, however - autoloaders lack this feature, and

Photo 3

Photo 5

Photo 4

on occasion any gun can fail to lock back.

When that happens, the support hand comes off the gun to retrieve a fresh magazine. Note that the shooter continues to look at the target (or threat) as the shooting hand starts to bring the gun back into the the body's "workspace" - the area in front of the chest where strength and agility are at their greatest. (Photo 2)

As the gun is being brought back into the workspace, the shooter releases the magazine by pressing the magazine release button or lever. (Photo 3)

Holding the gun in approximately the normal shooting orientation allows gravity to assist in the magazine falling free from the gun. In the rare case that it doesn't, a swift downward jerk of the gun will usually dislodge it. In extreme cases it may be necessary to use the support hand to remove the magazine.

Photo 6

Photo 7

Photo 8

Photo 9

By the time the empty magazine has been jettisoned, the support hand should have located the spare magazine. (Photo 4)

The gun should now be in the shooter's workspace; at this point the magazine is retrieved and, keeping close to the body, brought toward the gun. (Photo 5)

The magazine is inserted into the grip. (Photo 6)

The new magazine is pushed firmly home with the palm, with enough force to make sure that it is solidly latched. (Photo 7)

The support hand rotates up to grasp

Photo 10

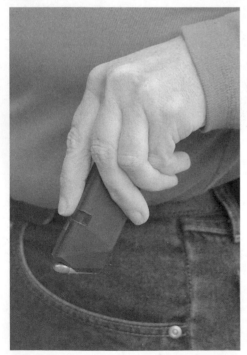

Photo 11a

Photo 11b

the top of the slide behind the ejection port. (Photo 8)

The slide is pulled sharply back, then released and allowed it to close on its own. (Photo 9) (Resist the urge to ride it forward - that's how misfeeds start!)

The gun is now reloaded and ready to shoot again.

VARIATIONS

There are an incredible number of variations in this basic reload sequence and many people champion different methods. Here are some of the more common variations and the reasons for them.

To look or not to look? Self-defense trainers often recommend that the reload be accomplished without looking at the gun. Part of the rationale is that it's better to be watching the threat, allowing the shooter to take evasive action while the gun is being reloaded

Competition shooters, on the other hand, don't have an adversary with which to be concerned, and so they often reload gun not in front of the chest, but in front of the face so that they can see the reload being done. (Photo 10) This is said to allow for the fastest reload possible, as sight is used to positively align magazine with the magazine well.

Bullets forward or backward? Another source of variation regards how the spare magazine is carried. The most prevalent method, particularly in the various types of competitive shooting games, is to carry the magazines with the bullets facing forward; when the magazine is retrieved the forefinger is on the front of the magazine and is pointed toward the magazine well, guiding the magazine home. (Photos 11a and 11b)

The other method is to carry with the bullets facing backwards so that on retrieval the thumb is on the back of the magazine. (Photos 12a and 12b) The thumb is used in the

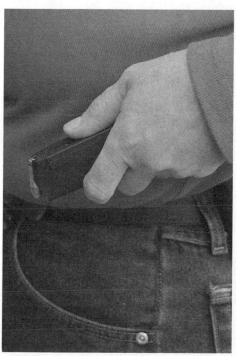

Photo 12a

Photo 12b

Photo 13

Photo 14

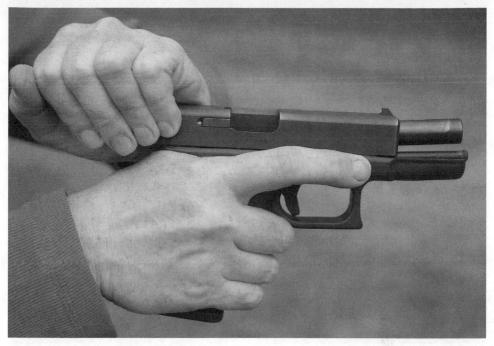

Pulling back the slide and releasing to chamber a round may be more reliable, works with guns that lack a slide lock function.

same way that the forefinger is used in the other method, pointing at the magazine well and guiding the magazine.

Supporters of the bullets forward technique point out that all of the best competitive shooters use that technique, which suggests that it is the fastest. The bullet backwards technique, however, requires less manipulation to perform as the magazine doesn't need to be flipped before it's inserted into the gun. With practice, most shooters find either works well.

Guns with magazine releases on the heel. Some guns, usually those with military or European origins, have their magazine releases on the heel of the gun butt. These aren't quite as efficient as the more common button-release type and require slightly different technique.

When the gun runs empty the support hand slides down to the butt instead of immediately retrieving the spare magazine.

The magazine release is pushed with the support thumb, either forward or backward, depending on how the gun is designed.

The magazine will eject only partway; the support hand grabs the protruding portion of the magazine and pulls it free. The rest of the reload is then completed the conventional way. (Photos 13 and 14)

Run the slide or use the slide lock? Defensive shooting teachers point out that using the slide lock lever to release the slide requires tactile sensation that may not exist in the stress of a lethal encounter, and often recommend the procedure shown. In addition, running the slide by hand has the virtue of working with all guns, even those without a slide lock lever. It's not dependent on the location of such a lever, and tends to work better in cold or wet conditions.

Competitive shooters, interested in the last bit of speed and not needing to worry about the natural loss of sensation due to

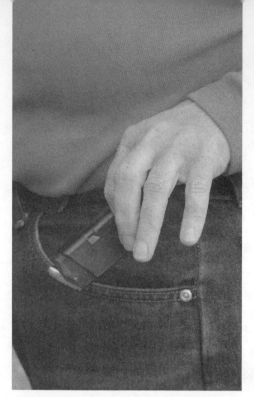

Photo 15a

Photo 15b

Photo 16a

Photo 16b

stress, find that using slide stop lever is faster and brings the support hand closer to the position it needs to be to re-establish the two-hand firing grip.

TACTICAL RELOAD

There is another kind of reload generally referred to as a "tac-load," short for "tactical reload." The concept is to reload at a convenient point before the gun runs empty, retaining the unused rounds in the magazine in case they're needed later. The concept of the tactical reload is not universally accepted, and many defensive shooting trainers no longer teach the technique. It is still often used in some of the shooting sports like IDPA, however.

There are many tac-load techniques espoused, and it would take an entire chapter to catalog all of the variations. The most commonly taught tac-load brings the gun into the working area, usually in front of the face and just below eye level, without ejecting the magazine.

The support hand retrieves the spare magazine, leaving the current magazine in the gun. As the spare magazine is retrieved it's grasped between the thumb and forefinger finger of the support hand and brought to the butt of the gun. (Photos 15a and 15b)

The partially empty magazine is ejected from the gun onto the heel of the palm, where it's grasped between the heel and the ring and pinky fingers of the support hand. It's held in this position as it's removed from the gun. (Photos 16 a and 16b)

The support hand, now holding both magazines, rotates to bring the new magazine into the magazine well. (Photo 17)

Photo 17

Photo 18

The new magazine is pushed into the gun with enough force to latch solidly. (Photo 18)

The partially depleted magazine is then stored in a pocket or other convenient place.

There are many, many variations on this technique. A common variant that some trainers recommend is to retrieve the new magazine as shown, but grasp the ejected mag between the pinky and ring fingers. (Photos 20a through 20d)

Photo 20a

Photo 20b

The tactical reload in all its variations is highly dependent on the user's anatomy and needs to be practiced extensively to be done smoothly.

Finally, it's important to note that many defensive shooting trainers don't recommend practicing any sort of tac-load at all, preferring instead that the student concentrate his or her limited training time on the emergency reload.

Photo 20c

Photo 20d

DOUBLE ACTION REVOLVER

There are more variations in revolver reloading techniques than there are in auto-loader techniques. The following is referred to as the "universal revolver reload," because it works exactly alike on all major types of revolvers: Smith & Wesson, Ruger, and Colt. It even works with the oddball Dan Wesson revolver!

When the need to reload is recognized, the gun starts to move backward, toward the body, while the trigger finger goes to its safe position on the frame. (Photo 21)

The support hand moves forward so that the thumb is on the frame in front of the cylinder and the two middle fingers touch the cylinder on the opposite side. (Photo 22)

The shooting hand thumb is pointed straight forward, toward the muzzle, regardless of whether the gun is a Colt, Ruger, or S&W. As that happens the wrists and forearms are twisted to rotate the gun to the

Photo 21

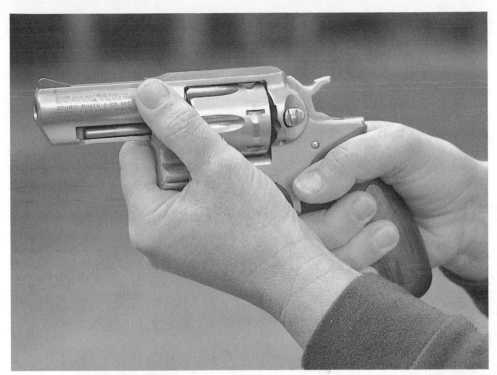

Photo 22

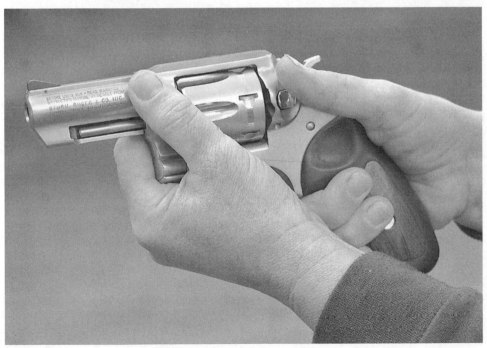

Photo 23

right. The gun will rotate in the hands into a muzzle-up position, and as that happens, the cylinder release will make contact with the shooting thumb. (Photos 23 and 24)

As the gun continues to rotate it will push the release into the stationary thumb, and the release will be depressed to unlatch the cylinder. A S&W will release very early in the

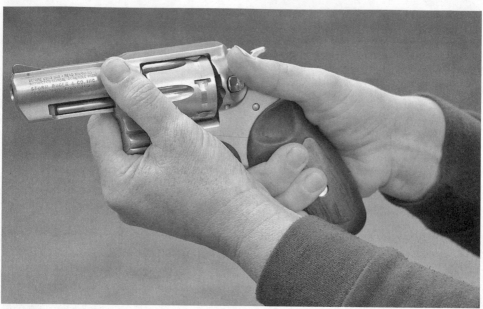

Photo 23

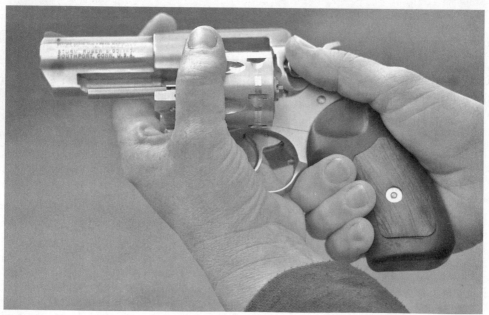

Photo 24

rotation, a Ruger a little later, and a Colt very late. As the cylinder unlatches, the fingers of the support hand will naturally apply pressure to open the cylinder. (Photo 25) It's the movement of the gun against the fingers that does the work!

As the muzzle starts to come to the vertical position, the gun rotates around the middle fingers of the support and the cylinder is pushed fully open. The cylinder is grasped between the thumb and fingers to immobilize it. The shooting hand comes off the grip, leaving the gun held by the support hand, and moves to eject the empty casings. (Photo 26)

The firing hand is flattened and the palm

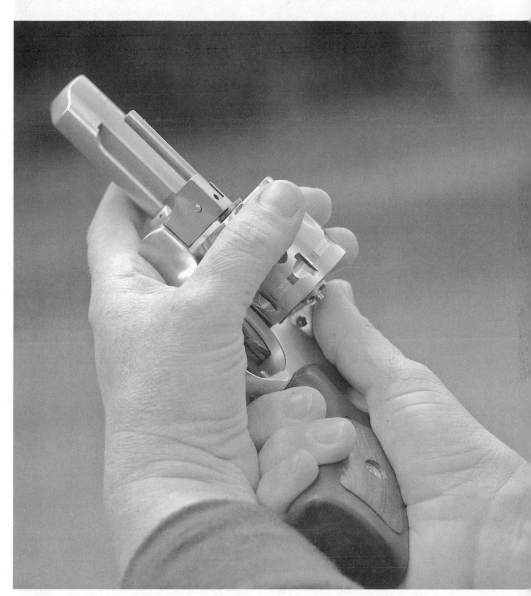

Photo 25

Photo 20

swiftly strikes the ejector rod. This accelerates the brass and tends to throw it clear of the cylinder, even with short ejector rods. Velocity is more important than force, and it's important that the ejector rod is struck one time. (If there are any cases which fail to clear the cylinder, multiple ejections will not clear. They will, however, significantly raise the risk of a case-under-extractor jam. If there are cases that don't clear, they should be picked out of the cylinder before spare ammunition is retrieved.)

After ejection the muzzle is rotated toward the ground and the gun drops to the mid-abdominal level. The shooting hand is now free to retrieve the spare ammunition, and inserts the fresh rounds into the cylinder. (Photos 27 and 28)

Once the rounds are in the cylinder, the shooting hand reestablishes its firing grip. The hands are now rolled together, as if closing a book. Ready to shoot again!

SINGLE ACTION REVOLVER

There are many ways to reload the single action, but this method has shown itself to be adaptable to the widest variety of hand sizes and dexterities.

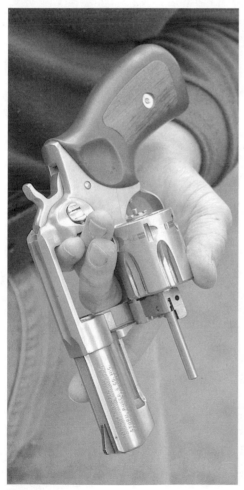

Photo 27

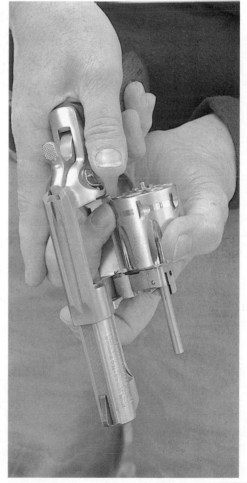

Photo 28

Photo 29

Photo 30

Photo 31

Safety note: a few modern single actions are able to be loaded to their full capacity, but older guns (and their modern reproductions) cannot. For those guns the hammer must rest on an empty chamber; if that's not done, a surprisingly small force on the hammer spur can cause the gun to fire. Many authorities suggest that all single actions be treated in the "empty under the hammer" manner to avoid tragic mix-ups, and this has been the standard practice for many years. The following reloading procedures respect this longstanding practice.

When all rounds have been fired, the hammer is brought to half-cock and the loading gate opened with the shooting hand. (Photo 29) (Some single action designs, such as the Ruger Blackhawk and Super Blackhawk, do not require the hammer to be place in half-cock; opening the loading gate itself releases the cylinder to rotate.)

The gun is held by the shooting hand and the muzzle is brought to vertical. This allows the spent cases to easily drop from the cylinder when ejected. The support hand reaches under the barrel to locate the head of the ejector rod. (Photo 30).

The ejector is swiftly depressed, ejecting the first empty case. (Photo 31)

The support hand rotates the cylinder until the click of the cylinder pawl is heard; the rotation must be stopped at just the point the click is heard. At that point the next chamber should be in alignment with the ejector rod and the loading gate. (Photo 32)

The case is ejected, and the process is repeated until all chambers are empty.

After all the casings have been ejected, the

Photo 32

support had cradles the gun and the muzzle is dropped to point at the ground. (Photo 33)

The shooting hand is now free to retrieve the spare ammunition and insert the first round into the waiting chamber. (Photo 34)

When the first chamber has been loaded, the support hand rotates the cylinder twice - bypassing the second chamber and leaving it empty. The third chamber is loaded, the support hand rotates the cylinder to the next

Photo 33

Photo 34

chamber, and the remaining three rounds are loaded in the same manner. (Photo 35)

After the last chamber is loaded, the loading gate is closed. DO NOT ROTATE THE CYLINDER AT THIS POINT! (Photo 36)

The shooting hand re-establishes a firing grip and brings the hammer to full cock. This advances the cylinder once, which brings the second chamber - the one left unloaded - under the hammer. (Photo 37)

Photo 35

Photo 36

The hammer is then lowered safely by holding the hammer spur as the trigger is pulled. The hammer is allowed to slowly come to the rest position on the empty chamber. (Photo 38)

LEFT HAND VARIATIONS

Some guns, it seems, were designed to torture left hand shooters by making some manipulations very difficult! There are generally workarounds, however, and in some cases they actually have advantages.

Photo 37

Photo 38

On autoloading pistols without ambidextrous magazine releases, the left hand shooter is advised to push the release with the trigger finger.

AUTOLOADERS

There are two concerns about reloading the autopistol left-handed. First is the magazine release; while there are a few guns on the market with ambidextrous release buttons or levers, not all have them. The best course of action is for the left handed shooter to release the magazine with either the trigger finger or, depending on the exact spacing of the magazine release, the middle finger of the shooting hand. The support hand retrieves the magazine and inserts it in the same manner as a right-hander.

Releasing the slide is another matter, as very few guns have ambidextrous slide locks. This is where recommended method of pulling the slide back and releasing it with the support hand is the best solution.

DOUBLE ACTION REVOLVERS

The hardest part of doing a left-handed reload with a double action revolver is getting the cylinder unlatched. With some attention to technique, however, it's not all that difficult. (Photo 39)

When the gun is empty, the support hand

is brought forward so that the cylinder can be "pinched" between the thumb, fore- and middle fingers. (Photo 40)

The forefinger of the shooting hand operates the cylinder release. Many shooters find it helpful to use the side of the forefinger

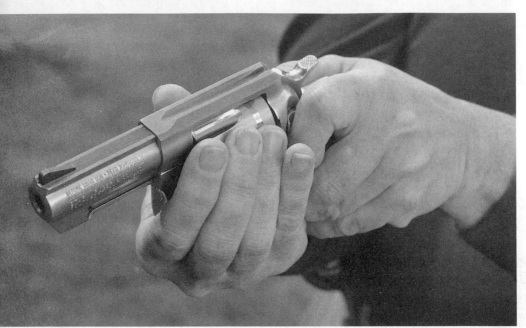

Photo 39

Photo 40

to do so, supported where necessary by the thumb on the opposite side of the frame.

As the cylinder unlatches, rotate the frame around the right thumb, so that the thumb ends up sticking through the frame to help grasp the cylinder. The cylinder should be held firmly by the right hand fingers. (Photo 41)

Strike the ejector rod swiftly with the left palm, once only. (Photo 42)

Rotate the muzzle toward the ground, retrieve the spare ammunition with the left hand and insert into the cylinder. (Photo 43)

Re-establish a firing grip; pull the right thumb out of the frame, and close the cylinder with the fingers. (Photo 44)

Go back to a two-handed grip to resume shooting. (Photo 45)

Photo 42

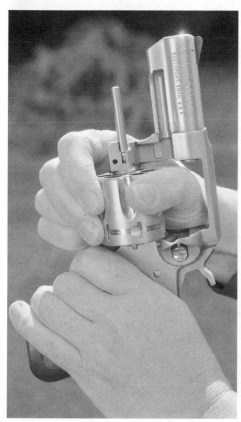

Photo 41

Photo 43

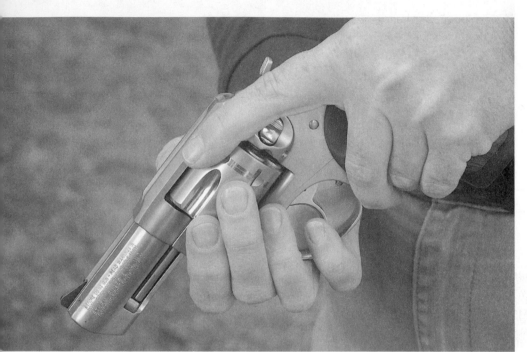

Photo 44

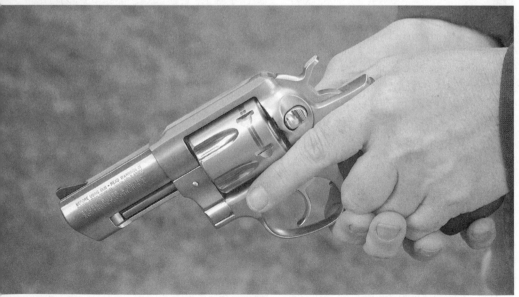

Photo 45

Photo 46

Photo 47

Photo 48

SINGLE ACTION REVOLVERS

The shooting hand stays on the grip and thumbs the hammer back to half cock, while the support hand thumb opens the loading gate. (Photo 46)

The shooting hand thumb rests on the hammer spur so the loading gate remains clear, while the support hand rotates the cylinder and operates the ejector. Tilting the gun slightly to the right may help the eject cases drop free. (Photo 47)

The ejector is pushed swiftly to drive the spent cases from their chambers. (Photo 48)

The support hand rotates the cylinder to the

Photo 49

Photo 50

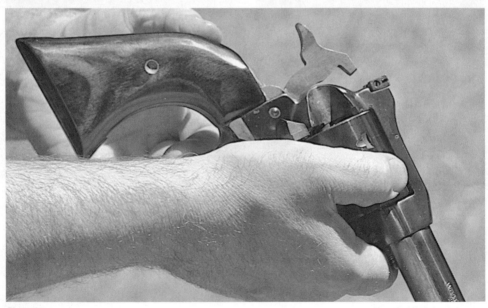

Photo 51

next chamber, and the process is repeated until all the cases have been ejected. (Photo 49)

When the cylinder is empty the support hand cradles the gun and drops the muzzle toward the ground, while the shooting hand retrieves the spare ammunition.

The first round is inserted, and just as in the right-hand reload the cylinder is rotated twice to leave the #2 chamber empty. As each further round is inserted, the support

Photo 52

Photo 53

hand rotates the cylinder to the next chamber. (Photo 50 and 51)

On loading the last chamber, the gate is simply closed. (Photo 52)

The shooting hand brings the hammer to full cock and restrains the hammer while the trigger is pulled. The hammer is slowly and safely lowered on the empty chamber. (Photo 53)

Photo 54

RACKING THE SLIDE FOR THOSE WITH STRENGTH ISSUES

One of the common complaints leveled against the autoloader is the force required to operate the slide. Many people feel they lack the hand and/or upper body strength to easily rack the slide against the heavy recoil spring. As it happens, racking the slide isn't a matter of strength, it's a matter of technique.

First, it's important to pull the gun into what's called the "workspace" - that area in front of the body, somewhere around the bottom of the ribcage, where strength and dexterity are at their maximum. The shooting hand maintains a firm grip on the gun with the finger extended along the frame, above the triggerguard, for safety. (Photo 54)

The shooting elbow is tucked into the side of the body, locking the shooting arm and the torso together. (Photo 55)

The support hand cups over the top of the slide, being careful not to cover the ejection port. (Photo 56) (It's possible for a live round in the chamber to detonate when being ejected, and the result can be extreme hand injury. Keep the hand in back of the ejection port!)

The support hand grasps the slide tight-

Photo 55

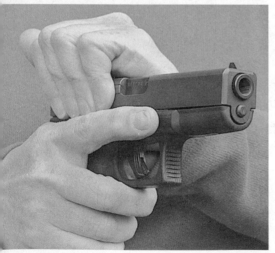

Photo 56

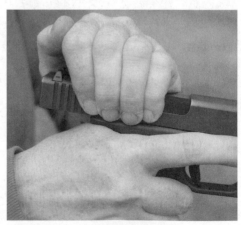

Covering the ejection port, even partially, while racking slide is dangerous - live rounds can be detonated as they eject, causing severe injury. Safest position is with the hand on the very back of slide, covering rear sight.

Photo 57

Photo 58

ly, and the shooting hand will push the gun forward. The key to this technique is to use the power of the hips to do this; as the support hand holds the slide, the shooter rotates his/her hip, driving the gun forward as the slide is held firmly. Notice that the slide isn't pulled back, it's simply held in place while the rest of the gun goes forward under the tremendous power of the leg and torso mus-

cles. (Photo 57)

If the gun is being loaded, the slide is simply released to chamber a round. If the gun is being unloaded, or a malfunction cleared, the slide is locked back. The easiest way to do this is usually to apply upward pressure on the slide lock as the gun's frame is pushed forward. This requires a little bit of coordination, and needs to be practiced to

Want to Know More?

Gun Digest Book of the Revolver by Grant Cunningham. ISBN 978-1440218125. Krause Publications, (855) 864-2579 www.gundigeststore.com

Defensive Handgun Skills by David Fessenden. ISBN 9781440213816. Krause Publications, (855) 864-2579 www.gundigeststore.com

The Complete Illustrated Manual of Handgun Skills by R.K. Campbell. ISBN 978-0760341056. Zenith Press, 400 First Avenue North Suite 300, Minneapolis, MN 55401. (800) 458-0454 www.zenithpress.com

Stressfire, Vol. 1 by Massad Ayoob. ISBN 978-0936279039. Police Bookshelf, www.ayoob.com

The Tactical Pistol by Gabriel Suarez. Paladin Press, 7077 Winchester Circle, Boulder, CO 80301. (303) 443-7250 www.paladinpress.com

The Cornered Cat by Kathy Jackson. ISBN 978-0982248799. White Feather Press, 3170 52nd Street, Hamilton, MI 49419. (269) 838-5586 www.whitefeatherpress.com

The Modern Day Gunslinger:
The Ultimate Handgun Training Manual
by Don Mann. ISBN 978-1602399860. Skyhorse Publishing, www.skyhorsepublishing.com

Modern Technique of the Pistol by Gregory Morrison. Gunsite Press, www.gunsite.com

The Encyclopedia of Bullseye Pistol (website). www.bullseyepistol.com

CHAPTER 7

SIGHTS AND SIGHTING

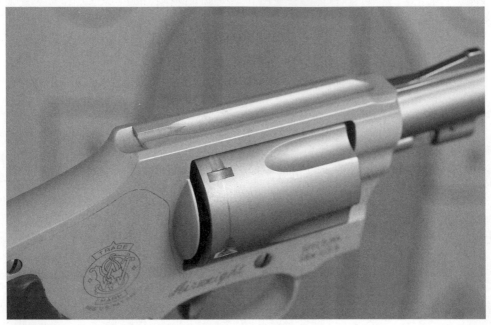

Fixed sights are usually machined into the gun itself, are not easily adjusted.

In theory, shooting a handgun is easy. All you have to do is get the gun aligned on target and pull the trigger without disturbing anything. In practice, as most people quickly discover, it's a lot harder than that - but it does start with getting the gun aligned on target, which is the job of the sights.

Any sighting system is really just a precision alignment guide. Some types have higher precision than others, and some help compensate for eyesight limitations, but at the end of the day they're just alignment guides. Keeping that in mind will help you cut through much of the hype which surrounds sight selection.

FIXED SIGHTS

The standard handgun sighting system is the blade and notch. On the barrel is a vertical blade, while at the rear of the handgun is a notch into which the blade is aligned. Once done (called "sight alignment"), the sights are then superimposed on the target ("sight picture").

The simplest version of the blade and notch are the solid, non-adjustable sights typically found on short-barreled revolvers. These are machined directly from or into the gun itself. The front blade is part of the barrel, and the rear is a simple notch milled into the frame. If the bullets aren't hitting where

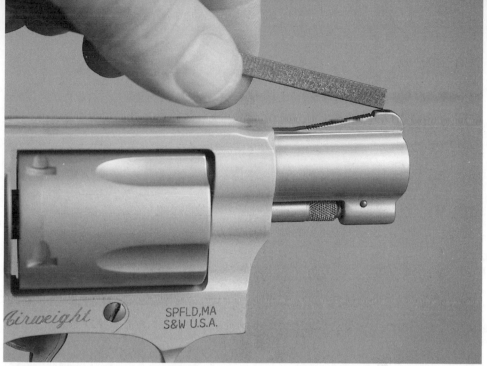

If a fixed-sight gun is shooting low, the solution is to file a very small amount from the front blade and test. Repeat as needed until the gun is shooting to point of aim.

the sights are pointed, physical changes to the gun are necessary. *n*

To adjust elevation (the vertical position of the bullet strike) the front sight blade is filed or machined. Adjusting the left and right position of the bullet, called windage, calls for the barrel to be screwed slightly into or out of the frame. This tilts the blade to the left or right, which causes the bullet impact to change.

Filing down the sight blade can be done by anyone as long a great care is exercised with the file, but adjusting the windage requires special tooling - making it a gunsmith-only proposition.

These are by far the most rugged types of sights, as they're almost impossible to accidentally dislodge. That ruggedness comes at the price of flexibility. If your handgun has fixed sights, it's generally easier (and cheaper) to find an ammunition load that agrees with the sights, rather than trying to make the sights agree with the bullets.

Another issue with fixed sights is that they're not easily changed. If the shooter doesn't like the style of the sights it usually requires the services of a gunsmith and his machine shop to get them changed. Since the sights are part and parcel of the gun, making any modifications means modifying the gun itself.

For instance, the front sight can be modified to have a colored insert, a tritium vial can be installed to make the sights visible at night, or that blade may be able to be milled away altogether and replaced with a completely different shape. The rear of the frame can be machined to accept a higher and more visible sight notch, or the existing notch can be flanked with glow-in-the-dark tritium vials. None of these is a do-it-yourself project.

Many revolvers have front blades that are held in place with cross pins. This makes it easy to exchange the blade for a taller, shorter, narrower, or wider style. This makes it easy for a handy gun owner to change out

Sight blades that are held in place with a cross pin are easily changed by driving out the pin, inserting new blade, and replacing the pin.

the sights at home.

Some guns have front sight blades that are designed to be easily interchangeable by the user. This isn't a common feature, being offered on very few guns, but they give the utmost ease of sight changes no tools (or extremely simple ones). Replacement can be done in the field, making it easy to match the sights to the shooting conditions. These sights are by their nature proprietary to the manufacturer, but some of the specialized sight companies make blades to fit the most popular models.

Fixed sights on autoloading pistols are often adjustable for windage. The rear sight, and sometimes the front as well, are often installed in a dovetail slot. This allows for the sight to be moved (called "drifting") from side to side. Most are a very tight friction fit, requiring a brass punch and a hammer to move. There are specialized tools, called sight pushers, which make that job much easier and more precise.

Sometimes, particularly on autoloading pistols, these sights are held in place with a setscrew. Drifting them requires only a hex key or a screwdriver to loosen the sight screw and tighten it again, though care must be taken to tighten them very firmly or recoil can send them out of adjustment - or off the gun altogether!

Some fixed sights are held in place via friction in dovetailed joints. Adjustments are often made with a brass punch and hammer.

Both autos and revolvers are available with fully adjustable (windage, elevation) sights.

ADJUSTABLE SIGHTS

Adjustable sights are those where the rear sight is fully adjustable for easy and precise changes to the bullet's point of impact. An adjustable rear sight can be moved left and right for windage corrections, or up and down for elevation changes. The adjustable rear may be combined with any of the front blade types, though most of the time the front blade is pinned in place. The adjustable sight eliminates the need to rotate the barrel for windage corrections or to file the blade for elevation changes. These types of sights are by far the most flexible, allowing the gun to be easily zeroed without any special tools (other than a screwdriver).

This flexibility comes with a price, how-ever. While they are generally fairly reliable, they are also less durable than a fixed sight. Whenever there are moving parts there is the chance that they'll break or be moved unintentionally.

Adjustable rear sights are often available in several blade types. While plain black is the most common, some makers have sights with colored outlines, V-shaped openings, and even round peeps. Some need special gunsmith tools to install, but many require nothing more than a screwdriver and pin punch to change.

An autoloading pistol with fixed sights can often be machined to accept fully adjustable sights. This involves cutting a dovetail into the slide, along with taking a small amount of metal off to clear the sight body.

A gunsmith can modify the slide of an autoloading pistol to accept adjustable sights. This requires precision work on a milling machine, as master gunsmith Todd Koonce demonstrates.

COMPETITION ADJUSTABLE RIBS

A specialized version of the adjustable sight can be found on some revolvers designed for a particular kind of competitive shooting. The rib sight, often called an "Aristocrat" after the most popular brand, is a single piece sight that extends from the back edge of the frame to the muzzle.

The rib sits on top of the barrel and frame and has integral rear notches and front blades. The rear is adjustable like any other adjustable rear, while the front can be either a fixed blade or a special click-stop blade for preset elevation changes. They're used in formal events like the NRA Police Pistol Competition. Installation usually requires extensive gunsmithing.

RED DOT SIGHTS

Red dot sights are optical devices that sit on top of the handgun. The shooter looks through the sight glass and sees a red dot (or a circle or a triangle or almost any other shape imaginable) superimposed on the target. Like a rifle or handgun scope, the dot and the target appear to be in the same plane; in other words, they're both in focus. This makes the red dot easy to use for people who have close-focus issues. Unlike a rifle (or handgun) scope, however, the red dot sight offers no magnification - targets appear the same size through the sight as they do in open air.

The red dot is also very fast, because the shooter can locate his target and fire an accurate shot without having to shift focus from the target to the sights. For this reason the red dot has come to dominate those pistol competitions where they're allowed.

The competition rib sight is a staple of precision revolver shooting events, requires special barrel and extensive gunsmithing to fit properly.

Some red dot sights, like this Trijicon RMR, are small enough to fit on a pistol slide for concealed carry. The red dot is projected onto the clear screen and is simply placed on the target where the shooter wants the bullet to land. Photo courtesy of Trijicon Inc.

Red dots were originally large affairs, the size of a traditional handgun scope, but over the years that's changed as small units using holographic technology have come on the market. Some of them are small enough to be practical for concealed carry and mount in place of the rear sight.

Most red dot sights use batteries that must be replaced periodically. There are some models that use radioactive tritium gas for illumination, eliminating the issue with batteries, but require that the gas tubes be replaced every ten years or so.

Though the newest models appear to be extremely robust, many people have lingering concerns about the red dot's durability in harsh environments. Since all red dots have optics in some form, they must be kept clean for best efficiency.

HANDGUN SCOPES

A handgun scope, like a rifle scope, has a reticle which the shooter simply places on the target. The reticle appears in the same plane as the target, which means that the target and the reticle are both in focus at the same time.

A scope on a hunting handgun greatly increases the effective range of the shooter. Photo courtesy of Sturm, Ruger Co.

Handgun scopes are usually low-magnification devices, often no more than 4x (four power, or four times the magnification without the scope.) Many are adjustable, offering continuous magnification changes. Some specialized handgun competitions, such as metallic silhouette shooting, often use higher magnification scopes.

The major difference between a rifle scope and a handgun scope is the eye relief, or the distance between the scope and the eye when a proper sight picture is achieved. A rifle scope may only have a couple of inches of eye relief, where a handgun scope - because they're usually held at arm's length - need to have an eye relief from 10" to as much as two feet.

The reticle in a handgun scope can be of the traditional crosshairs, but other styles are available. Red dots can be incorporated into a handgun scope reticle as well, making it easier to shoot as the sun starts to set - an important consideration for handgun hunters.

SCOPING A HANDGUN

Since most handguns, except for the single shot variety, aren't set up for scope mounting, it's necessary to buy specialized mounts, modify the gun, or sometimes both.

Revolvers are usually easy to deal with. If a revolver has an adjustable rear sight there are "no-gunsmith" scope mounts which will install simply in its place. Normally all that's needed is to remove the rear sight and attach the scope mount.

Some no-gunsmith mounts clamp to the barrel. These mounts should be tightened very securely, as a heavy-recoiling gun is likely to jar them loose. They often result in marring and scratching where the clamps attach to the barrel.

Most revolvers can have a scope mount screwed to the top strap. Some guns come from the factory drilled and tapped for those mounts, but many don't. If so, a gunsmith can easily drill and tap the necessary holes.

"No gunsmith" mount attaches in place of rear sight, uses threaded holes originally used to hold sight in place.

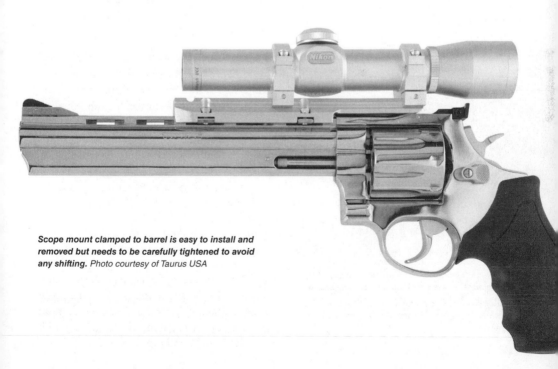

Scope mount clamped to barrel is easy to install and removed but needs to be carefully tightened to avoid any shifting. Photo courtesy of Taurus USA

The Desert Eagle gas-operated autoloader has rails built into the gun to which rings or an elongated mount (to adjust eye relief) can be attached. *Photo courtesy of Magnum Research*

Some Ruger revolvers come with cuts to accept Ruger-specific rings. This is a very strong mounting method which is quickly and easily removed when desired. *Photo courtesy of Sturm, Ruger Co.*

These are usually much more durable, and more likely to hold zero, than the "no gunsmithing" styles. The barrel, if it has a pronounced rib which is flat on the top, can also be drilled and tapped to accept a scope.

Some Ruger revolvers come from the factory with Ruger's proprietary mounting cuts in the barrel and frame. These take special Ruger scope rings, are exceptionally durable and easy for the shooter to mount and dismount as needed.

Scoping an autoloading pistol is a little trickier. The scope cannot be mounted on the slide, for a couple of reasons. First, the reciprocation forces would quickly destroy the scope (perhaps in one or two shots), and second the added weight would cause the slide to slow and the gun to malfunction.

Autoloader scope mounts must attach to the frame in some manner. One such mount, which does not require a gunsmith, replace a grip panel with the mount coming up over the top of the gun. The mount has a rail to which the scope rings are attached.

Another option is a scope mount which attaches to the side of the frame, above the trigger. There are no-gunsmith options here as well, with the mounts utilizing take-down pins or the front rails common to many newer guns.

These require drilling and tapping several holes in precise places, to match both the mount and to avoid interfering with internal mechanisms. This is a gunsmith-only proposition.

The big Desert Eagle autoloading pistols have rails built in, making them (along with the Ruger revolvers) the easiest from-the-factory guns on which to mount a scope.

The laser shoots a dot of concentrated light in line with the barrel; bright dot in middle of target shows where bullet will land. Photo courtesy of LaserMax

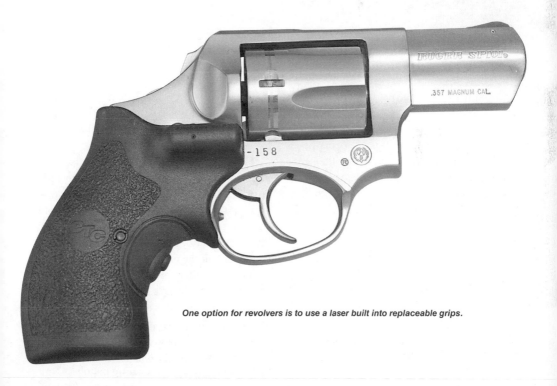

One option for revolvers is to use a laser built into replaceable grips.

Another option is this unit from LaserLyte, which attaches to the sideplate of this Smith & Wesson revolver.

LASERS

In the last couple of decades lasers have been miniaturized to the point that they can easily fit on a handgun. The laser emits a very concentrated beam of light that projects a small bright dot on the target, making it an ideal way to mark where on the target the bullet will hit.

Modern laser sights attach to the gun and are aligned with the barrel. If the target is at a distance which is close to that for which the laser is adjusted, the laser dot will precisely mark the point at which the bullet will hit. This makes the laser sight a powerful tool for self defense and law enforcement.

There are many different ways to mount a laser sight. For revolvers, lasers are available built into the grips or in housings that attach to the side of the frame.

Some autoloading pistols may also use lasers built into their grips, but if the gun doesn't have replaceable grips there are options: lasers that mount in place of the rear sight, in place of the guide rod, to the front of the triggerguard, and even styles that attach to the back of the grip via the takedown pins.

There are very few handguns which cannot be equipped with a laser sight.

Most lasers project a red beam, but there are now a few lasers on the market with green beams. There are also lasers built into clip-on flashlights which attach to the forward rail on many autoloading pistols.

Laser sights run on very small lithium

Many autoloading pistols have rails in front of the trigger guard, for which small laser units are made.
Photo courtesy of Crimson Trace

Small polymer pistols like this Ruger LCP are ideal candidates for lasers which attach to the front of the trigger guard. Photo courtesy of Crimson Trace

Lasers can even be mounted inside the guide rod of an autoloading pistol. Photo courtesy of LaserMax

batteries, many of which last can a year or more in use.

Like a scope, a laser needs to be precisely zeroed to insure that the bullet goes where the dot does. If the laser is removed - for cleaning or battery replacement - it must be readjusted.

The laser makes a good auxiliary sight, but even their makers insist that they are not intended as a primary sighting device. Unless attached to or accompanied by a flashlight, the laser will not illuminate a target in the dark sufficiently to be able to identify it.

The laser is a specialty tool whose use must be carefully considered.

One practical use for the laser is in trigger control training. Because the laser emits a continuous beam when activated, it can be useful to diagnose trigger finger issues. Simply dry firing at a target and watching the beam dance is often enough to help shooters steady their aim as the trigger is pulled.

SIGHT PICTURES FOR IRON SIGHTS

Using iron sights boils down to two things: sight alignment and sight picture.

They are related, but different concepts.

Sight alignment refers to the relationship between the front and rear sight. With most blade-and-notch sights, the blade is centered in the rear notch, with the tops of both sights even and and equal amount of light coming through on either side of the front blade. (Photo 1)

If the front sight's top is above the top of the rear sight, the shot will hit high on the target. (Photo 2a) If it's lower, the shot will go low. (Photo 2b)

If there is less light on one side of the blade than the other, the shot will track to that side. (Photos 3a and 3b)

It's only when the alignment is correct that the bullet will land where the shooter intends.

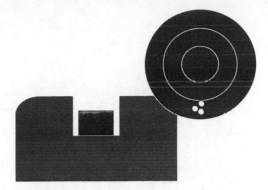

Photo 2b

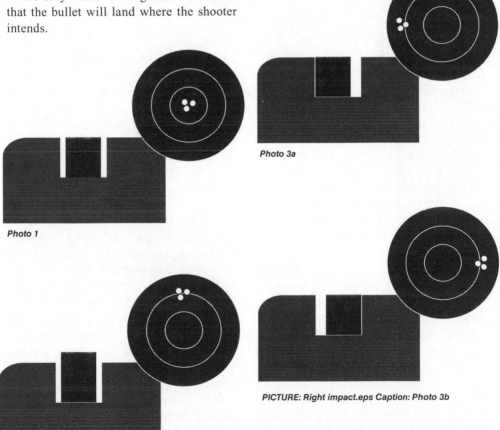

Photo 3a

Photo 1

PICTURE: Right impact.eps Caption: Photo 3b

Photo 2a

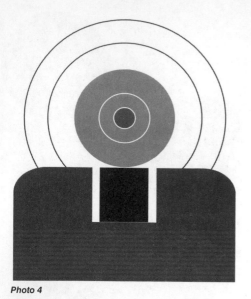

Photo 4

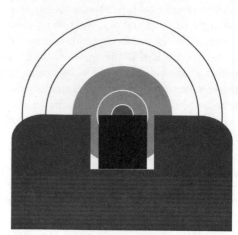

Photo 5

Sight picture refers to how the aligned sights are placed on the target. There are two common sight pictures: the "six-o'clock hold" and "point of aim/point of impact."

The six-o'clock hold is an old holdover from bullseye shooting. The sights are adjusted so that when they are held on the bottom edge of a target - the point where the number "6" would be on a clock face - the rounds will impact in the center of the target. In other words, the sights are intentionally adjusted to hit very high.

The six-o'clock hold allows the shooter to have a very defined edge onto which his sights can be placed, making precision placement easier. (Photo 4) That wouldn't be the case if the sights were placed into the center of the black target, where it's much harder to judge where exactly they're pointed.

This works well as long as the target size and distance are the same each time. Any change in size or distance will result in the bullet hitting a different spot - how different being dependent on how great the change is. Because of this, the six-o'clock

hold is only really useful for shooting at targets of known size and at known distances.

The point of aim/point of impact sight picture places the sights where the bullet is expected to hit. (Photo 5) The sights are usually adjusted so that the bullet hits in the center of the top edge of the front sight, when the sights are properly aligned. (Some people use front blades with small dots, and prefer to have the impact point be the center of the dot instead of the top of the blade.)

Point of aim/point of impact is not dependent on any given target size or distance. Until the target gets so far away that the bullet starts to drop noticeably, all the shooter has to do is put the aligned front sight where he/she wants the bullet to hit. This is the preferred sight picture for virtually all kinds of shooting, from plinking to self defense to most types of competitive shooting.

Unless the shooter is going to be competing in formal bullseye matches, it's recommended to adjust the sights for point of aim/point of impact.

ADJUSTING SIGHTS

It's easy to get confused about adjusting sights! If the rear sight is being adjusted, the sight is moved in the direction that the bullet needs to go. Let's say the bullet is hitting to the right of the point of aim; that means that the impact point needs to move to the left, so the rear sight is adjusted to the left. If the bullet is hitting low, its impact point needs to be raised - which requires the rear sight to go up.

Adjusting the front sight is exactly the opposite - the sight is moved in the opposite direction that the bullet needs to go. If the bullet impact needs to be moved to the left, the front sight is moved to the right; this makes the impact move shift leftward. If the bullet is hitting low and needs to be moved up, the front sight is lowered.

LASER TARGET TRAINING AIDS

There's no substitute for getting out to the range and practicing the proper sight alignment and sight picture. That's not always possible, and with increasing ammunition prices may not be economically feasible - at least not as often as we might like.

Luckily technology has come to the rescue. There are now relatively inexpensive laser training systems on the market which allow the shooter to get that important shot placement feedback without the need to fire a shot. These devices typically consist of a small laser barrel insert that projects a laser beam - instead of a bullet - with the trigger is pulled. The shooter can see the laser dot and determine if the round impacted where he or she expected.

The more sophisticated systems have a special electronic target that displays the shot, and even recall past shots to get a feeling of how good the "group" would have been. Though they don't replicate the recoil of the gun, and thus aren't suitable for all facets of shooting practice, they do help with mastering the use of the sights. Plus, they're a lot of fun!

Want to Know More?

RED DOT OPTICS

C-More - very popular with competitive shooters, they have several models commonly mounted on handguns, including a model small enough for concealed carry. C-MORE Systems, PO Box 340, Warrenton, VA 20188. (540) 347-4683. www.cmore.com

Trijicon - small to large red dot sights, popular with law enforcement and military but also commonly seen in competitions. Their RMR sight is particularly popular for concealed carry. Trijicon, P. O. Box 930059, Wixom, MI 48393-0059. (800) 338-0563 www.trijicon.com

Docter - makes a very small red dot sight that can be mounted on handguns. Docter USA, www.docterusa.com

Aimpoint - one of the original makers of red dot sights has models to fit handguns that have scope mounts installed. Popular with competitive shooters. Aimpoint Inc., 14103 Mariah Court, Chantilly VA 20151-2113. (703) 263-9795 www.aimpoint.com

Eotech - very popular line of red dot sights, some of which are ideal for mounting on handguns. Eotech, 1201 E. Ellsworth, Ann Arbor, MI 48108. (734) 741-8868 www.eotech-inc.com

BSA - big selection of red dot scopes; all are designed to mount to Weaver scope bases. BSA Optics, Inc., 3911 SW 47th Ave. Suite 914, Ft. Lauderdale, FL 33314. (954) 581-2144 www.bsaoptics.com

Burris - well established scope makers also produce the FastFire red dot optic, small enough to fit into the rear sight dovetail on an autoloading pistol. Made to fit a wide variety of handguns. Burris Company, 920 54th Avenue, Greeley, CO 80634. (970) 356-1670 www.burrisoptics.com

Simmons - makes several conventional styled red dot scopes, suitable for handguns using conventional scope mounts. Simmons Outdoor Products, 9200 Cody, Overland Park, KS 66214. (913) 752-3400 www.simmonsoptics.com

Zeiss - famed lens maker also has two styles of top quality red dot sights. Carl Zeiss Optical, LLC., 13005 North Kingston Avenue, Chester, VA 23836-8333. (800) 441-3005 www.zeiss.com

Weaver - makes a unique red/green reticle dot scope. ATK Onalaska Operations, N5549 County Trunk Z, Onalaska, WI 54650. (800) 635-7656 www.weaveroptics.com

HANDGUN SCOPES

Leupold - famed maker of rifle scopes, also offer a line of fixed and variable power long eye relief handgun scopes. Leupold & Stevens Inc., 14400 NW Greenbrier Parkway, Beaverton, OR 97006. (800) 538-7653 www.leupold.com

Burris - well established scope maker has several handgun scopes in their line. Burris Company, 920 54th Avenue, Greeley, CO 80634. (970) 356-1670 www.burrisoptics.com

Simmons - has a good selection of handgun scopes in both fixed and variable magnification. Simmons Outdoor Products, 9200 Cody, Overland Park, KS 66214. (913) 752-3400 www.simmonsoptics.com

BSA - value-priced line of handgun scopes; fixed and variable power, black and silver. BSA Optics, Inc., 3911 SW 47th Ave. Suite 914, Ft. Lauderdale, FL 33314. (954) 581-2144 www.bsaoptics.com

Weaver - Long time maker of handgun scopes, guaranteed to stand up under the heaviest magnum recoil. ATK Onalaska Operations, N5549 County Trunk Z, Onalaska, WI 54650. (800) 635-7656 www.weaveroptics.com

MOUNTING SYSTEMS

Aimtech - huge selection of mounting systems for both revolvers and autoloaders; most do not require a gunsmith for installation. Aimtech Inc., (229) 226-4313 www.aimtech-mounts.com

B-Square - specializes in "no gunsmith" mounts for revolvers and autopistols. BAE Systems Inc., 13386 International Parkway, Jacksonville, FL 32218. (800) 347-1200 www.b-square.com

Ruger - while there are several sources for rings to fit their specialized mounting systems, the original Ruger rings are among the best available. Sturm, Ruger Co., 411 Sunapee Street, Newport, NH 03773. (603) 865-2442 www.ruger.com

Weaver - makes the Pistol Mount system for a variety of handguns; also makes scope bases for drill-and-tap installation. ATK Onalaska Operations, N5549 County Trunk Z, Onalaska, WI 54650. (800) 635-7656 www.weaveroptics.com

Warne - produces the Maxima mount system for S&W, Dan Wesson, and some Ruger revolvers. Warne Scope Mounts, 9500 SW Tualatin Road, Tualatin, OR 97062. (800) 683-5590 www.warnescopemounts.com

Leupold - famous for their scopes, they also make mounts

Weigand - highly regarded source of handgun parts, including scope mounts for a wide range of autoloading pistols and double- and single-action revolvers. Weigand Combat Handguns Inc., 1057 South Main Road, Mountaintop, PA 18707. (570) 868-8358 www.jackweigand.com

LASERS

LaserLyte - specializes in frame and rail mount lasers for revolvers and autopistols. LaserLyte Corp., 30 N Alamos Drive, Cottonwood, AZ 86326. (928) 649-3201 www.laserlyte.com

Crimson Trace - the inventors of the grip-mounted laser, they also have a wide range of frame and rail mounted options for guns that don't have grip panels. Both red and green lasers available. Crimson Trace Corporation, 9780 SW Freeman Dr., Wilsonville, OR 97070. (800) 442-2406 www.crimson-trace.com

LaserMax - innovative company that makes a wide range of lasers: mounted in guide rods for many different autopistols; on the frame for S&W revolvers, Glock, and pocket pistols; and rail mounts for those newer pistols which have them. LaserMax, 3495 Winton Place Bldg. B, Rochester, NY 14623. (800) 527-3703 www.lasermax.com

Viridian - specializes in green rail-mount lasers and laser/flashlight combinations in several configurations. Laser Aiming Systems Corporation, 5929 Baker Road Suite 440, Minnetonka, MN 55345 (800) 990-9390 www.viridiangreenlaser.com

Want to Know More?

LASER TRAINING AIDS

Laser Devices - makes a bore-sighted laser training pointer for many different calibers. Laser Devices, Inc., 70 Garden Court, Monterey, CA 93940. (831) 373-0701 www.laserdevices.com

LaserLyte - bore-mounted laser pointer plus electronic target that registers "hits." LaserLyte Corp., 30 N Alamos Drive, Cottonwood, AZ 86326. (928) 649-3201 www.laserlyte.com

SIGHTS

XS Sight Systems - makers of the "Big Dot" Express style handgun sights; tritium illumination optional. 2401 Ludelle, Fort Worth, Texas 76105. (888) 744-4880 www.xssights.com

Kensight - Formerly known as Champion Gunsight, Kensight products are used on many factory guns and by custom gunsmiths. Fixed, adjustable, and night sight varieties to fit a wide range of guns. KFS Industries Inc., 875 Wharton Drive SW, Atlanta, GA 30336. (800) 848-4671 www.kensight.com

HiViz Sights - fiber optic sights for many revolvers and autoloading pistols, both front and rear. HiViz Shooting Systems, Div. of North Pass Ltd., 1941 Heath Parkway, Ste. #1, Fort Collins, CO 80524. (800) 589-4315 www.hivizsights.com

Bowen Rough Country Sights - the most rugged adjustable rear sights for S&W and Ruger revolvers; front blades for select models. Bowen Classic Arms Corp., P. O. Box 67, Louisville, TN 37777. (865) 984-3583 www.bowenclassicarms.com

Gemini Customs - fiber optic and gold bead front sights for Smith & Wesson and Ruger revolvers. Gemini Custom, 717 Botkins Lane, Frankfort, KY 40601. (502) 226-1230 www.geminicustoms.com

Tooltech - custom night sight installation for revolvers and autopistols for which there is no ready-made alternative. Tooltech Gunsight, Inc., 20 Church Street, Oxford, Michigan 48371. (248) 628-1811 www.tooltechgunsight.com

SDM sights - gold bead and fiber optic front sights, rugged rear sights for S&W revolvers. SDM Fabricating Inc., 3775 Foskett Road, Medina , Ohio 44256. (330) 723-3098 www.sdmfabricating.com

Cylinder & Slide - Extreme Duty fixed rear sights for S&W revolvers. Cylinder & Slide Inc., 245 E. 4th Street, Fremont, NE 68025. (402)721-4277 www.cylinder-slide.com

Ameriglo - specializes in night sights, but also makes plain and fiber optic front and rear sights and sets. AmeriGlo Inc., 31 Waterloo Ave, Berwyn, PA 19312. (610) 296-8915 www.ameriglo.net

Novak - makers of one of the most popular line of pistol sights. Plain, fiber optic, gold bead, and tritium varieties. Novak Designs Inc., PO Box 4045, Parkersburg, WV 26104. (304) 428-2676 www.novaksights.com

Ed Brown - makes adjustable and low-profile fixed sights for autoloading pistols. Has a tritium option on the fixed varieties. Ed Brown Products, Inc., PO Box 492, Perry, MO 63462 (573) 565-3261 www.edbrown.com

Truglo - tritium and fiber optic sights for autoloading pistols. TRUGLO, Inc, 710 Presidential Drive, Richardson, TX 75081. (972) 774-0300 www.truglo.com

Meprolight specializes in tritium night sights, both front and rear, for pistols and revolvers. Imported through Kimber Mfg, Inc., 555 Taxter Road Suite 235, Elmsford, NY 10523. (914) 909-1941 www.meprolight.com

Trijicon - one of the first makers of tritium night sights for handguns. Trijicon, P. O. Box 930059, Wixom, MI 48393-0059. (800) 338-0563 www.trijicon.com

Heinie Sights - front and rear sights for popular autoloading pistols, including the famous "Straight 8" tritium night sights. Heinie Speciality Products, 301 Oak Street, Quincy, IL 62301. (217) 228-9500 www.heinie.com

Hex sights - unique front and rear handgun sight said to be faster and easier to use. Goshen Enterprises, Inc., 1355 Lee Mountain Road, Sedona, AZ 8635. (928) 284-1483 www.goshen-hexsite.com

Advantage sights - unusual trapezoidal sight system said to provide faster target acquisition. Available in various colors to fit many pistols. WrenTech Industries, LLC, 7 Avenida Vista Grande B-7, Santa Fe, NM 87508. (310) 316-6413 www.advantagetactical.com

CHAPTER 8

CLEANING AND MAINTENANCE

One of the messy facts of shooting life is guns need cleaning and lubricating after they've been shot. It's a dirty job, and one which many gun owners dread, but with a little preparation, care, and the right materials it's not an overwhelming task.

A handgun - any gun, actually - should be cleaned as soon after shooting as is practical. It keeps the gun in proper condition for immediate use, reveals potential maintenance issues before they become serious problems, and generally allows for a better understanding of the gun and how it functions. It's still a dirty job, but a necessary one.

SAFETY FIRST!

The first thing to do is to check that the pistol or revolver is unloaded, then double check it. It's amazing the number of people who claim their gun just "went off" while they were "cleaning it." Accidental shootings while cleaning guns are so common as to be fodder for late-night comedians. Don't be one of those people - make doubly sure that your handgun is empty before ever starting.

A good way to prevent cleaning "accidents" is to make sure that there is no ammunition in the proximity of the cleaning area. This is an important and often overlooked safety procedure, one which ensures that no live round can inadvertently make its way anywhere near the gun being cleaned. It's best to do the cleaning in a separate room from where the gun is unloaded, a room which has

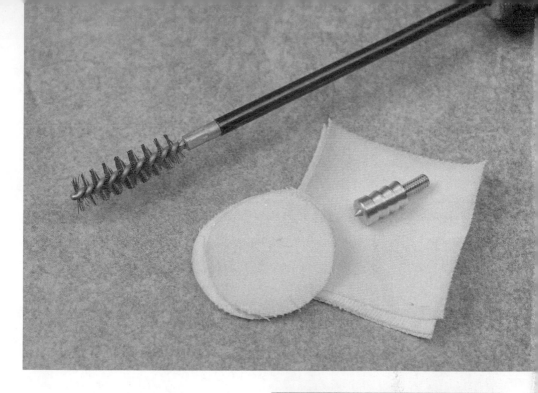

been checked and confirmed to have no ammunition present.

Seemingly obsessive attention to safety is the mark of the professional.

STEP ONE:
GATHER TOOLS AND MATERIALS

Revolvers and single shots are generally pretty straightforward to clean and only require that their actions or cylinders be opened. The autoloader, on the other hand, has to be "field stripped" – partially disassembled or "taken down" into large component groups.

If you're not familiar with how your autoloader is taken down, consult the gun's owner's manual. If the original manual isn't available, Gun Digest has disassembly/reassembly guides for many models available at reasonable cost.

First, a short bore rod, approximately nine inches in length, will be needed to push brushes and patches through the barrel. The bore rod is constructed so that it rotates in its handle, which allows the brush or patch to follow the twisted rifling. There are a number

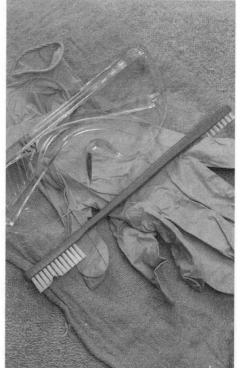

In addition to bore rods, brushes, and cotton swabs, it's helpful to have a GI Toothbrush, shop towel, gloves, and goggles.

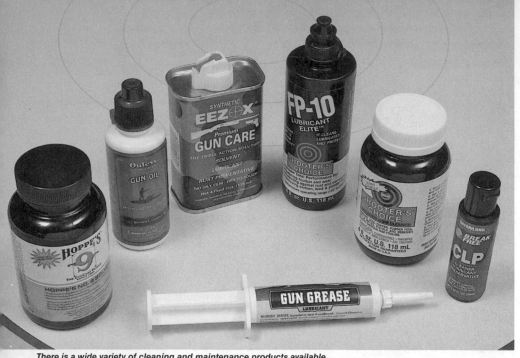

There is a wide variety of cleaning and maintenance products available.

of brands to choose from, but most people find the larger the handle, the more comfortable the rod is to use.

The bore brushes and patches do the actual work inside the barrel. There are nylon, bronze, and stainless steel brushes available, but the all-around best choice is bronze. Stainless steel is used for extremely stubborn deposits, but is thought to scratch the barrel's bore and is recommended only in severe cases. Nylon brushes are useful primarily to apply copper cutting cleaners in high precision single-shot handguns chambered for rifle rounds. For most handgun cleaning they aren't needed. Brushes are made in various sizes to precisely match the caliber of the gun being cleaned.

Patches are small pieces of cloth that are passed down the barrel on a jag. Patches come in various sizes to fit a wide variety of calibers and are usually made of cotton twill that both holds cleaning solution and provides a bit of a scrubbing action. (Patches can also be cut at home from used cotton t-shirts.) The jag, which carries them down the bore, is generally purchased to fit the specific caliber, though there are some universal-fit styles available.

A most useful cleaning tool is the "GI Toothbrush," more precisely known as an M16 cleaning brush. This specialized tool has bristles at both ends of the brush; long on one end, short and stiff on the other. They're cheap, widely available, and amazingly handy - buy several, as you'll find many uses for them.

Cotton swabs and a cotton washcloth or shop towel will prove useful as well, and latex or nitrile gloves are highly recommended when cleaning any gun. The chemicals in cleaners can damage skin, and the lead residue from cleaning is toxic. Disposable gloves eliminate all these concerns and make clean-up quick and easy. It's also a good idea to wear safety glasses to prevent splashes from ending up in your eyes.

Wherever the gun is cleaned it's a good idea to put down some sort of surface cover to catch spills and prevent damage to the counter surface. Many people find that plasticized baby changing pads work well for this; similar products are sold as disposable bed pads for incontinent patients or as training pads for dogs.

In a pinch, a folded bath towel works well, but it must be remembered that gun cleaning solvents and oils will stain - don't use one expecting to be able to hang it in the bathroom after laundering!

There are a bewildering number of gun cleaning solutions on the market, each one claiming to be better than the last. These come in two primary forms: cleaners or solvents, and combination cleaner-lubricant-rust protectants (called "CLP" for short).

Photo 1

The CLP products are sold as all-in-one solutions to gun care, but there is some debate as to their effectiveness at lubricating and rust prevention. The author prefers a standard cleaner/solvent and separate lubricants, as his experience has been that the CLP products usually need supplementation with oil or grease to maintain proper functioning.

The last step in maintenance is lubricating the gun. Generally a bottle of gun oil is sufficient, but autoloading pistols can benefit from having their slide rails lubricated with a very light grease, one that is almost a liquid at room temperature. The grease doesn't migrate out of the gun and is not thrown off when the slide moves back and forth during shooting.

Photo 2

STEP TWO: DISASSEMBLE THE GUN

Before starting any cleaning project, remember to unload the gun in a separate area and keep all ammunition away from the cleaning area. Unload the gun in a separate room, double-check that it's unloaded, and only then bring it in to be cleaned.

Revolvers need only have their cylinders opened for cleaning, but autoloaders need to be field stripped. Check once again that the gun is unloaded - chamber empty and magazine out - and if necessary refer to the manufacturer's instructions for takedown procedures.

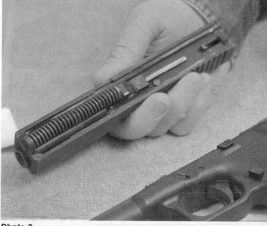

Photo 3

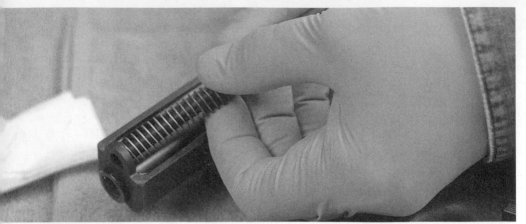

Photo 4a

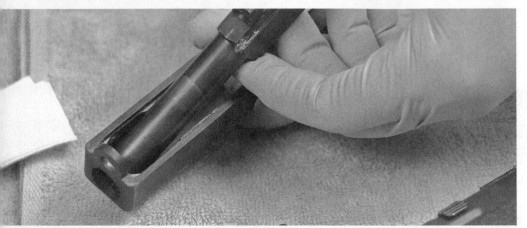

Photo 4b

Photo 5

Lay the pistol's parts on a pad or towel, in the order they were removed, is especially helpful with those guns that have a lot of parts.

Generally speaking, a typical centerfire autoloading pistol is disassembled by first removing the slide assembly. Some guns require the removal of a slide stop lever or pin, while many - like this Glock - require only that a disassembly catch be released. Whichever method the gun uses, pull the slide off the frame. (See photos 1 and 2.)

The slide will usually contain the recoil spring (or the recoil spring guide rod) and the barrel. (See photo 3.)

Take the recoil spring out, and then remove the barrel. (See photos 4a and 4b.)

The slide and barrel are now ready to be cleaned. (See photo 5.)

Some find it helpful to the reassembly process to lay the parts out on the pad or towel in the order that they were removed.

STEP THREE: GENERAL CLEANING

Attach a clean patch to the jag, dip it into the cleaning solution, and run it down the barrel. (See photo 6.)(Revolvers should also have the wet patch run through the chambers in the cylinder.) Let the barrel sit and soak while the rest of the gun is cleaned.

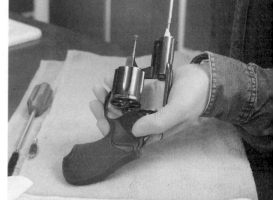

Photo 6

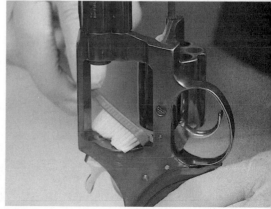

Photo 7a

Photo 7b

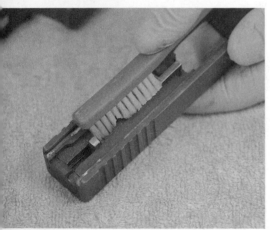

Photo 8a

Photo 8b

For revolvers, take the M16 brush and dip it in the cleaning solution. The brush should be damp, not wet, so shake off the excess. Use the brush to scrub the inside of the frame, where the cylinder normally sits. Pay particular attention to the tight area between the topstrap and the barrel, as this is where carbon and other ignition residue likes to collect. (See photos 7a and 7b.)

Be careful when scrubbing this area; don't let excess solvent get into the firing pin hole or the slot where the hand (the piece which rotates the cylinder) resides. Some seepage is inevitable, but too much is detrimental to the lubricants inside the gun - prevention is the best cure. After scrubbing, a cotton swab is helpful to remove the grimy film that the brush leaves.

Once that's done, wipe the brush on a shop towel or rag. Don't use paper towels for brush cleaning, as they leave fibers in the brush bristles and can end up in the works of the gun.

For autoloaders use a damp brush to clean the underside of the slide, paying particular attention to the recesses which are in contact with the frame rails. The area where the barrel sits tends to be a magnet for soot and needs special attention. Also clean the grooves which mate with the frame. (See photos 8a and b.)

When cleaning the slide of a striker-fired gun, it's important that no cleaners or oils be allowed down into the channel where the striker resides. (See photo 9.) It's best to clean this area with a nearly-dry brush (dipped in cleaner and thoroughly blotted on the shop towel.) Use cotton swabs or a towel to remove any loosened dirt that the brush doesn't pick up.

The extractor, which grabs the rim of the cartridge to pull it from the chamber, needs to be cleaned as well. A build up of dirt under the extractor is a common cause of malfunctions, so it pays to keep it clean. If there is hardened debris that the brush won't remove,

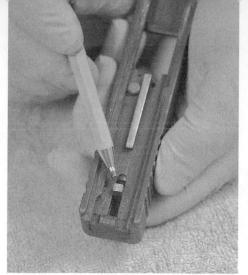

Photo 9

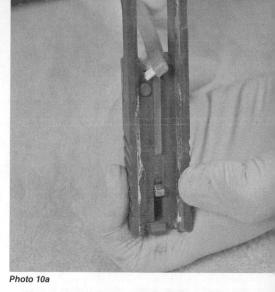

Photo 10a

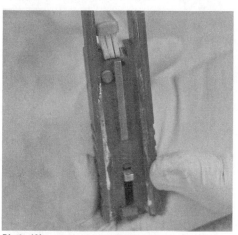

Photo 10b

Photo 11

Photo 12a

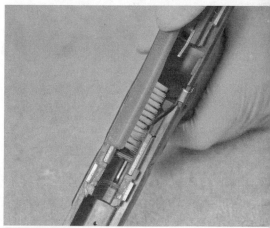

Photo 12b

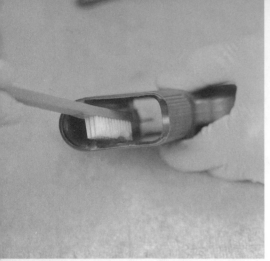

Photo 13

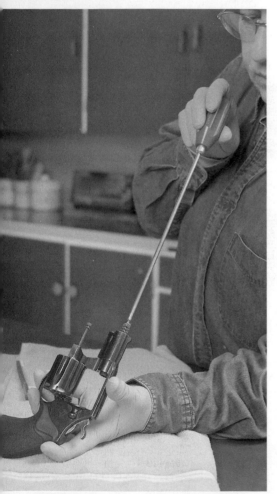

Push the brush all the way through the barrel before reversing.

a toothpick may dislodge it enough to brush away. The short, stiff bristles on the small end of the M16 brush come in handy for this task. (See photo 10a.)

Finish with the large end of the brush to clean the area around the firing pin hole (called the breechface). (See photo 10b.)

The area where the barrel locks into the slide often gets grimy. Inserting the brush through the front of the slide, as on this 1911-pattern pistol slide, often makes it easier to clean this area. (See photo 11.)

The frame rails should also be cleaned thoroughly, and the inside of the frame given a general brushing to remove any loose dirt or soot. (See photos 12a and 12b.)

The magazine well in the grip often gets very dirty, and often presents openings for that dirt to make its way into the action of the gun. A baby bottle brush makes quick work of this job, but the M16 brush will suffice in a pinch. (See photo 13.)

For both autoloaders and revolvers, dampen the corner of a rag with cleaner and do a general scrubbing of the exterior surfaces. Follow up with a clean, dry rag. Many shooters will put a small amount of oil on a clean cloth and apply it to the exterior surfaces of the gun to prevent rust. Stainless guns don't really need that, nor do most of the modern guns that have rust resistant finishes, but blued guns do benefit from oiling, particularly in damp climates.

With some familiarity, this can all be done in just a few minutes.

STEP FOUR:
BARREL AND CHAMBER CLEANING

The barrel (and cylinder on a revolver) has been soaking while the other parts were being cleaned, and should now be ready for some attention.

Attach a brush to the cleaning rod and dip it into the cleaner, shaking off any excess. Push the brush all the way through the barrel, then pull it back out; never reverse the

How Clean is Too Clean?

There are lots of opinions on bore cleaning, with some people insisting that clean patches should be run through the bore until they show absolutely no trace of dirt. It's certainly possible to clean a barrel that well, but the author has seen no benefit to doing so in most cases. Clean thoroughly, but there's no need to go overboard!

direction of the brush while it's in the barrel. Repeat the procedure a half-dozen times.

Autoloader barrels should always be cleaned from the chamber end; revolvers, out of necessity, can only be cleaned from the muzzle end.

Take the brush off the rod and replace it with the jag; attach a clean patch and dampen it with cleaner. Run the patch through the bore several times.

Replace that patch (which should be quite dirty) with a clean one, also wetted with cleaner. Push it through the barrel a couple of times, then replace with a clean dry patch. Run the dry patch through the barrel once and inspect; ideally the dry patch should have no more color on it than that of a light pencil streak on white paper. The patch doesn't need to be absolutely spotless, but if the residue it picked up is any darker repeat the wet patch procedure and check again.

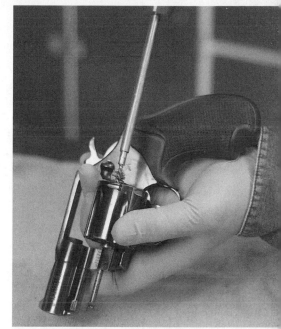

Clean a revolver's chambers just like the barrel.

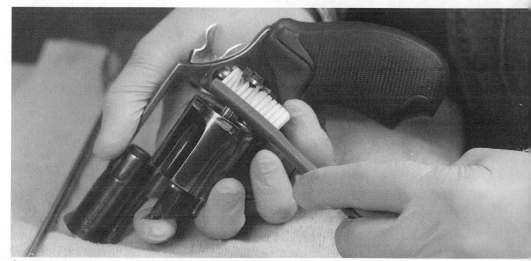

A nearly-dry brush is the best tool for cleaning under a revolver's extractor.

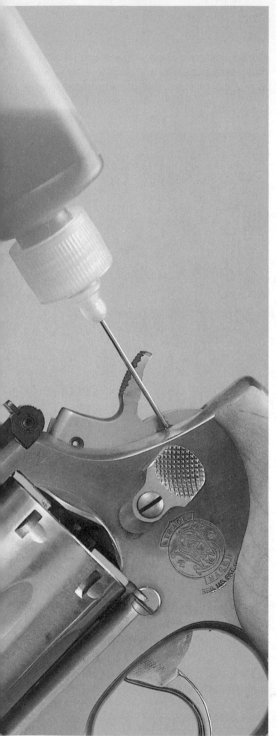

Photo 14a

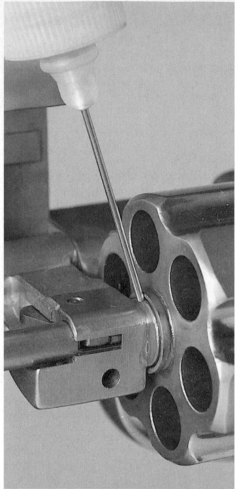

Photo 14b

A revolver's chambers need to be cleaned as well. The procedure is exactly the same as the barrel: start with a wet patch down each chamber; brush thoroughly; use another wet patch and follow up with a dry patch.

The brush for revolver chambers should be one size larger than the bore of the gun for best results. This is because the chamber is a larger diameter than the bullet, because it has to accommodate the larger brass case. Picking a larger brush will result in easier and more thorough cleaning. For instance, if you're cleaning a .38/357 revolver a .40 caliber brush is the perfect size for the chambers.

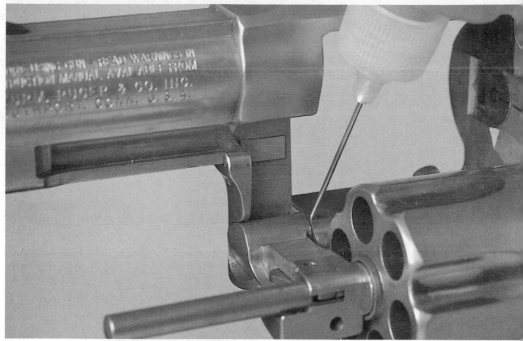

Photo 14c

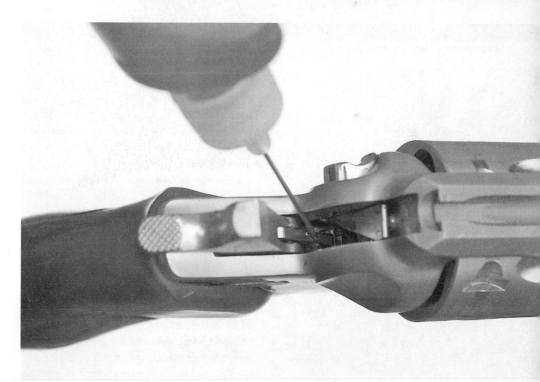

Photo 14d

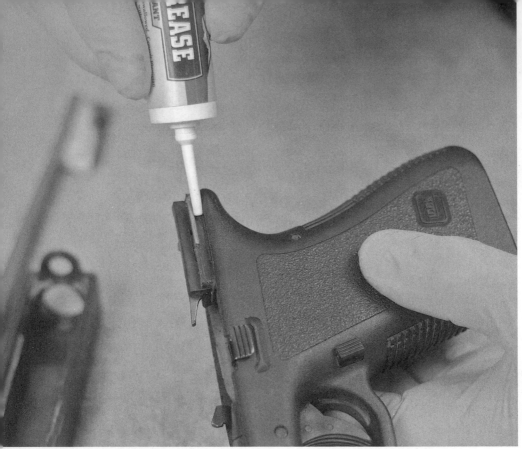

A light grease is perfect for the frame rails.

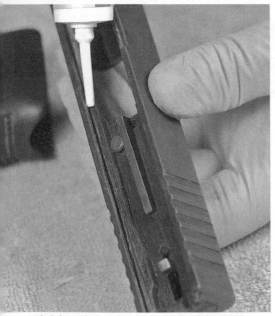

Lubricate the matching areas on the slide as well.

The final step in cleaning a revolver is to brush underneath the extractor star, a common place for dirt and debris to build up, which can cause the cylinder to bind up when turning. Be sure to brush the matching recess in the cylinder.

The gun is now ready for lubrication and re-assembly.

STEP FIVE: LUBRICATION

It's not necessary to use a lot of oil or grease on a handgun. A little lube in the right place is all that's needed to keep any gun running for many years.

For revolvers, put a drop of oil on the front of the cylinder, where it rotates, and one on the joint where the cylinder opens. A drop inside the lockwork, applied with the hammer cocked, and another drop on each side of the hammer is all that's really needed. (See pho-

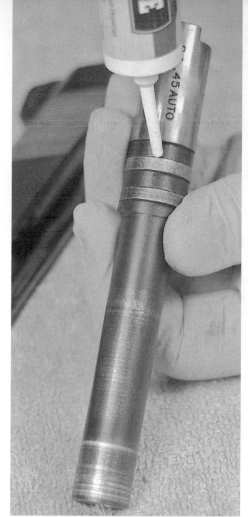

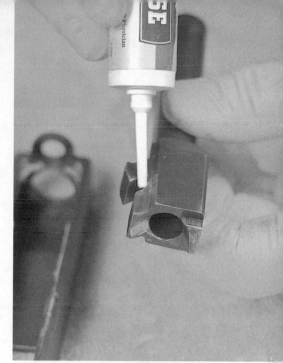

If the gun has locking lugs on the barrel, apply a small amount of oil or grease. Do the same with the matching lugs in the slide.

tos 14a through 14d.)

The main points of lubrication on an auto-loader are the frame rails. They're the surfaces on which the slide runs, and are a source of malfunctions and increased wear if not properly lubed. As mentioned at the beginning of this chapter, the best thing is a light grease. For the technically inclined, a grease with an NLGI grade of #0 will generally work best, though in hot climates a #1 can be used successfully.

If grease isn't available any decent gun oil will suffice, though it will be thrown off more

The barrel will usually have a cam surface, or a pivoting link, which should be lubricated.

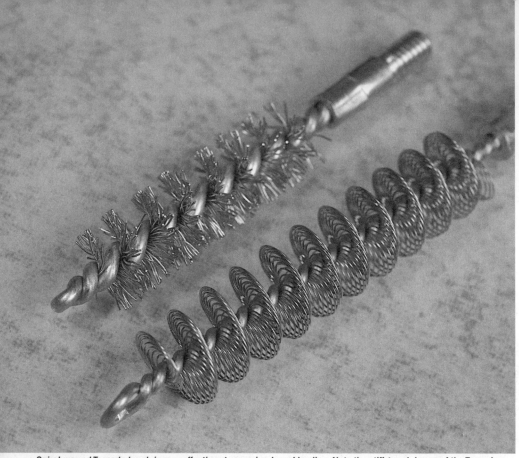

Spiral-wound Tornado brush is very effective at removing barrel leading. Note the stiff, tough loops of the Tornado brush compared to a standard brush.

rapidly when the gun is fired. Whether oil or grease, apply just a dab onto the frame rails and spread it evenly across the surfaces. Be sure that any bright spots, which signify wear points on a used gun, have lubricant on them.

The grooves in the slide which ride on the frame rails should also have a small amount of grease or oil applied, and spread over their length.

The area of the barrel where it locks into the slide should also receive a very small amount of oil or grease.

The part of the barrel that runs on the gun's cam or slide stop should also be lubricated.

Pistols with exposed hammers may have a drop of oil applied to the hammer sides and left to run down into the pivots.

While these guidelines are suitable for most common revolvers and autoloaders, certain guns may have special cleaning or lubrication procedures that can be found in the owner's manual.

SPECIAL CLEANING ISSUES: REMOVING LEAD DEPOSITS

If plain lead bullets are shot in a handgun it's just a matter of time before they leave metallic residue in the barrel. There is no such thing as a lead bullet which leaves absolutely nothing in the bore, but some do leave less than others. Proper maintenance has a lot to do with that.

If the barrel is carefully cleaned and kept that way, most of the lead deposits will come out with normal cleaning. Occasionally, however, a nasty layer of lead plates the bore and must be removed. Lead fouling raises gas pressures and lowers accuracy, and once it has started it worsens very quickly.

The easiest method to clean a stubborn barrel is to use a spiral-wound brush called a "Tornado." Available in bronze and stainless steel, the Tornado bristles touch the bore with the rounded side of their wires, as opposed to a standard brush, which touches with the sharp cut end. This allows them to be much stiffer without fear of bore damage.

A bronze Tornado brush will generally remove most leading without risk of damage to the bore, and there are also stiffer stainless steel Tornado brushes available that will remove all but the very worst leading.

To use, dip the Tornado in cleaner and run it through the bore like any other brush. Run it through the bore and pull back out; if small silver flakes show up on the wire windings,

Pure copper Chore Boy scrubber wrapped on brush will remove stubborn dirt and lead deposits. Be sure to get only the pure copper variety to avoid damage to bore.

Lewis Lead Remover, here being readied to pull through revolver barrel, is an expensive tool necessary only for the worst leading.

the brush is doing its job. All that's necessary is to repeat the process until successive passes show no lead flakes.

Another tactic for lead removal is to use a kitchen scouring pad made from pure copper. The most common brand is the Chore Boy "Ultimate Scrubber." These copper wool balls will clean stainless appliances without

scratching, and they do the same thing to a barrel. (Some scrubbers are copper plated steel, which can damage the bore. Be sure to get a scrubber that is marked very clearly as being made from pure copper.)

To use, a small piece of Chore Boy is torn off the ball and wrapped around a brush. Dip into bore cleaner and push down the bore;

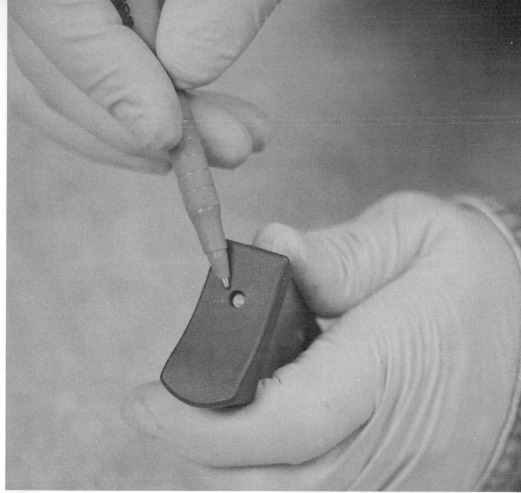

Photo 15a

it should be a very tight fit requiring some force. The Chore Boy can remove large amounts of lead with each pass and leave a completely clean bore in just a minute or so of work. It's rare to find a leaded bore which can't be cleaned with the Chore Boy trick.

Extreme cases of leading require a special tool called the Lewis Lead Remover. It's comprised of fine bronze mesh disks wrapped around a conical rubber sleeve which expands when tightened. The expanding sleeve forces the mesh into the walls of the bore, conforming to the rifling and increasing the scrubbing action.

The Lewis tool will remove the worst leading imaginable, but it's not a cheap tool.

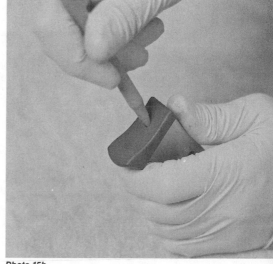

Photo 15b

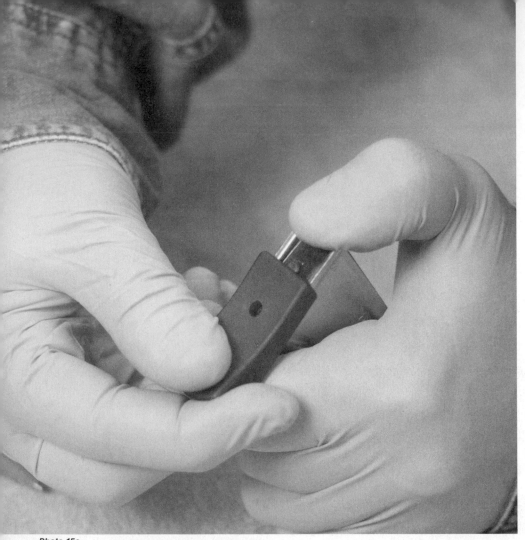

Photo 15c

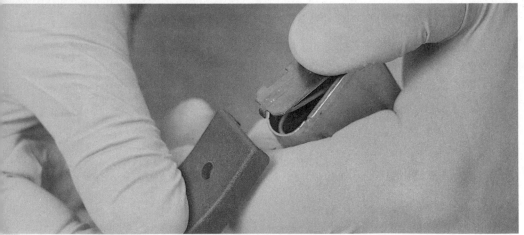

Photo 15d

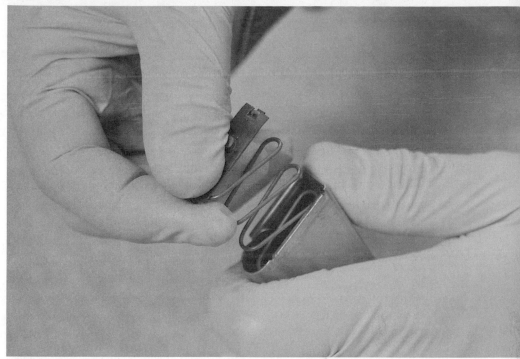

Photo 15e

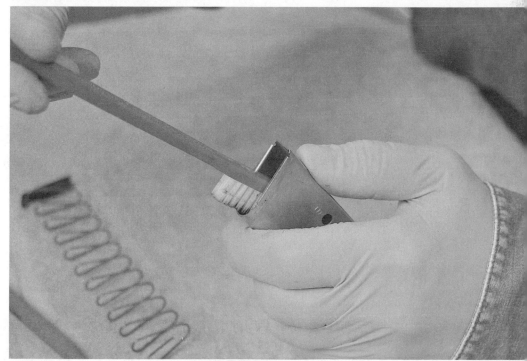

Photo 15f

Do not use a cleaner which claims to remove copper fouling on a nickeled gun!

Some gun clubs and ranges will have them available for member use, and most gunsmiths have one on their shelf as well.

CLEANING AUTOLOADER MAGAZINES

Most autoloader shooters forget about their magazines until it's too late. Magazines get quite dirty, and when they do they can cause feeding failures. It's not necessary to clean them after every outing, but magazines should be disassembled and cleaned occasionally to prevent jams caused by improper feeding.

Most magazines can be disassembled by removing the baseplate and pulling the magazine spring out. Baseplates are most commonly removed by pressing in on a small locking tab, sliding the base off, and removing the spring (photos 15a through 15c). Be careful - the spring comes out like a jack-in-the box! Use a thumb to restrain it as the baseplate comes off (photos 15d and 15e).

Some magazines do not have locking tabs or buttons; consult the owner's manual for the gun, or one of the resources listed at the end of the chapter, for instructions on disassembling specific magazines.

There are specialized brushes and mops which are designed to go fit the magazine like a bore brush fits a barrel. They're ideal for removing dirt and accumulated grime and make the job much easier, but if not available the handy M16 brush will work (photo 15f).

It's best to clean magazines without the use of solvent; if some is needed to remove stubborn dirt, denatured alcohol is the best choice. Do not oil a magazine or use any of the cleaner/lubricant products in them.

MAINTAINING FINISHES

The chemicals used in gun cleaners are generally safe for the finishes that are used on the metal parts of the gun. The major exception is nickel plating, which can be damaged by cleaning solutions containing chlorine or ammonia.

Bore cleaners that claim to remove copper fouling usually contain ammonia, which attacks the copper underneath the nickel plate. This causes the plating to develop a frosted appearance, and in extreme cases can cause the nickel to peel.

The solution is to use a cleaner that doesn't contain those compounds. If the cleaner in question says anything about removing copper fouling, don't use it on nickel plate. Unsure? Take a cotton swab and dip it in the cleaner, then rub on an empty brass casing. If the casing darkens after a few minutes, it shouldn't be used on a nickel plated gun.

Smith & Wesson states in their owners manuals not to use cleaners which are "strongly alkaline" on any of their firearms. This is especially true for alloy framed guns, whose anodizing is usually covered by a clear coating which can be damaged by such solutions.

In all cases, do not leave cleaning solvents in prolonged contact with any finished surface. Clean the surface then immediately wipe away; follow with a light oiling to help neutralize any remaining chemicals.

Lead residue often builds up on the external surfaces of revolvers, particularly the cylinder face and flutes. This is often quite difficult to remove, but there are impregnated cloths designed to remove lead deposits and carbon rings. However, they are not to be used on blued guns - they will strip the finish!

RUST PREVENTION

Handguns with blued finishes are very susceptible to corrosion in the form of rust. While the problem is more common in humid areas, even those in dry climates may face the problem from perspiration and handling. Nothing is more disconcerting than pulling a finely blued gun out of storage only to find ugly red splotches of rust.

Bluing doesn't resist the corroding effects of moisture very well, and rust prevention is all about getting the moisture away from the gun and keeping it away.

Owners of stainless steel guns may feel somewhat smug at this moment, but they should understand that stainless will in fact rust under the right conditions - and usually catches the unsuspecting owner by surprise. The stainless gun requires much less attention than does a blued steel gun, but that

doesn't mean it can simply be ignored!

Rust prevention starts with cleanliness. Fingerprints from a person who has been perspiring can quickly initiate rust. Even without sweat, some people's skin is more corrosive than others; ever wonder why collectors of fine guns wear white cotton gloves? To keep corrosive skin oils away from the finish.

Start by wiping the exterior of the gun thoroughly with a soft rag that's been moistened with a bore cleaner. (Note: do not use a copper-removing cleaner! The CLP type bore cleaners are a good choice as long as they do not say "cleans copper fouling" on the label.) Wipe the excess off with a clean rag. In areas with low humidity this may be all that's needed.

For more humid areas, especially along the saltwater coasts, it will probably be necessary to employ a specialized rust protectant. Picking a particular one can be a challenge, so it's important to know that corrosion protection varies in effectiveness depending on how the gun is used. For instance, what works well for a gun in long-term storage may not work well for a gun that's handled daily; what works for a gun carried in a holster may not be suitable for a gun that sits in a nightstand.

Corrosion protection products can be roughly classified into four categories: oils, dry film products, greases and waxes, and vapor inhibitors.

Corrosion-resistant oils are generally good for guns that see frequent or daily use. They're easy to apply, aren't easily rubbed off with normal handling or holster carry, and provide very good protection against severe but not prolonged conditions (a rain shower, as opposed to being constantly damp.) Even the best oils will eventually oxidize and leave the metal unprotected, so they're not ideal for guns in long-term storage.

This is the basis for the time-honored tradition of wiping a freshly cleaned gun down with an oil-soaked cloth, and it works pretty well for carry guns in most climates.

Vapor inhibiting paper must be used in enclosed environment; wrapping gun in paper, then placing in sealed freezer bag, works well.

Dry film protectants are very popular. These are sprays or aerosols that evaporate leaving the metal dry. They're easy to apply and generally resist wear, though not quite as well as oils in the author's experience. They generally give good protection against short duration exposure, but their greatest strength is in extended mixed duty (some use, some storage) in damp environments.

Greases and waxes are the heavy hitters of rust prevention. Their greatest strength is their ability to resist corrosion in long-term storage in humid environments. They're almost universally messy to apply and can be very messy to remove, and must usually be removed before the gun can be used. They're sticky and often require some sort of wrapping to keep dirt and dust from adhering to their surface. These are "old school" products that still have modern application because they work well.

Vapor inhibitors are the brownish paper in which new guns come wrapped. Gun manufacturers rely on this stuff, called "vapor corrosion inhibitor" or VCI, to keep their new guns from rusting while sitting in a warehouse. VCI products are most often an impregnated paper, though they're also available as small chips of a felt-like material. The big advantage of a VCI is that it lasts for years and is reusable. VCI paper is usually used in conjunction with a case or plastic bag to provide a sealed environment in which the paper's vapors can effectively displace moisture; it is significantly less effective in an open environment. It's a little hard to find, but gun specialty companies usually carry it. It is also often found on the shelf at industrial tool distributors, as it's used to protect cutting and precision measuring tools.

Want to Know More?

INSTRUCTION MANUALS

The Gun Digest Book of Firearms Assembly/Disassembly Part I - Automatic Pistols by J.B. Wood.
ISBN 978-0873417839. Krause Publications, (855) 864-2579 www.gundigeststore.com

Steve's Pages - online trove of gun manufacturer's owner manuals.
Virtually every maker is represented, and there are manuals for vintage guns you can't find anywhere else. www.stevespages.com

The Gun Owner's Handbook: A Complete Guide to Maintaining and Repairing Your Firearms by Larry Lyons.
ISBN 978-1592287420. Globe Pequot Press, P.O. Box 480, Guilford, CT 06437. (203) 458-4500 www.lyonspress.com

CLEANERS, OILS, AND GREASES

Hoppes
Their "#9" is an old favorite bore cleaning product, which some call "shooter's cologne" because of the distinctive smell. They also make an autoloading handgun solvent, said to be ideal for modern pistols, along with oils and greases ideal for gun use. Bushnell Outdoor Products, 9200 Cody, Overland Park, KS 66214. (800) 423-3537 www.hoppes.com

Outers
The other "old guard" cleaner, Outers today makes a variety of cleaners and lubricants. Their foaming bore cleaner is effective and easier to use than traditional liquid cleaners. Also makes specialized gun oils and greases. Outers, N5549 County Trunk Z, Onalaska, WI 54650. (800) 635-7656 www.outers-guncare.com

Shooter's Choice
One of the largest selection of cleaning chemicals and lubricants, including one of the few solvents guaranteed safe for polymer frames and internals and lead removing chemicals.

Shooter's Choice Gun Care Products, (440) 834-8888 www.shooters-choice.com

M-Pro 7
Well regarded line of cleaners, oils, and cleaning kits; popular with military and law enforcement shooters. Their oil is said to repel dirt. M-Pro7 Weapon Care Products, 225 W. Deer Valley Rd., Phoenix, AZ 85027. (888) 608-7888 www.mpro7.com

KG Products
Specialized cleaners and lubricants; has varieties for cleaning carbon build up and lubricating triggers. KG Industries, (512) 352-3245 www.kgcoatings.com

Gunslick
Known for high quality and wide selection of both cleaners and lubricants, including foaming bore cleaners and a unique foaming gun oil. Popular with professional competitive shooters. Gunslick Products, N5549 County Trunk Z, Onalaska, WI 54650 (800) 635-7656 www.gunslick.com

Birchwood-Casey
Produces lead removal cloths, as well as a line of cleaners and lubricants. Birchwood Laboratories, Inc., 7900 Fuller Road, Eden Prairie, MN 55344-2195. (800) 328-6156 www.sport.birchwoodcasey.com

BreakFree
Popular line of cleaners and lubricants, including several CLP (clean-lubricate) options. Break-Free Inc., 13386 International Parkway, Jacksonville, FL 32218 (800) 347-1200 www.break-free.com

Kleen-Bore
Makes a variety of solvents, as well as the Lead-Away lead removing cloths. Kleen-Bore, Inc., 13386 International Parkway, Jacksonville, FL 32218. (800) 433-2909 www.kleen-bore.com

Want to Know More?

CLEANERS, OILS, AND GREASES

D-Wipe towlettes
Personal cleanliness is important too! Removes lead residues from hands and face, after shooting or cleaning. Highly recommended to keep lead from entering the bloodstream. ESCA Tech, Inc., 3747 North Booth Street, Milwaukee, WI 53212. (414) 962-5323 www.esca-tech.com

BORE BRUSHES, MOPS AND RODS

Hoppes
Has a wide choice of gun cleaning kits, including the BoreSnake: a one-piece cloth rope which is pulled through the bore for quick and easy cleaning in the field, as well as brushes and patches. Bushnell Outdoor Products, 9200 Cody, Overland Park, KS 66214. (800) 423-3537 www.hoppes.com

Otis
Full line of gun cleaning kits and accessories that are ideal for field use. Otis Technology, PO Box 582, Lyons Falls, NY 13368. (315) 348-4300 www.otistec.com

Dewey rods
Top quality cleaning rods and brushes, one of the few sources for non-rotating rods that make chamber cleaning easier. Dewey Manufacturing, PO Box 2014, Southbury, CT 06488. (203) 264-3064 www.deweyrods.com

Tornado brushes
Hoppes, div. of Bushnell Outdoor Products, 9200 Cody, Overland Park, KS 66214. (800) 423-3537 www.hoppes.com

Chore-Boy
Makers of the pure copper Chore Boy Ultimate Scrubber. Chore-Boy Products, (866) 288-0414 www.choreboyscrubbers.com

Lewis Lead Remover tool
A product of Brownell's Inc., 200 South Front Street, Montezuma, Iowa 50171. (800) 741-0015 www.brownells.com

Kleen-Bore
Large line of rods, brushes and patches. Kleen-Bore, Inc., 13386 International Parkway, Jacksonville, FL 32218. (800) 433-2909 www.kleen-bore.com

RUST PREVENTION PRODUCTS

EEzox
Popular line of rust preventing cleaners and greases. Warren CustomOutdoor Products, 3034 Aris St. NW, Warren, Ohio 44485-1601. (330) 898-1475 www.warrencustomoutdoor.com

Boeshield T9
Effective rust preventative, originally designed to protect Boeing planes. A favorite in the damp Pacific Northwest. PMS Products Inc., 76 Veterans Dr. #110, Holland, Michigan 49423. (800) 962-1732 www.boeshield.com

RIG grease
An old favorite that still works, RIG rust inhibiting grease is ideal for long term storage. Birchwood Laboratories, Inc., 7900 Fuller Road, Eden Prairie, MN 55344. (800) 328-6156 www.birchwoodcasey.com

VCI paper
One of the few sources for small quantities of rust-preventing impregnated wrapping paper is Brownell's Inc., 200 South Front Street, Montezuma, Iowa 50171. (800) 741-0015 www.brownells.com

Metal Seal
From Outers, said to drive out moisture and leave a protective film to prevent corrosion. Often used to prevent damage to a gun that has already been exposed to moisture (such as rain.) Outers, N5549 County Trunk Z, Onalaska, WI 54650. (800) 635-7656 www. outers-guncare.com

CHAPTER 9

CUSTOMIZING THE HANDGUN

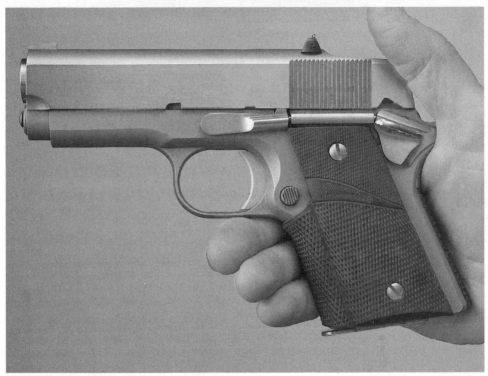

Soft rubber grips are very tacky, and can help with recoil control.

E veryone likes something that's their very own. We customize cars, motorcycles, kitchens, skin (via tattoos), so why not handguns?

Customization can be done to make the gun function better, fit the shooter better, or simply look better. While some customizations are easy for the owner to do at home, others require the skills of a professional - and sometimes a quantity of money.

GRIPS

If the gun has removable grips, the fastest and easiest modification is to swap them out for something more functional, better fitting, or better looking. There are a wide variety of grips, in an array of materials, available for a huge number of guns.

Grips can be had in a startlingly large number of materials. Of course wood is the historical favorite, but grips are also made in hard nylon, soft and hard rubber, various kinds of animal horn, varieties of polymers,

Many shooters like the extra control of finger grooves, but care must be taken to make sure that they fit properly. A mismatch like this can actually reduce control.

metal, and even industrial materials like micarta and Corian (typically used for countertops), even recycled bowling balls!

From a functional standpoint, replacement grips are an easy way to fit a gun to the shooter. For those cases where a gun is too big or small for a particular shooter's hands, there are often larger or smaller grips available to customize the fit. This is especially true of revolvers and single shot handguns, but some autoloaders can benefit as well. For the venerable Colt 1911, for example, there are grips that are thicker, for larger hands, and thinner, for smaller hands.

Perhaps the major thing that grips provide is friction, traction, so the shooter can maintain his or her grasp on the gun as it recoils. The material that the grips are made of has a large bearing on how much traction they provide. Soft rubber grips, for instance, will

give more traction than will smooth wood.

For harder grip materials it's possible to roughen the surface to increase the hand-to-gun friction. A typical way to do this is with checkering. Checkering makes for a rougher yet decorative surface and can increase shooter control.

Another surface treatment, more popular in Europe that in the U.S., is stippling - making minuscule craters in the surface that dramatically increase friction and control. Many of the European competition pistols utilize this high-traction grip treatment and have for many years.

Many shooters feel that finger grooves in the front of the grip help with recoil control. The grooves surround individual fingers, increasing the surface area of contact and providing a solid stop for each finger, keeping the gun from rolling backward in the hand.

These grips, by Herrett's Stocks, were specifically made to fit the owner's hands. Photo by Jim Amato

The grip of a polymer-framed gun can be modified to better fit the shooter. This Glock, from master gunsmith Lou Biondo, has had the grip reduced in size and heavily stippled for better traction. Photo courtesy of Lou Biondo/ Business End Customs

This works fairly well, but if the groove size and spacing don't precisely fit the fingers they can actually give less control than a grip which didn't have them to begin with.

Grips can also have a bearing on the shooter's ability to tolerate the handgun's recoil. Today there are grips made from ex-tremely soft rubber compounds which absorb a noticeable amount of recoil. For extremely hard-kicking guns, such as the very lightweight revolvers, these recoil-absorbing grips can make the difference between merely unpleasant and downright painful.

For shooters who are hard to fit, or for a

gun for which grips aren't readily available, there are many custom grip makers. Often one-person shops, these people can make grips that fit the shooter's hand perfectly, and often work in the more exotic and hard-to-find materials.

It's not just about the fit, of course - custom grips can be downright beautiful and are often used to add the finishing touch to a good-looking gun.

Custom grips are not inexpensive, but for a special gun or a special shooter, they may be the perfect solution.

Autoloading pistols with polymer frames that don't have removable grips or panels can often be radically altered to reduce the size or increase the gripping traction. The work is much like sculpting in plastic, and the results can be dramatic. Many people with smaller hands, who have been left out of the high-capacity polymer pistol era, have been able to get their guns altered to fit their hands perfectly.

Keep in mind that this work likely voids any manufacturers warranty, so anyone considering this kind of modification is advised to consider the ramifications before proceeding.

SIGHTS

The typical handgun today comes with sights which have not changed over many decades: the simple post and notch. For most applications those work well - after all, if they didn't they'd have gone the way of the dodo bird long ago - but for some applications they're less than ideal. In those cases there are aftermarket sights available.

The most common aftermarket sight installation is a set of glow-in-the-dark tritium sights, often generically referred to as "night sights." They feature very small glass vials, filled with tritium gas, which glow continuously. In dark conditions they make it easy to align the sights, while in daylight they function like normal, everyday post-and-notch sights. The front sight is usually configured as a dot, while the rear can have dots or bars,

Many defensive shooters like night sights, like these from Ameriglo, for precise sight alignment in diminished lighting. Small glass vials containing luminescent tritium gas are inserted into the front and rear blades. Photo courtesy of Ameriglo

depending on the owner's preference. Some defensive shooting experts consider the tritium night sights to be extremely important to shooting in low light conditions.

Even in the daylight, some people have trouble seeing their sights. Fiber optic sights feature a light-gathering plastic rod inserted into a sight blade. These rods serve as light pipes, taking the light that comes along their length and channeling it to the ends - where the user sees a very bright glowing dot. The effect is much like neon! Fiber optic sights are available in a variety of different colors to suit the shooter's preference, though green, red and orange are the most popular.

An old sighting arrangement that has been regaining favor in recent years is the gold bead sight. The front sight blade is inset with a gold-colored bead; the shooter sees a gold dot on the front sight. In use, the gold bead is placed on the target and simply "dropped" into the rear notch. Many compe-

Fiber optics inserted into a front sight blade are bright in a wide range of lighting conditions, are easy to spot even shooting at high speed. Available in several neon colors.

Shooter's view of "safari" or "express" sighting system.

tition shooters feel that the gold bead sight is the fastest of all conventional sight arrangements.

In recent years we've seen the introduction of numerous specialized sighting arrangements for handguns. One such system is the safari or express sight, taken from rifles used on African safaris. Popularized by Ashley Emerson, the express sight consists of a large dot in the front combined with a very shallow "v" notch in the rear sight.

What is Tritium?

Tritium is a radioactive isotope of hydrogen. Tritium is produced in small quantities as a byproduct of nuclear fission, and in larger quantities as an intentional isotope for certain uses in nuclear weapons. Tritium gas itself is not luminous, but as it decays it causes phosphors to glow; the tritium vials in night sights are coated on the inside with a phosphor, then filled with the tritium gas. As the gas decays, it causes the phosphors to glow continuously. Tritium has a half-life of just over 12 years, which is also the general useful life of sights made using the material.

Users of these sights report that the large dot is very easy to see and fast to align in the shallow notch, making rapid target acquisition easier. The system has some prominent supporters who praise its speed and accuracy.

There are other such systems with non-standard sight configurations. While the jury is still out on many of the claims, some shooters may find that these unusual products do in fact help them shoot better.

Some sights are user-replaceable, while others require the use of special tools. Ruger revolvers, in particular, are well known for their easily interchangeable front sight blades, which are available in a wide variety of colors. It's possible to have an interchangeable sight system installed on some guns, but this requires machining work by a skilled gunsmith.

ACTION WORK

Action work usually means smoothing the internal parts of a handgun to improve the trigger action. Variously referred to as "trigger jobs," "action jobs," or "trigger tuning" (there is no general agreement on terminology), this work helps make the gun easier to shoot well.

Action work involves taking the gun completely apart and finding areas of friction or roughness, then polishing the parts to eliminate them. The result is a trigger which moves without roughness and often with less force as well. A good action tuner can change how much weight the trigger presents, as well as making it release more cleanly and predictably.

Action work is usually performed by a gunsmith, though it's possible for someone with reasonable mechanical aptitude along with some simple tools to do the work at home. The experienced gunsmith, however,

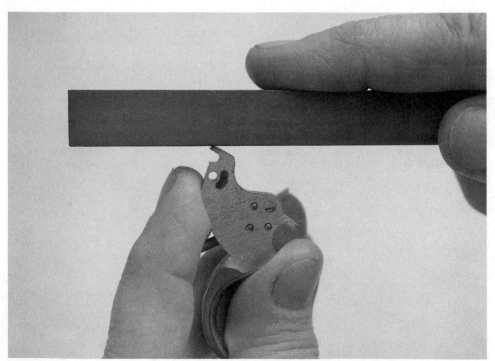

A skilled gunsmith can smooth the action of a revolver or autoloader, making it easier and more pleasant to shoot.

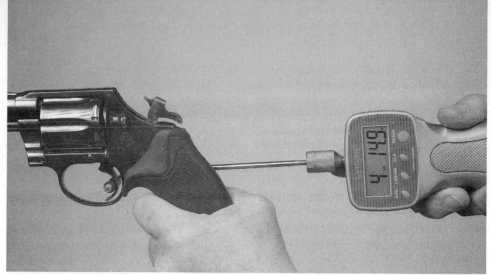
The amount of effort to operate a trigger is measured in pounds with a special gage. This trigger takes nearly five pounds of force to release.

will usually be able to tune an action more precisely simply because of experience. Knowing all the little points where the action's feel is compromised, and how to adjust them, makes the difference between a good action and a great one.

WHAT MAKES A GOOD TRIGGER?

There are several aspects of a trigger's operation that, taken together, comprise the feel of an action. For single actions, they are weight, creep, feel, letoff, and over-travel. For a double action, they are weight, consistency, feel, letoff, over-travel, and return.

Weight is simply the amount of force required to move the trigger. While many people worry (or brag) about the weight of their trigger, it's only one part of the equation, and probably not the most important part (within reasonable limits, of course.) For single action handguns lighter is generally better, to the point that it affects either reliability or safety. (A hammer that won't stay cocked on its own, or one that is released so easily that it is almost accidental, is a danger to both the shooter and the people around him/her.)

Reducing pull weight in double action guns often results in misfires, and it also affects how positively the trigger returns. Very light double action triggers on revolvers

often have very slow, hesitating trigger returns. A trigger that doesn't return positively can stick, causing the gun to jam.

Overly light triggers can also mask an otherwise bad action. People often think that the best trigger job is lighter springs, because when the action is lightened the trigger doesn't transfer as much of the gritty feel through the trigger to the finger. The trigger is still awful, it's just that the shooter doesn't notice it as much. There is an old mantra with regard to double action trigger weight: smooth, not light. It's easier to shoot a smooth but heavy trigger than a light but gritty one.

Creep in a single action trigger refers to the amount of movement the trigger makes before the sear releases. A gun with no creep seems to break like the proverbial "glass rod" - regardless of how heavy the trigger is, it seems to release instantaneous when the shooter wills it to. In contrast, a trigger with lots of creep will move quite a bit before the sear breaks.

In general, a very slight amount of creep is acceptable but excessive amounts are the sign of sloppy trigger work. Exactly where the line between "slight" and "excessive" is drawn depends on the individual shooter. Competition shooters in the long-range games like handgun silhouette, or the accuracy-intensive matches like bullseye, will generally be more critical of creep in a trigger. A small amount of creep does give a bit of a safety margin, and is the solution to what some people call a "hair trigger."

"Consistent" in a double action trigger means that it has the same pull weight from start to finish. Some triggers continually increase their pull weight toward the end of the trigger travel, an effect called "stacking." Some triggers have a slight decrease in pull weight before the sear releases, while others start out at one weight, increase in the middle of the pull, then decrease at the end. In general, the more consistent the pull the easier it is to shoot.

However, some people like a bit of "stacking" in their actions and shoot best that way. A gun with decreasing pull weight is slightly harder to shoot, and those with a "hump" in their pull are usually the hardest of all to shoot. A good trigger will have as consistent a pull weight as possible, within the limitations of the gun's design (and the shooter's desire).

The feel of the trigger is probably the most important characteristic. A trigger that feels as if there is sand in the action, or a trigger that feels like running a stick down a picket fence are both examples of bad action feel. This happens as the parts of the action slide and rotate against each other. The elimination of those artifacts in the feel is a true test of a gunsmith's ability. Whether single or double action, a good trigger should not have any roughness or hesitation in its travel regardless of pull weight.

When the sear releases, which is called letoff, it should do so predictably and without abruptness. Many triggers release with what can only be described as jerk, which makes holding the sights steady at the moment of the bullet's exit much more difficult.

After the sear breaks, the trigger should stop moving. Trigger movement after the sear releases is called over-travel, and has an

effect similar to a bad letoff: it can result in the gun moving slightly when the bullet exits the muzzle. Some guns, because of their design, have no over-travel; others control it through the use of trigger stops. (Interestingly, correcting over-travel can often make up for an abrupt letoff.)

Jerry Miculek, one of the best competitors with any handgun and considered the best revolver shooter in the world, points out that the trigger pull is only half - or even less - of the equation. Trigger return is at least as important to successful double-action shooting. Whether revolver or autoloader, the double action trigger return should be judged much like trigger pull: no hesitation, no grittiness or roughness. It should also return at a consistent speed, and should be fast enough to keep up with the trigger finger. A good double action trigger should have a return as good as its pull.

PERFORMANCE MODIFICATIONS

Some modifications are made to enhance the performance of the gun: making it faster or easier to shoot or handle. Most such modifications come to us from the world of competition and have made their way into common use because they have value to many shooters outside of the shooting games.

MAKING RELOADING FASTER

In the early days of IPSC competition it was discovered that a substantial amount of time could be saved by speeding up the re-

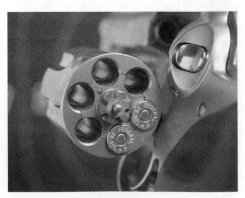

loading sequence. Someone (several people claim credit) figured out that by making the opening of the magazine well larger it would shave time getting the magazine inserted. Originally the corners of the well's mouth were ground away, but it wasn't long before someone made a larger one out of metal and attached it to the gun's grip. Today many guns come from the factory with beveled magazine wells, but there are still aftermarket oversized magazine wells to fit many kinds of autoloading pistols.

For double action revolvers, the equivalent is to have the edges of the chambers beveled or chamfered. It doesn't take a lot to make a huge difference, and having it done makes reloading smoother, easier and faster. Despite the value of this modification, very few revolvers today come with chamfered chambers. Luckily, any decent gunsmith can do this relatively inexpensively. *DSC04420*

REDUCING MUZZLE RISE

One of the issues shooting powerful rounds out of a handgun - in competition, hunting, or self defense - is the force with which the muzzle jumps during recoil. It slows down follow-up shots and makes

The magazine well acts like a funnel to make rapid magazine changes. *Photo courtesy of Dawson Precision*

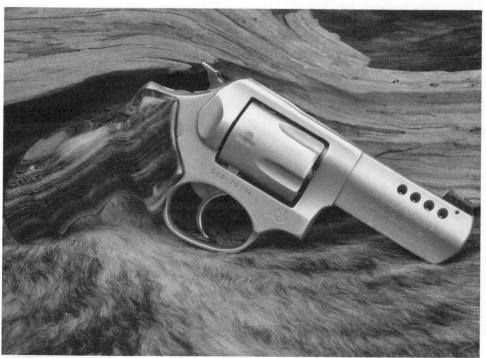

This revolver barrel shows one type of muzzle compensator; in this case, gunsmith Marc Morganti has machined ports on either side of the barrel which act as jets to keep the muzzle from climbing. *Photo courtesy of Gemini Customs*

shooting heavy loads uncomfortable. The solution is to install a muzzle brake or compensator on the gun.

The principle behind these devices is the redirection of the combustion gases exiting the muzzle so that they counteract the recoil and muzzle rise. The usual method is to machine ports (guns so equipped are often referred to as being ported), which are simply holes in the end of the barrel. The holes may be round, oblong, or even narrow slits, but the concept is the same: use the power of the escaping gas to push the muzzle down. The ports act like little jets to apply a downward force to the barrel, helping to counteract the natural tendency of the muzzle to arc upward.

There are a number of different approaches to the design of a muzzle brake or compensator. Some simply have the ports cut into the barrel, while others have a chamber machined into the end of the barrel - the chamber having the ports. The chamber method allows the gases to expand before they exit the compensator and are said to be more efficient than simple porting without an expansion area.

For revolvers, the ports are usually cut into the barrel near the muzzle. For autoloaders it's generally easier to install a special barrel with a compensator added to the end, though there are compensation systems which have ports cut into the barrel with the slide machined away above them to allow the gases to escape. Single shot handguns often have provision to thread a muzzle brake onto the end of the barrel, and remove it when it's not needed. The variations are almost endless.

In general, the more powerful the round the better muzzle compensators work. In revolvers they're usually reserved for the Magnum rounds; in autoloaders they work best with higher-pressure rounds such as the .357 SIG and .40 S&W. Any single shot handgun chambered in a rifle cartridge can benefit from compensation.

There are a couple of downsides to brakes or compensators. First, they're louder from the shooter's perspective than a gun that doesn't have one. This is because instead of being blown away from the shooter, the gases are directed up or to the sides. This means more noise at the shooter's position, and directly to either side, but less noise downrange.

The other negative is that the burning gases are capable of inflicting severe wounds to any flesh that is nearby, and the jet which comes out of the compensator can contain small particles of combustion material. These particles can be forced into an unprotected eye, causing severe pain and sometimes permanent damage. For this reason compensators aren't usually recommended for self defense guns, where they might be fired in close quarters. Any compensated gun should be used only when wearing proper safety glasses.

MAKING THE GUN GO FASTER

In many kinds of competition it's desirable to have the gun cycle as quickly as possible so that the shooter can trigger the next shot in a shorter period of time. On an autoloader this is often done by machining the slide to reduce its mass. Reduced mass means that it moves faster under the same amount of recoil force; a side benefit is that recoil is slightly reduced, making the muzzle come back on target faster.

Guns with lightened slides generally must be used only with specific ammunition, where the bullet weight and muzzle velocity have been carefully chosen to operate the slide without doing damage because of the higher slide velocity. As a result, doing this modification should only be done for competition purposes, and only by a gunsmith who understands the job.

For revolvers the usual method to reduce cycle times is to reduce the amount of force needed to operate the trigger. Lighter springs are installed to reduce the trigger effort, and sometimes the hammer is machined to reduce its weight and the time it takes between when the sear releases and the round ignites (called lock time.) Most such modified revolvers are very picky as to what ammunition they will fire, and usually the shooter is required to handload ammunition specifically crafted to fire with very little firing pin force. Revolvers so modified are not suitable for self defense use.

COCKING SERRATIONS

Autoloading pistols usually have cocking serrations or notches on the rear of the slide, where the hand can grab onto them to pull the slide back. Many competition shoot-

Lightened slides are popular in such shooting competitions as the Steel Challenge. This "Steelmaster" gun from Dawson Precision has it all: lightened slide, big magazine well, and red dot sight. Photo courtesy of Dawson Precision

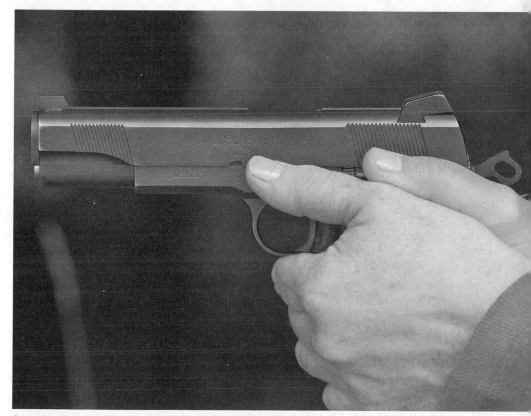

Forward cocking serrations, as on this customized Springfield 1911A1 pistol, are a popular modification.

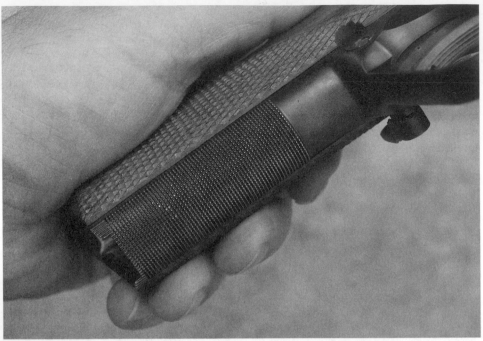

Checkering, as on the front of this grip, is another method to improve the traction on handguns.

Stippling is an attractive, affordable alternative to checkering.

ers like to do a "press check," a procedure where the slide is pulled back very slightly to allow the shooter to see if there is a round in the chamber. To make this maneuver easier, some gunsmiths cut cocking serrations in the front of the slide, near the muzzle, to make the press check easier. Some very well-optioned factory guns today include forward serrations.

It's important to note that many self defense shooting instructors believed that this is an unsafe practice and do not recommend the installation or use of forward cocking notches.

INCREASING TRACTION

In the discussion about grips and gripframe modifications it was mentioned that a side benefit of those modifications was increased traction and control. Sometimes these modifications are done specifically to gain traction without changing the grip size. Increased traction means better control over recoil, especially when hands are wet or cold.

On metal autoloading pistols, the usual way to increase traction is to roughen the front or back of the gripframe (frontstrap or backstrap, respectively). Like with the grips, this is usually done by checkering or stippling the metal.

Checkering metal is an art unto itself, and is usually considered the more elegant of the two. Stippling has a unique look of its own and is usually faster, easier and cheaper to apply.

The straps can also be machined with grooves or divots to achieve the same effect. Some custom gunsmiths have their own distinctive machining patterns for this modification, and some factory guns also have a distinctive machining pattern.

A revolver's backstrap can also be checkered or stippled, though the former is less

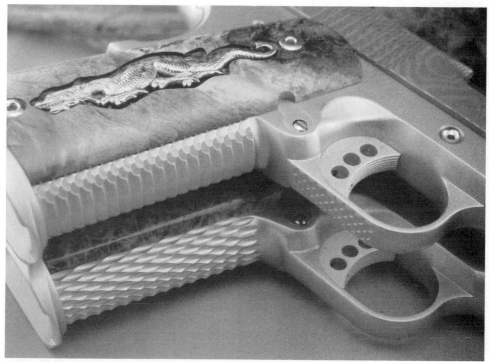

Some custom gunsmiths can machine the front strap into an attractive pattern that looks good and provides great traction. *Photo courtesy of Gemini Customs*

Skateboard tape adds significant traction to an otherwise smooth gun, can be used on autoloaders, revolvers, and single shots.

common. The compound curves of a revolver's grip make doing the checkering a very time-consuming and delicate task, one which very few gunsmiths today are willing to attempt. The usual choice is some sort of stippling, which achieves the goal at a substantially reduced cost.

Polymer framed autopistols usually have some sort of grip enhancement molded in, but sometimes it's less aggressive than the owner would prefer. For those people it's possible to have the surface grooved or stippled to increase the grip traction. This is usually done in concert with a grip reduction, but some gunsmiths offer it as a separate service.

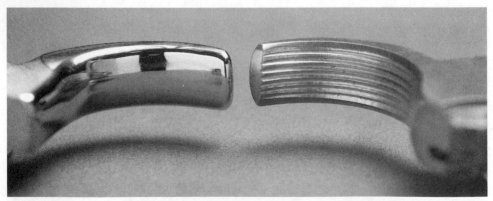

Smooth trigger was once serrated like the example on the right. Removing serrations and polishing to a bright shine makes a big difference in shooter comfort.

An extreme example of dehorning a gun is the "melt job," where all edges and corners are removed. "Meltdown" photo courtesy of Clark Custom Guns

No matter what the gun, there is a user-installed alternative that works well: skateboard tape. Skateboard tape is, for all intents and purposes, is a weather-resistant pressure-sensitive sandpaper which can be applied to any smooth, clean surface. (Some types will even adhere to a textured surface.) Skateboard tape is extremely effective as a friction enhancer, is cheap and easy to apply, and can even be had in different colors. It's a cost-effective way to experiment with increased grip stability.

COMFORT MODIFICATIONS

Handguns are machined implements, and because of that often have sharp edges and pointy corners that are not friendly to human skin. Many handgunners prefer to have those sharp edges removed to aide in comfort; a gun that's pleasant to shoot will get shot more often, which means that it's easier to become proficient with it.

Some triggers, for instance, have rough serrations or sharp edges that rub on the trigger finger. Many shooters complain of blisters or sore skin on their trigger fingers after long shooting sessions, and having such a trigger smoothed can make a huge difference in shootability. Rounding and polishing the surface of a double-action trigger, in particular, makes a huge difference in shooter comfort.

The rest of the gun can often benefit from some attention. For instance, autoloading pistols often have edges on the slide or on controls - safety, slide lock, or decocker - that become uncomfortable after shooting even a small number of rounds. Those parts can be taken out, polished and smoothed, and reinstalled for a big boost in comfort.

The slide itself often has sharp edges as well, sometimes sufficient to cause lacerations in the shooter's palm. Sharp corners and edges on autos and revolvers, can cause injury but are easily removed.

Photo courtesy of VZ Grips

Photo courtesy of Gemini Customs

The process of removing these protrusions and edges is called "dehorning"; extreme dehorning, where the edges aren't just blunted but dramatically rounded, is called "melting." A melted gun has a feel that's been likened to a bar of soap, with no defined edges or corners to cause any pain. It's also a unique look that people either love or hate.

AESTHETIC CUSTOMIZATION

Guns are tools - but sometimes it's nice to use a tool that looks as good as it performs. Some modifications are done simply to enhance the visual appeal of a handgun, and there's certainly nothing wrong with that.

GRIPS

We talked about grips earlier, but from a functional perspective. From an aesthetic standpoint, a nice set of grips can dramatically alter the appearance of a gun; a blued steel pistol with highly figured wood grips, for instance, is frequently held to be the epitome of firearm styling. Wood grips offer the widest variety of colors and patterns, from the traditional walnut to exotics like bloodwood and bocote. There are even makers

Bluing is a chemical process that requires both equipment and expertise. Gunsmith Todd Koonce pulls a disassembled gun from the 270 degree bluing bath.

using polymer-stabilized and colored woods for a very different look.

REFINISHING

A worn-looking but still serviceable handgun can be brought back to life or given a completely different look through refinishing. Most manufacturers offer refinishing services for their guns, but generally won't change from one finish type to another. There are a number of reputable refinishers that can give the gun's owner just about any finish he/she desires.

A blued gun can always be easily reblued, and in the process have small scratches and pitting polished out. The epitome of bluing is the mirror polished finish, a time-consuming but stunning alternative offered by the

Modern polymer finishes are durable, resistant to moisture, and come in a wide variety of colors to make patterns like camouflage and even flames! Photos courtesy of Custom Digital Designs

better refinishing shops.

One downside of bluing is that it does wear over time, though many people see a worn blue finish as a badge of honor, comparing it to a pair of well-worn blue jeans. The other downside is that blued guns will rust pretty easily in the presence of moisture, making maintenance more difficult and more important.

In recent years there's been a boom in polymer-based finishes for guns. These are usually applied and baked on, and can be had in a variety of colors as well as many different camouflage patterns. Some of these companies can even craft custom, one-of-a-kind camouflage patterns. Many handgun hunters take advantage of these services, because the finishes are both moisture resistant and help hide the gun from wary prey.

These new polymer finishes are generally tough, but under extreme use can wear on edges or corners. They're resistant to abrasion, but it is possible that a severe scratch can pierce the coating down to the metal. As mentioned, they're quite resistant to water and salt air unless compromised by wear or damage.

Stainless guns can be easily refinished in a variety of surface textures.

Electroplating is a time-honored finish for pistols and revolvers. The brightly polished nickeled revolver is a staple of old crime novels, and nickel plating is still available. Unfortunately nickel plating tends to peel over time and is adversely affected by cleaners that contain ammonia compounds, such as those found in bore cleaners designed to remove copper fouling. It's also soft, wears easily, and is expensive to redo when it starts to look shabby.

There is a version of nickel plate that's applied chemically, rather than electrically, and shares almost none of it's cousin's weaknesses. Called electroless nickel, or sometimes abbreviated to "e-nickel," it is quite tough, very hard, resistant to moisture, and doesn't peel. It has the same slightly warm color as the plated version, and can be applied over a wider variety of metals. Some manufacturers offer new guns in e-nickel, although they're becoming fewer each year. For some reason the nickel color is falling out of favor with today's gun buyers.

One handgun finish that's popular is hard chrome. A favorite of many custom gunsmiths, hard chrome can be applied to polished or matte surfaces and the resulting finish matches the original surface. Chrome is durable, hard, and resists moisture and chemical damage. It also has a cold, slightly bluish tinge which some people find objectionable.

Physical Vapor Deposition (PVD) coatings are beginning to become popular. PVD uses a vacuum chamber to deposit minuscule layers of vaporized material onto a surface. These finishes are very thin, very hard, and generally have good wear characteristics. They're also available in colors other than black (dark earth, gray, and dark green are popular). PVD coating is still fairly expensive, but the cost is coming down as more gun manufacturers adopt the technology. PVD is an excellent option for darkening stainless steel.

Stainless guns can be easily refinished and given a brushed, beaded, or polished appearance. While the surface will wear over time, having the gun refinished is a relatively inexpensive proposition.

Any decent gunsmith should be able to

Engraving is the ultimate personalization given to a handgun. Since this is an art form, it pays to research the various styles and artists before picking one. Engraving by Weldon Lister. Photo by Paul Goodwin

Gold inlays, often in animal form, are extremely unique - though costly. Photo courtesy of engraver Weldon Lister

Engraving is priced depending on the coverage. This Colt, by master engraver Weldon Lister, shows 100% coverage - including the hard-to-engrave hammer. Photo by Gary Hess

offer at least a couple of alternatives to the owner of a stainless handgun.

ENGRAVING

The most personal of all handgun modifications is engraving. While engraving has become less popular in recent years, it's still available from a surprisingly large number of true artisans. An engraved gun can be as simple or as ostentatious as the owner desires, and can incorporate symbols of his/her life and interests to become a true personal reflection.

There are numerous styles of engraving, from traditional scroll to art deco to "bulino" scenic illustration. Most engravers tend to specialize in one or two styles, though they may be able to produce others. The engraving style has to be something the owner likes, but it also has to fit the gun. Some styles don't look right on some guns, and a working knowledge of the art is helpful in understanding why.

One of the first choices to make is how much of the gun will be engraved. Called "coverage," it's usually expressed in terms of the percentage of the gun's surface. Obviously the more engraving, the more it costs! Certain parts, such as hammers and triggers, are sometimes billed separately because their hardened surfaces require extra effort on the part of the engraver.

If the gun to be engraved is blued it will need refinishing once the engraving is complete. Even if the gun has a good blued surface prior to the work being done, the engraving will expose unprotected metal which will quickly rust. Rebluing (or other finishing) after engraving is a necessary precaution.

In addition to (or sometimes instead of) the engraving, gold inlays can be incised into the gun's surface. Inlays can be as simple as a narrow decorative band around the muzzle or as ornate as engraved plaques of animals or busts of people. Gold inlays incur not just the cost of the engraving, but of the gold as well - and with the price of gold as this is written, that can run into very serious money!

It's important to understand that engraving is art, and like all art there are those who are merely competent and those who are truly gifted and expressive. All engraving is not equal. Picking an engraver needs to be done carefully. There's a lot of money at stake, and it should only happen after seeing the work of several who engrave in the desired style.

Engravers are a rare breed, and those who are accomplished tend to have waiting lists measured in years. The work is really a collaboration between the owner and the artist; there are many decisions to be made along the way, and the owner will need to budget both money and time.

An engraved gun is a big undertaking, both financially and chronologically. If the idea of commissioning an engraved arm is appealing, a good start is to study quality work and common motifs. Since engraved guns are not common, the best method is to research via pictures. One of the best books on the subject is "Steel Canvas: The Art of American Arms" by R. L. Wilson, highly recommended for anyone interested in highly embellished guns.

Want to know more?

REPLACEMENT GRIPS - see Chapter 4

REPLACEMENT SIGHTS - see Chapter 8

CUSTOM GUNSMITHS

Clark Custom Guns - originators of the "Meltdown", an extreme dehorning process for autoloading pistols. CCG, Inc., 336 Shootout Lane, Princeton, LA 71067. (318) 949-9884 www.clarkcustomguns.com

Dawson Precision - one of the most popular custom gunsmith shops for professional competitive shooters. Dawson Precision, 3300 CR 233, Florence, TX 76527. (866) 300-1911 www.dawsonprecision.com

Robar - best known for their synthetic finishes, Robar also offers extensive custom gunsmithing services. The Robar Companies, Inc., 21438 N. 7th Ave Suite B, Phoenix, AZ 85027. (623) 581-2648 www.robarguns.com

Gemini Customs - custom work on revolvers and autoloaders; specialist in Ruger revolvers. Marc Morganti, Gemini Custom, 717 Botkins Lane, Frankfort, KY 40601. (502) 226-1230 www.geminicustoms.com

Cylinder & Slide - well known for a wide range of custom work on both autoloading pistols and revolvers. Bill Laughridge, Cylinder & Slide Inc., 245 E. 4th Street, Fremont, NE 68025. (402)721-4277 www.cylinder-slide.com

Glenn Custom - renowned for action work and competition guns, one of the few qualified Colt revolver gunsmiths. Autoloaders too. Frank Glenn, Accuracy Unlimited, 11012 N. 32nd Street, Phoenix, AZ 85028. (602) 978-9089 www.glenncustom.com

Bowen Classic Arms - specializes in custom revolvers and restorations. Hamilton Bowen, Bowen Classic Arms Corp., P. O. Box 67, Louisville, TN 37777. (865) 984-3583 www.bowenclassicarms.com

Business End Customs - specializes in the newest polymer-framed pistols. Lou Biondo, Business End Customs Inc., 662 Clark Rd Unit #8, Tewksbury, MA 01876. (978) 642-9096 www.businessendcustoms.com

Apex - best known for competition modifications on revolvers and select autoloaders. Randy Lee, Apex Tactical Specialties, Inc., 715-D Santa Maria Ave., Los Osos, CA 93402. (805) 528-5250 www.apextactical.com

Koonce Custom - custom gunsmithing and refinishing on a wide variety of handguns. Precision machining a specialty. Todd Koonce, Koonce Custom Gunworks, 2325 Hoyt St SE, Salem OR 97302. (503) 364-0100 www.kooncecustom.com

REFINISHERS

Custom Digital Designs - specialists in Duracoat finishes, especially decorative patterns and camouflage. Custom Digital Designs, 115 Enterprise Dr. Suite 115A, Cumming, GA 30040. (770) 886-9900 www.CDDonline.com

Robar - famous for their NP3 and Roguard synthetic finishes. The Robar Companies, Inc., 21438 N. 7th Ave Suite B, Phoenix, AZ 85027. (623) 581-2648 www.robarguns.com

Turnbull - Doug Turnbull is the authority on fine gun finishes like bluing and case hardening. Many gun manufacturers and gunsmiths utilize Turnbull finishes on their best guns, but they also offer refinishing and restoration services to the general public. Turnbull Manufacturing Co., PO Box 471, Bloomfield, NY 14469. (585) 657-6338 www.turnbullmfg.com

Black-T - developed by W.E. Birdsong, Black-T is a proprietary metal coating that is durable and very resistant to corrosion. A favorite of gun and knife manufacturers, it is available in green, tan, and brown as well as their signature black. W. E. Birdsong & Associates, Inc., 1435 Monterey Road, Florence, MS 39073. (601) 939-7448 www.black-t.com

Want to know more?

DuraCoat - a proprietary synthetic finish from Lauer Weaponry, renowned for its durability and resistance to water and chemicals. Available in a wide variety of colors from mild to wild. Available only through their certified appliers; list available on their website. Lauer Custom Weaponry, 3601 129th St., Chippewa Falls, WI 54729. (800) 830-6677 www.lauerweaponry.com

IonBond - supplier of PVD coating services, offers DiamondBLACK coating specifically engineered for firearms. Springer Precision LLC, 60053 Minnetonka Ln., Bend, OR 97702. (541) 480-5546 www.springerprecision.com

APW/Cogan - offers hard chrome, nickel, black nickel, bluing, titanium nitride, and ceramic polymer coatings. Extensive gunsmithing abilities too. Accurate Plating and Weaponry, Inc., 5229 County Road 99, Newville, Alabama 36353. (334) 585-9488 www.apwcogan.com

Metalife - respected firearms plating and bluing shop. Mahovsky's Metalife, 2327 Eureka Road, Grand Valley, PA 16420. (814) 436-7747 www.mahovskysmetalife.com

TechPlate - wide range of gun plating and coating, from hard chrome titanium nitride, matte to high polish. TechPlate, Inc., 1571-H S. Sunkist St., Anaheim, CA 92806. (714) 634-9254 www.techplate.com

Cerakote - developers of ceramic/polymer gun finishes that are extremely hard and wear resistant, available in a wide range of colors through certified appliers nationwide. CERAKOTE™ Firearm Coatings, 7050 6th Street, White City, OR 97503 (866) 774-7628 www.cerakoteguncoatings.com

ENGRAVING

Firearms Engravers Guild of America - the one-stop source of contact information for the best engravers in the country. 1452 Ivanhoe Rd., Ludington, MI 49431. (616) 929-6146 www.fega.com

Weldon Lister - a member of the FEGA and a renowned artist, Lister works on all types of handguns. Engraving, gold inlays, and refinishing. (210) 269-0102 www.weldonlister.com

Steel Canvas: The Art of American Arms by R. L. Wilson. ISBN 978-0785818915. Quayside Publishing Group, 400 First Avenue North Suite 300, Minneapolis, MN 55401. (800) 458-0454 www.booksalesusa.com

BARREL PORTING

Mag-na-port - long term reputation for quality work and effective recoil reduction. Magna-port International, Inc., 41302 Executive Drive, Harrison Township, MI 48045-1306. (586) 469-6727 www.magnaport.com

Gemini Customs - exclusive source for jack Weigand's "Hybra-Port" system. 717 Botkins Lane, Frankfort, KY 40601. (502) 226-1230 www.geminicustoms.com

POLYMER GRIP REDUCTIONS

Business End Customs - quality grip reductions and stippling. Lou Biondo, Business End Customs Inc., 662 Clark Rd Unit #8, Tewksbury, MA 01876. (978) 642-9096 www.businessendcustoms.com

GripReductions - does reductions, stippling, and extensive modifications like flared magazine wells and beavertail extensions. Grip Reductions c/o Dale Hunnicutt, 21515 Hufsmith-Kohrville Rd., Tomball, TX 77375. (832) 457-1562 www.gripreductions.com

Bowie Tactical - grip reductions, texturing, grip shortening. David Bowie, Bowie Tactical Concepts, 124 Roy Pence Rd., West Union, OH 45693. (937) 544-4606 www.bowietacticalconcepts.com

Robar - polymer grip reductions and texturing. The Robar Companies, Inc., 21438 N. 7th Ave Suite B, Phoenix, AZ 85027. (623) 581-2648 www.robarguns.com

USING YOUR HANDGUN

The handgun, contrary to the panicked pronouncements of the gun control crowd, is a versatile tool that is adaptable to a wide variety of activities. If you're looking for something new to do with your pistol, revolver, or single shot you'll probably find it in this chapter.

HUNTING

Handgun hunting has become very popular in the last few decades, partially thanks to advances in ammunition and the introduction of cartridges specifically designed for hunting.

Small game hunting, such as for squirrel and rabbit, is usually done with smaller calibers - the various rimfires and the .32 caliber centerfires. Since the targets are small and are generally shot at distances of up to 50 yards or so, handguns with barrels that give a longer sight radius are usually preferred. Scoping a handgun reduces the need for a long sight radius, but the resulting shorter barrels may not give sufficient velocity for the longest shots.

The .22 Long Rifle is by far the most popular small game round. It's easy to shoot, makes reliable kills at normal handgun distances (say, up to 40 yards or so), and is available with a wide variety of bullets to suit any game. Pest control is efficiently handled with a high-velocity hollowpoint round, while meat hunters will usually choose a solid standard velocity slug to maximize the amount of edible meat.

Serious shooters of small pests often choose one of the extremely high velocity rounds such as the .17 HMR or the .22 Magnum, which offer quick and sure kills even at longer distances.

Hunters of small meat animals who choose a small centerfire cartridge usually choose slower rounds with solid round-nose bullets, which don't destroy an excessive amount of edible meat. Solid bullets in the various .32 calibers result in reliable knockdown and maximum meat yield at ranges beyond the .22 Long Rifle.

Autoloaders, revolvers and single shots are all well suited to small game hunting. A scoped .22 autoloader is a common sight amongst squirrel hunters, and long-barreled .17 HMR revolvers and single shots are favorites for pest control.

Since many small game animals such as squirrels inhabit dim forests, low power scopes that transmit maximum light to the eye are called for. Illuminated reticles are also very helpful, as a black crosshair can be difficult to see amongst tree branches.

As the size of the animal increases, often the caliber of the handgun does as well. Many hunters of the larger varmints and predators - badgers up to coyotes - start with rounds such as the .32 H&R Magnum or the .327 Federal and go up from there.

The .357 Magnum loaded with high performance hollowpoints seems to be a particular favorite among western coyote hunters, as it assures reliable kills at any reasonable distance. Autoloading rounds such

The long-barrel .357 loaded with high performance hollowpoints is a popular varmint combination, may be legal for deer in some states.

as the 9mm are also reasonable choices, if a little uncommon, and the .357 SIG is making something a name for itself as a long-range coyote killer.

The major limitation with centerfire autoloading pistols is the difficulty of scoping them, a must for any long-range hunting. As a result custom barrels for the single-shot pistols, chambered in the hot autoloading cartridges, are very popular.

Where the pelt is to be kept, such as with fox or bobcat, bullets are chosen for minimal fur damage. The ideal is a single entry hole that is easily patched. Many hunters swear by the .17 HMR for pelt hunting, as the rounds make a very small entry hole and almost never exit the larger bodies of these animals. The .22 Magnum is also a popular choice for the same reason.

Fur hunters using centerfire cartridges usually select solid bullets which make small entry and exit wounds. The power of the round must be carefully controlled if a good pelt is to be realized, and the excessively powerful Magnums with hollowpoint bullets are not usually chosen. Some pelt hunters make do with round nose .38 Specials, though they are on the large side for such use.

Big game hunting, for animals of deer size and up, is done with centerfire cartridges exclusively. (No state currently allows rimfire cartridges for any large game animals.) The emphasis is on clean, quick kills, and this is where the large Magnums come into their own.

The .357 Magnum is generally the smallest cartridge legal for the larger animals, but not in all states. Fired from a handgun it is generally at the bottom edge of what is considered powerful enough for deer. Where the .357 is legal to use, it's generally recommended that the hunter load it with heavy bullets; 158 grain slugs at a minimum, with 180 grains considered preferable. Modern controlled expansion hollowpoint bullets are the best choice for reliable kills on deer.

Big game hunting really comes into its own with powerful cartridges like the .41 Magnum. Eminently suitable for deer at reasonable distance, the .41 has a very dedicated following among handgun hunters.

Heavily loaded, the .45 Colt makes a fine deer cartridge and is also suitable for elk at reasonable distances. The same can be said of the .44 Magnum as well; both of these are commonly encountered in the field during deer and elk seasons.

Longer range deer and elk hunting, as well as hunting of the more dangerous species such as bear, is best handled with the larger magnums such as the .454 Casull, .460 S&W, and the .480 Ruger. They're suitable for anything that walks in North America, and have been used successfully on African species as well.

Autoloading cartridges are limited because of the aforementioned scope issues, but also because of barrel length limitations in some states. Still, certain autoloading rounds have developed good reputations for large game, especially when chambered in a single shot handgun. The 10mm Auto is suited for the same kind of game that the .41 Magnum is, and makes a fine deer cartridge. The .50 AE is also occasionally found in pursuit of deer (and elk at shorter ranges), and has the advantage of being available in the long-barreled, easily scoped Desert Eagle pistol.

The powerful .500 S&W Magnum is best suited for the largest game at extended distances, and is said to work extremely well for that use. It's also not a gun that most shooters can handle well, so it should be reserved for the experienced shooter and hunter.

Anyone wishing to hunt with a handgun should be well practiced in shooting from different field positions, including standing, kneeling, sitting, and prone.

The handgun hunter should be familiar with a variety of field positions. Kneeling, especially against a tree for stability, is most useful in the woods. Practice with various kinds of support, such as leaning on a tree stump or resting the shooting hands on a convenient log, will greatly increase the range at which game can be humanely taken and is strongly encouraged.

A convenient support, such as this very low branch, is a field-expedient method to ensure an accurate shot.

COMPETITION

Handgun competition is a rapidly growing area of the shooting hobby, and there are a wide variety of shooting events that appeal to just about anyone who owns a handgun.

BULLSEYE

Many people get started in handgun competition through what is generically referred to as "bullseye." Both rimfire and centerfire guns are used, though rimfire seems to be the most prevalent at the local level. Bullseye is formal target shooting, where shooters vie to produce very small groups on their targets under generous time limits. Bullseye is the basis for most Olympic shooting sports.

Bullseye is shot mostly from the standing position, and there is no drawing or movement on the part of the shooter. The emphasis is on precision, whether using rimfire or centerfire.

The NRA is the primary sponsor of bullseye competitions around the country. They also run, in conjunction with the Civilian Marksmanship Program, the annual National Rifle & PIstol Championships at Camp Perry, where handgun shooters compete in bullseye matches for several prestigious awards.

A bullseye league is generally easy to find anywhere in the U.S., with many of them sponsored by the local gun club. All that's needed to get started is a suitable gun and some ammunition; match costs are reasonable too.

PPC

Another precision-oriented pistol competition is called "PPC," which stands (depending on who is asked) for Police Pistol Course, Police Pistol Combat, or Practical Pistol Course. Most people call it PPC or sometimes "1500 shooting" (1500 being the perfect score in a sanctioned match, which requires shooting 150 rounds with each round being worth a possible 10 points).

PPC shooting is said to have originated in the 1930s with the FBI, who developed as a training tool for agents and police officers. Over the years it has developed into a sport of its own, with local matches all over the country and an annual national match.

PPC was for many years limited to police officers, but today many private citizens are eligible to participate in local matches. PPC is generally shot with revolvers chambering .38 Special and autoloaders in 9mm, .40 S&W, and .45 ACP. The course of fire includes shooting from standing, kneeling, sitting, prone, and from behind barricades, at distances of up to 50 meters. Other than getting in or out of a shooting position, there is no movement required. All shooting is done from the holster.

Guns are divided into divisions. "Duty Gun" is for stock revolvers and autoloading pistols and allows virtually no modifications. "Distinguished" allows certain small modifications, while "Open" guns can be completely custom within certain limits. There is also an "Off Duty" division for short-barreled revolvers and auto pistols.

The freedom of the Open division has resulted in a specialized type of customized revolver called a "PPC gun." They usually feature extremely thick barrels (over an inch in diameter and extremely heavy), specialized rib sights, and very light and precisely honed double action triggers.

The annual National Police Championships are the top event in PPC shooting and are run through the NRA. Entry is limited to police officers only.

NRA ACTION PISTOL (BIANCHI)

An outgrowth of PPC shooting was an annual match that has grown into a sport of its own. The Bianchi Cup, started by former lawman John Bianchi, was intended as the ultimate handgun shooting competition. It combined accuracy and speed under a variety of shooting conditions, and borrowed

Guns for the open class in PPC competition are highly customized, with heavy barrels and special high-precision sights.

from PPC as well as some other combat shooting sports.

The Bianchi Cup quickly became the most prestigious handgun competition in the country and spawned local matches that used the same courses of fire. The sport was eventually absorbed into the NRA Competition Division, and today is officially called NRA Action Pistol competition. The Bianchi Cup is the annual championship of NRA Action Pistol.

Action Pistol/Bianchi Cup competition is made up of several events and uses both paper and steel (reactive) targets. There are sixteen possible courses of fire defined in the NRA Action Pistol rule book, which are combined at the match director's discretion. The annual Bianchi Cup, for instance, uses the same four courses every year: the Practical, Barricade, Moving Target, and Falling Plate events.

Action Pistol competition tests a wide va-riety of shooting skills under controlled, re-peatable circumstances. The various Action Pistol courses of fire have shooting ranges from five to 50 yards, from various shoot-ing positions and sometimes from behind barricades. Some courses of fire have targets that move laterally across the firing line as the competitor shoots at them, while others require combinations of strong hand/weak hand shooting or speed reloading.

Like PPC, Action Pistol has divisions for both stock guns and highly customized pis-tols. Both double action revolvers and auto-loading pistols can be used as long as they are within the caliber limits and fit the modi-fications authorized in their division. All events start with the gun in the holster, so the ability to draw quickly is an important skill.

STEEL CHALLENGE

Steel Challenge is the annual champion-ships in speed steel competition, and today local speed steel matches are often referred to by the name of the championship match.

Steel Challenge matches consist of a number of pre-defined events, called stages, that use five steel targets called plates: four standard plates and one "stop" plate. The object is to hit each standard plate with one round, and only after that has been done may the stop plate be hit. The shooter's score is strictly the amount of time it took from the start command to the stop plate being hit.

The plates are of several shapes and sizes, and are arranged in a specific ways and at specific distances for each stage. The shooter is usually required to draw from a holster, though some gun divisions allow for the shooter to start in a "low ready" condition with the gun held at a 45-degree angle to the ground. At the sound of a buzzer, the shooter attempts to hit each plate as fast as he or she can. It's been described as "drag racing with a pistol", which isn't too far from reality: championship shooters regularly draw and shoot five targets in well under two seconds on some stages.

Each shooter gets several runs at each stage, and the slowest time is thrown out. The score for the stage is the total of the counted times, and the match score is the shooter's total time on all the stages.

Steel Challenge has divisions for nearly any kind of handgun, from rimfires to single action revolvers to highly customized and red-dot-sighted autoloaders. It's easy to follow, easy to understand, easy to get started in, and delightfully difficult to shoot.

HANDGUN SILHOUETTE

Steel Challenge isn't the only place to shoot reactive targets. Handgun Silhouette uses steel plates cut in the shape of various animals and placed at long distances. Meant to simulate handgun hunting challenges, Handgun Silhouette originated in Mexico. Called Siluetas in Spanish, it was conceived as a competitive game for handgun hunters. It soon became popular in this country as well, and can now be found around the world.

There are two main sanctioning bodies for Handgun Silhouette in the U.S.: the International Handgun Metallic Silhouette Association (IHMSA), and the ubiquitous NRA. Their rules and matches are slightly different, but the general object is to topple a number of metallic animals at distances ranging from 25 to 200 meters. Handgun Silhouette is a precision event, as the animals are quite difficult to hit with a handgun at those distances.

There are divisions for both centerfire and rimfire guns, and (depending on the sanctioning body and the kind of match) shooters may stand or go to a stable position on the ground. The open divisions for centerfire cartridges are one of the main domains of the powerful single shot pistols, where their accuracy and ability to deliver enough force to tip a heavy steel target of its stand are prized. Single action revolvers are also extremely popular for this kind of competition, as are the Magnum pistol cartridges.

Handgun Silhouette matches are generally relaxed affairs, but the concentration required to knock down 40 steel animals at long distance is enormous!

USPSA

While PPC was originally derived from a training exercise for police officers, it was not universally available to the general public. In the 1950s and '60s a series of informal "combat" shooting matches were held in California, the result of which was the formation of the South West Pistol League (SWPL). By the 1970s the SWPL had become well enough known around the country that a need for more codified rules, and an organization to administer them, was deemed necessary. In 1976 the International Practical Shooting Confederation (IPSC) was born and the sport of "practical shooting" was born. (This does sometimes cause a little confusion with those PPC competitors who call their sport "practical pistol competition.")

By the 1980s IPSC was active in many countries, and the organization moved into administering the world wide aspects of the sport, leaving individual countries to form their own organizations. In the U.S., that organization became known as the United States Practical Shooting Association (USPSA). Despite the technical division, the sport is often referred to by its original name and pronounced "ip-sick."

USPSA/IPSC matches are noted for their movement and athletic skill in addition to an emphasis on marksmanship. Often called "run and gun," a typical stage may have the shooter doing things such as drawing his or her gun and shooting a couple of targets, then running to a stage-prop doorway to shoot more targets, then running some more to crouch down behind a barrel to shoot more targets. It's not unusual for a stage to have 15 or 20 targets and for the competitors to fire 40 or more rounds.

Targets can be a mix of paper and steel, and reactive targets that release other targets are common. The stages are often elaborately designed and can be quite complicated to the uninitiated.

Chris Tilley shoots a USPSA match with a typical open class "race gun." Photo courtesy USPSA/Dave Thomas

In the early days of the sport, the emphasis was on guns that might actually be useful in defensive shooting. Over the years, as competitors experimented with equipment to help them win matches, the guns evolved into very specialized devices just for this kind of shooting.

Today there are opportunities for everything from stock revolvers to very highly modified autoloading pistols, each arranged in its own division so the playing field is kept reasonably level. Most competitors, however, congregate in the divisions for stock autoloaders or "open" autoloaders - the latter being the most specialized, featuring such things as recoil compensators and red dot optics. The highly modified open-class pistols are collectively called "race guns."

All shooting is done after drawing from a holster, and there are many specialized holsters and belts to help the shooter reduce the time needed to get on target.

There are USPSA clubs all over the United States, and most of them offer classes to help the new shooter get started. USPSA/IPSC shooting is a very dynamic and exciting type of handgun competition, and it's not necessary to spend a lot of money on a race gun starting out. Many USPSA clubs are more than willing to show the new shooter how to get started without breaking the bank.

IDPA

As the USPSA style of shooting was evolving, many felt that it had gotten away from its "practical" roots despite still having the word in their title. Some of the founding members of IPSC, along with some of their top shooters, decided that an organization devoted to their vision of realistic combat shooting was needed and in 1996 formed the International Defensive Pistol Association (IDPA).

From the beginning the IDPA was intended to be a shooting game where people could usc the same gun that they had for carry or home defense, and the rules were written to prevent the kind of equipment races that had come to dominate the USPSA. Stages would be designed to limit the number of targets presented and rounds needed, holsters would be of the type suited for lawful concealed carry, and all shooting would start with the gun concealed, in an effort to mimic the way that competitors were accustomed to carrying their sidearm.

The IDPA was an instant hit among shooters, and economy was a big reason: the average shooter could take the gun and holster he or she carried every day and compete with them, on a level playing field with others who wished to do the same thing. Today the IDPA has clubs all over the country and overseas as well.

IDPA shooting stages are often decorated with real props, such as furniture in a room or a car in a driveway. There are also matches held indoors to simulate low light conditions. The goal of the competition is to place winning hits on targets as fast as possible while still maintaining good accuracy.

Equipment for IDPA is modest: a gun, a few speedloaders or magazines, and a suitable holster for concealed carry are all that's needed. Like the USPSA, each type of gun has its own division so that shooters don't have any equipment advantages.

COWBOY ACTION SHOOTING

If USPSA and IDPA competitions are oriented to practical reality, Cowboy Action Shooting (CAS) is all about fantasy and fun. The organization which sanctions CAS

IDPA competitions attract many well known shooters like Massad Ayoob, shown here engaging targets from around simulated cover. Photo courtesy of Gail Pepin

matches is the Single Action Shooting Society (SASS). Started in 1981 by three friends who loved western action movies, SASS promotes the recreation of the days of the Old West.

In CAS, costuming is a requirement of the sport. Competitors must dress in period-appropriate clothing and use corresponding firearms. Most shooting is done with a combination of pistols, rifles, and shotguns, which takes it out of the realm of a handgun-only sport. However, there are matches and events within the organization where only handguns are used, such as the mounted (as in, "on horseback") events.

Competitors all use aliases that evoke the old west, and SASS members are issued brass badges, reminiscent of old-time lawmen, which carry their member number.

The emphasis may be on the costuming and historical recreation, but it is also about the shooting. It's also a true family sport,

and it's not uncommon to see Mom, Dad, and the kids participating in the matches. In fact, some of today's best USPSA and IDPA shooters started as kids shooting SASS matches!

SELF DEFENSE

One of the most prevalent reasons for acquiring a handgun is for self defense. Much of the progress in handgun and ammunition design in the last few decades has been because of the sharp increase in demand for concealed carry and home defense firearms.

While there is a wide range of opinion on many aspects of defensive shooting, most experts seem to agree on some basic principles and the first is that proper training is essential.

Knowing how to shoot under the conditions of a criminal attack is different than shooting bullseyes or plinking in the backyard, and defensive shooting instructors can

A defensive shooting course, like this Combat Focus Shooting class being taught by Rob Pincus, is the best way to learn the skills needed to use a handgun to protect yourself or your loved ones.

guide their students through the differences. It's necessary to learn how to shoot quickly and with the amount of accuracy needed to reliably stop an attacker.

Experts also agree on the need for regular and relevant practice. Learning the difference between target shooting and defensive shooting doesn't do much good if the students goes home and only practices target shooting. Being able to practice such basic skills as drawing from concealment, or retrieving a gun from a quick-access safe, is essential to maintaining proficiency for self defense.

This usually means finding a range where those things can be practiced. Many ranges and clubs forbid drawing from a holster or shooting in "rapid fire," which are a basic function of defensive shooting. The range that allows such things may entail some drive time, but it's a sacrifice that needs to be made if the student is to keep his or her skills sharp.

It's also necessary to have a good grounding in the laws and regulations regarding self defense and the use of lethal force. Knowing when and where concealed carry is allowed, understanding the legalities that dictate the circumstances where lethal force is appropriate, and being prepared to navigate the tricky waters of the legal system in the event of a shooting are all important. An instructor who knows the ethics and legalities of self defense can distill and make sense of the sometimes overwhelming legal mass.

When selecting a gun for self defense, whether in the home or on the street, it's important to remember that the goal is to stop the attacker, not to merely wound or expressly to kill. There seems to be a baseline of calibers which do this reliably, and they usually include cartridges from .380ACP to .45ACP. Lesser calibers are usually deemed to be unreliable at stopping people, and the larger or more powerful calibers may not be

more effective but are certainly more difficult to shoot.

This is not set in stone, however, and there are always exceptions. Someone whose physical condition is such that they have trouble handling the recoil of more mainstream self defense calibers may be better served with a light-recoiling .22 Long Rifle or .22 Magnum handgun, even though it's not as effective. Training to rapidly fire a half-dozen or more .22 rounds in rapid succession, and hitting the target, will have a more immediate effect on an attacker than a .357 Magnum that misses because the shooter flinched.

For home defense, the recommendation is usually for a centerfire handgun which any properly trained individual in the house can access and shoot. Common calibers for home defense include the .38 Special and .357 Magnum revolvers, and 9mm, .40 S&W, and .45ACP autoloaders. Since the size of the gun isn't limited by the need to tote it around constantly, larger capacity models are often chosen. Those with lasers and white lights attached are often suggested as good options, though one must be careful not to use the gun as a flashlight and risk pointing the muzzle at an innocent party.

Having a quick-access safe in which to store the home defense handgun when not in use is strongly recommended. Being able to bolt that safe to the floor, under a bed or in a closet, keeps the gun safe from theft (or inadvertent discovery by children) yet allows very fast retrieval when needed.

Concealed carry handguns need to be small and light enough to carry around all day, which requires some compromises not inherent in the home defense handgun. A full-sized pistol carrying 17 rounds may not be practical to conceal in an office setting, which is where the compact autoloaders and snub-nosed revolvers come in. A small auto or revolver can be carried inside the waistband of slacks or, if small enough, put into a pocket for discretion. Try that with a full-sized pistol!

Calibers for concealed carry usually mimic those of home defense, though pocket pistols in "lesser" calibers such as .380ACP and .32ACP are quite common. One of the trends today is to make ultra-small carry guns chambering more powerful rounds like the 9mm and .40 S&W. The tradeoff for those "pocket rockets" is shootability - they're harder to control, less comfortable in recoil, and much more difficult to shoot accurately.

A concealed carry handgun is always a compromise; it must be large enough to do the job required and be easy to shoot, yet it has to be small enough to hide on one's person. The prospective carrier is best counseled to go to a range which rents guns, where several models and calibers can be tested to see what works best for that individual.

There are many ways to carry a handgun. The most common is some sort of belt holster, though pocket holsters are very popular for the smaller pistols and revolvers. Shoulder holsters work well for those whose flexibility allows them to reach across their bodies. Surprisingly, more women than men are able to effectively use a shoulder holster, yet more men buy them.

Some people carry "off body," meaning in a purse or planner designed to hide a handgun. This is often the only functional choice in professional settings, but the downside is that the gun is easily stolen or misplaced. Most defensive shooting trainers agree that off body carry should be considered only when all other methods have failed.

The subject of self defense handguns is serious and warrants a book unto itself; the publisher has a number of excellent titles, from renowned experts, specifically on this subject.

Some reactive targets and a safe backstop are all that's needed for an afternoon of family fun.

PLINKING

Plinking is usually considered to be informal shooting at non-traditional but reactive targets: tin cans, watermelons, balloons, and the like. It is perhaps the only kind of shooting that doesn't have a goal or reason for existence, other than simply passing time in an enjoyable manner.

While any caliber handgun can be used for plinking, far and away the most common choice is the .22 Long Rifle in either revolver or autoloader.

Targets can be set on the ground, on a fence rail, or any other convenient place where bullet holes are not an issue. Of course, it must be safe! Plinking should only be done where there is a good backstop and no danger of ricochet.

In earlier days, when drink cans and bottles carried no deposit, it was common to use them as plinking targets. Today soup cans are a better choice, and many people enjoy filling transparent water bottles with colored water. These are especially reactive with .22 Magnum hollowpoints, .17 HMR guns, and centerfire pistols.

Lollipops, the flat kind with the looped "rope" handles, can be hung from a string between trees or thumbtacked to a cardboard box. They shatter impressively when hit, even with the lowest powered .22 "CB Caps," and are favorites with kids and grown ups alike.

A box of paintballs and some golf tees can be used for plinking. Simply push the golf tees into a cardboard box and sit a paintball on top of each one. They're difficult target to hit and a challenge to marksmanship, but when they're hit with a high-speed .22 Long Rifle round they disappear into a cloud of brightly colored water-soluble paint. It's hard to resist shooting another, and yet another - and the best part is that they're biodegradable!

Raw eggs and golf balls are a similarly addictive yet easier-to-hit alternative.

When plinking with a group, it's not uncommon to hold impromptu contests to see who can hit more targets, or targets further away, sometimes in a certain amount of time. The variations on the game are limitless.

Being a clean and courteous shooter is part of plinking etiquette. Clean up any mess, and especially pick up any broken glass if jars and bottles have been used. Always leave the shooting area better than it was found.

Want to know more?

COMPETITIVE SHOOTING

Your Competition Handgun Training Program: A complete training program designed for the practical shooter by Michael Seeklander. ISBN 978-1449966423. CreateSpace, 2010. www.createspace.com

Shoot: Your Guide to Shooting and Competition by Julie Golob. ISBN 978-1616086985. Skyhorse Publishing, www.skyhorsepublishing.com

Practical Shooting : Beyond Fundamentals by Brian Enos. The classic book on competition shooting. ISBN 978-0962692505. www.brianenos.com

National Rifle Association (NRA) - though best known for their political lobbying, they are the largest sanctioning body in the shooting sports and cover a wide range of shooting disciplines. Every gun owner should be a member! National Rifle Association of America, 11250 Waples Mill Road, Fairfax, VA 22030. (800) 672-3888 www.nrahq.org

International Handgun Metallic Silhouette Association (IHMSA) - sanctioning body for metallic silhouette shooting. IHMSA Inc., P.O. Box 95690, South Jordan, UT 84095. 801-733-8423 www.ihmsa.org

International Confederation Of Revolver Enthusiasts (ICORE) - sponsors revolver-only action shooting matches. ICORE Inc., P.O. Box 6898, Los Osos, CA 93412. www.icore.org

Steel Challenge Shooting Association (SCSA) - sanctioning body for the fast game of steel shooting. Holds an annual match, the Steel Challenge. SCSA, 826 Metcalf Street PMB 73, Sedro Woolley, WA 98284. (360) 855-2245 www.steelchallenge.com

International Defensive Pistol Association (IDPA) - the organization devoted to sport shooting with a self-defense approach, using typical concealed carry guns and gear. IDPA, 2232 CR 719, Berryville, AR 72616. (870) 545-3886 www.idpa.com

United States Practical Shooting Association (USPSA)- the United States organizing body for International Practical Shooting, the "king" of action shooting. USPSA sanctions hundreds (if not thousands) of matches all across the country every year. USPSA, P.O. Box 811, Sedro-Woolley, WA 98284. (360) 855-2245 www.uspsa.com

HUNTING

Handgun Hunting by Mark Hampton. ISBN 9780873493642. Krause Publications, (855) 864-2579 www.gundigeststore.com

The Ultimate Guide to Handgun Hunting by Clair Rees. ISBN 978-1585748204. Globe Pequot Press, P.O. Box 480, Guilford, CT 06437. (203) 458-4500 www.lyonspress.com

Safari Club International (SCI) - "First For Hunters", dedicated to the conservation of wildlife, education of the people, and the protection of hunters' rights. SCI International Headquarters, 4800 West Gates Pass Road, Tucson, Arizona 85745-9490. (520) 620-1220 www.safariclub.org

North American Hunting Club - resource for hunters of all kinds. Monthly magazine, many benefits. (800) 922-4868 www.huntingclub.com

National Rifle Association (NRA) - the NRA is also a major voice for hunters and hunting rights. National Rifle Association of America, 11250 Waples Mill Road, Fairfax, VA 22030. (800) 672-3888 www.nrahq.org

DEFENSIVE SHOOTING

Combat Focus Shooting: Evolution 2010 by Rob Pincus. ISBN 978-0979150876. I.C.E. Publishing Company, P.O. Box 752, Mays Landing, NJ 08330. (855) 468-4789 www.icetraining.us

Personal Defense for Women: Practical Advice for Self Protection by Gila Hayes.

ISBN 9781440203909. Krause Publications, (855) 864-2579 www.gundigeststore.com

The Gun Digest Book of Concealed Carry by Massad Ayoob. ISBN 9780896896116. Krause Publications, (855) 864-2579 www.gundigeststore.com

The Gun Digest Book of Personal Protection & Home Defense by Robert K. Campbell. ISBN 9780896899384. Krause Publications, (855) 864-2579 www.gundigeststore.com

Holsters For Combat And Concealed Carry by Robert K. Campbell. ISBN 9781581604375. Krause Publications, (855) 864-2579 www.gundigeststore.com

Combat Shooting with Massad Ayoob ISBN 9781440218576. Krause Publications, (855) 864-2579 www.gundigeststore.com

The Gun Digest Book of Combat Handgunnery, 6th Edition by Massad Ayoob. ISBN 9780896895256. Krause Publications, (855) 864-2579 www.gundigeststore.com

Defensive Use of Firearms by Stephen P. Wenger. ISBN 978-1581607352. Paladin Press, Gunbarrel Tech Center, 7077 Winchester Circle, Boulder, CO 80301-3505. (303) 443-7250 www.paladin-press.com

The Cornered Cat by Kathy Jackson. ISBN 978-0982248799. White Feather Press, 3170 52nd Street, Hamilton, MI 49419. (269) 838-5586 www.whitefeatherpress.com

SCHOOLS AND TRAINING

I.C.E. Training - one of the premier, leading-edge training companies, home of the Combat Focus Shooting program. Courses all over the U.S. and overseas. I.C.E. Training Company, P.O. Box 752, Mays Landing, NJ 08330. (855) 468-4789 www.icetraining.us

Firearms Academy Of Seattle (FAS) - respected in the training community, though not well known to the general public, FAS offers classes from simple firearm safety to the most advanced available. Firearms Academy of Seattle, Inc., PO Box 400, Onalaska WA 98570. (360) 978-6100 www.firearmsacademy.com

Massad Ayoob Group - famed teacher, writer, and deadly force expert Massad Ayoob travels the country teaching intermediate to advanced courses. His classroom course on the judicious use of lethal force is the standard in the field, and is considered a "must" by many other trainers. Massad Ayoob Group, P.O. Box 1477, Live Oak, FL 32064. www.massadayoobgroup.com

Rangemaster - one of the most progressive training academies in the country, founder Tom Givens frequently travels around the country teaching. Rangemaster LLC, 2611 S Mendenhall Rd, Memphis, TN 38115. (901) 370-5600 www.rangemaster.com

Gunsite - the first private-sector training facility dealing with defensive shooting in the country, founded by well known teacher and writer Jeff Cooper. Runs a wide array of shooting courses on their large desert complex. Gunsite Academy, 2900 W. Gunsite Rd., Paulden, AZ. 86334. 928-636-4565 www.gunsite.com

Thunder Ranch - home of renowned trainer and author Clint Smith. Courses from beginner to expert on their home range in Oregon. Thunder Ranch, 96747 Nwy 140 East, Lakeview, OR 97630. 541-947-4104 www.thunderranchinc.com

US Shooting Academy (USSA) - staffed by some of the country's best trainers, frequently featured on television shows about shooting. US Shooting Academy, 6500 E 66th St N, Tulsa, OK 74117. (918) 948-7856 www.usshootingacademy.com

Gander Mountain Academy - the most state-of-the-art training facilities in the private sector. Six locations around the country, with more coming. Gander Mountain, (888) 5GANDER gandermtnacademy.gandermountain.com

CHAPTER 11

BUYING A USED HANDGUN

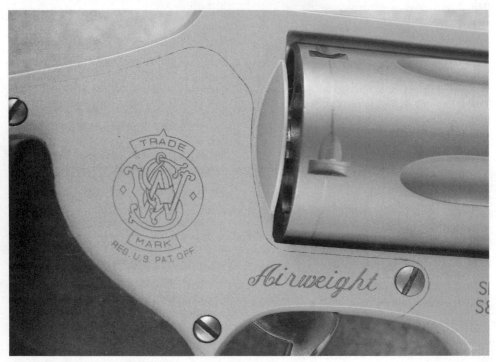

Exam the seam of the sideplate; it should fit tightly, with no gaps, all the way 'round.

Firearms are a superb illustration of the term "durable goods." With relatively modest care most guns will be perfectly serviceable for generations. It's not uncommon to go to a range on a nice sunny weekend and find more than one person shooting a hundred-year-old firearm. How many consumer products can boast that kind of service life?

Because guns have such long lives there are lots of them available for sale at any used gun counter or gun show. When buying a used handgun it's important to be able to determine if it's a gem, or a problem that someone else dumped on an unsuspecting buyer.

This guide assumes that the buyer wishes to be able to shoot the gun immediately, without putting money into repairs. It will help identify issues which make the gun unsafe, or which require the services of a gunsmith to correct. Of course if the gun is a rare model, or is being acquired as a collector's item, the buyer may wish to complete the transaction regardless of the need for any repairs.

Safety first! Before checking out any handgun, make sure that it is unloaded, then double-check. With revolvers, open the cylinder, point the muzzle up, and operate the ejector rod. Look at every chamber in the cylinder and make sure that they're all empty. Repeat the entire procedure! Yes, it sounds like overkill, but it is the best way to make sure that there are no accidents.

With an autoloader, operate the magazine release and take the magazine completely out of the gun. After the magazine is out, pull the slide or bolt back and lock it in the open position. On most autos there is a small lever on the left side of the gun, just under the slide, which is pushed up to engage the slide lock.

There are exceptions; the HK P7, for instance, has a small tab on the left side of the frame at the back of the triggerguard. It is pushed toward the back of the gun to engage the lock.

Some autos do not have easily accessible slide locks. Guns like the Walther PPK and many of its clones require an empty magazine be inserted in the gun as the slide is withdrawn. It's important to know ahead of time the manual of arms for the specific gun.

Once the slide has been locked back the chamber is checked. Look in the chamber and make sure it's empty; many instructors also recommend that a finger be inserted into the chamber to feel for a missed round.

Now the double check: feel and look at the magazine well to make sure that there is no magazine inserted, then look and feel the chamber one more time just to make sure that there's no live ammunition anywhere in the gun!

A single shot, whether it's a bolt or break action, is very easy to check: simply open the action and check - by sight and feel - for any round in the chamber. Close the action, open it again, and double-check the chamber; again, by sight and feel.

Should any ammunition be found it should be removed and put someplace where it's not easily accessible during the checkout. The entire clearing process is repeated just to make absolutely sure that the gun is truly unloaded.

Since the gun can be pointed in many different directions during the checkout, it's important to pay close attention to the muzzle direction. Always keep the muzzle pointed in a generally safe direction, which is one where - if the gun were to fire - it would not injure you or anyone else.

Of course, fingers should be kept out of the triggerguard unless a specific test makes it necessary to pull the trigger.

DOUBLE ACTION REVOLVER CHECKOUT

Begin by looking at the general condition of the gun. Look for rust in the barrel or chambers and on the exterior surfaces. Look at the condition of the screw heads; if they're damaged, it may indicate that there is internal damage as well. (If someone was so inept that the relatively simple exterior screws were damaged, there's no telling what may have happened to the more delicate interior mechanisms.)

Look at the seams where the sideplate is fitted. On a Colt or Dan Wesson, the sideplate is on the left side of the gun; on a Smith & Wesson, Taurus, and most other double actions it's on the right side. Look for any gaps in the seam; there should be none. The sideplates are normally fitted very tightly, and a gap may indicate a frame that was bent or has experienced damage from over-pressure ammunition.

Rugers don't have sideplates; instead the triggerguard carries most of the lockwork, and is removed by pulling down and out of the frame. There is a seam that is just above the trigger which follows the contours of the triggerguard; it too should have little to no gap.

Take a look at the muzzle and check to make sure that the crown is in good condi-

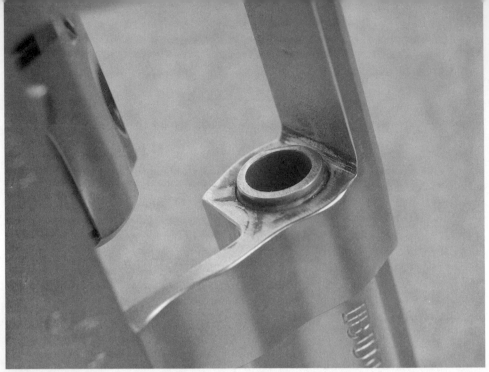

Examine the forcing cone - the part of the barrel where the bullet enters - for cracks. Area of frame directly above should be free of any damage from burning powder or gases. This gun, though a bit dirty, is fine.

tion. The crown should be even and free from nicks and burrs. The other end of the barrel, called the breech end, has a slightly tapered entry called the forcing cone. This end of the barrel should be square and clean. Be sure to check for cracking in this area, which makes the gun un-shootable and can be expensive to correct.

The area above the breech end of the barrel should be checked for damage as well. When the revolver is fired, hot gases escape from the barrel/cylinder gap in all directions, including up, toward the top strap. Sometimes those gases eat away at the metal, an effect called flame cutting. The deeper the cutting, the more rounds the gun has seen (and possibly, the more abuse it's endured.) Flame cutting weakens the top strap slightly, and a gun with noticeable cutting should be passed up. Cutting tends to be worse on lightweight alloy guns than steel guns, and is more of a concern.

Look in each chamber to check for car-bon build up and rust. If there are any pits in the chambers, the gun should be rejected unless it's extremely rare. Pits and rust can affect accuracy and result in cases sticking in the chambers. The bore should likewise be examined for any rust or pitting.

The next step is to close the cylinder and, keeping the muzzle pointed in a generally safe direction, check the gap between the cylinder and barrel. It should measure between .003" and .008". If a feeler (thickness) gage isn't handy, it can be approximated with a few sheets of copier paper. The gap should be enough to pass one sheet of paper easily, but should not allow three pieces (stacked on top of each other) to be inserted.

A small gap may indicate wear in the cylinder or the axle on which it rotates, and it undesirable because it can cause the cylinder to jam when dirty. A gap which is too large will allow excessive combustion gas escape and may harm accuracy, as well as making it hazardous to shoot (still-burning powder

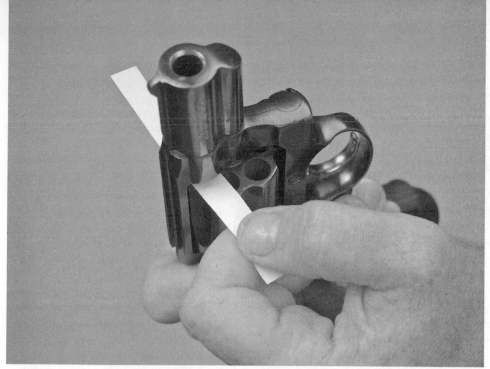

A strip of copier or printer paper makes a handy gap gauge. The strip should go in with no more than a slight amount of resistance.

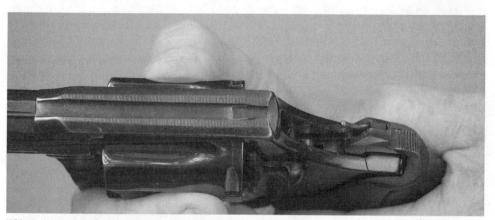

With the hammer cocked, try to rotate the cylinder. A Colt should have no play at all; for any other revolver, a very small amount is acceptable.

can escape at high velocity, which can cause damage to unprotected eyes).

The next check is for cylinder endplay. Again holding the gun so the muzzle is pointed in a safe direction, push and pull the cylinder back and forth. There should be not more than .003" of endplay, which is about the thickness of a piece of copier paper. Endplay is an important check for two reasons:

first, because it increase cylinder gap at the instant that the gun fires; second, because excessive endplay batters the frame and results in ejector star wear.

Checking endplay carefully is particularly important for Colt revolvers, which are more sensitive to the problem.

After the endplay has been checked, try to rotate the cylinder in both directions.

It should remain locked, though a small amount of rotational movement is acceptable. If the cylinder unlocks and rotates it can indicate a worn bolt or cylinder catch - the little piece that snaps into the cylinder's notches to provide locking. A cylinder that unlocks is unsafe, and the gun should not be fired until repaired.

Cock the hammer on each chamber and pull the trigger (guns with hidden hammers are simply dry-fired). Hold the trigger back after the hammer drops, and attempt to rotate the cylinder with the other hand. On a Colt, the cylinder must not move at all - it should be locked tightly. On any other revolver a very small amount of rotational play is acceptable, but the amount should be just perceptible. If the cylinder rotates and locks with a "click," the gun is severely out of time and should not be shot until it can see the gunsmith.

Timing on a revolver is critical. A revolver is "in time" when the chamber is aligned with the barrel when the shot is fired. If it isn't, the bullet can shave lead or copper

jacket material as it enters the barrel. This material is forcibly ejected from the cylinder gap and can cause injury. A timing problem can also ultimately result in cracking of the forcing cone, which is an expensive repair, and increased wear on internal parts.

To check the timing, a finger is placed very lightly on the cylinder; the idea is to keep the cylinder from accelerating faster than the hammer or trigger is being operated. If that happens it can make the gun appear to be in time, when it really isn't. The finger should add just a hint of drag to keep the cylinder under control, and no more.

With drag applied to the cylinder, cock the hammer (if the gun is so equipped) very slowly. If the cylinder locks into place with an audible "click" before the hammer reaches the cocked position, that chamber is in time. If the hammer drops into its cocked condition before the cylinder is locked, the gun is out of time and should be repaired before being shot. Check every chamber the same way.

If the gun passes the hammer cocking

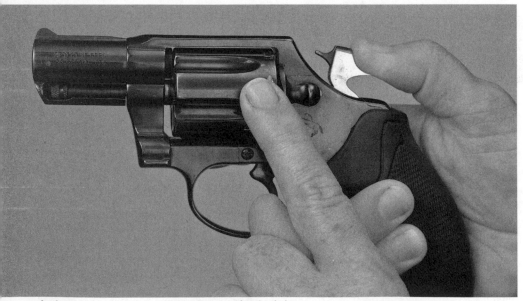

Apply very faint pressure on cylinder when checking the timing.

Checking for "push-off" - cock the gun and push on the hammer. It should stay cocked; if not, it needs to see the gunsmith.

test, repeat using the double action trigger instead of cocking the hammer. (Guns that can't be cocked, of course, will only be tested using the trigger.) Pull the trigger extremely slowly and listen (and watch) for the telltale "click" of the cylinder locking before the hammer drops. Ruger revolvers tend to lock very early in the trigger pull; Smith & Wesson (and most others) lock just before the hammer drops, while a Colt should lock just as the hammer falls. Again, check every chamber the same way.

If the gun fails any timing test, it should be repaired before shooting. Timing issues are a normal part of revolver maintenance, much like the timing on a car. Because it's a common service item, most revolvers can have the timing repaired fairly inexpensively. The exception is for a Colt that is out of time; it may be quite expensive to repair. That cost needs to be factored into the purchase price.

Finally, if the gun has an exposed hammer, cock it and, with the finger out of the triggerguard, try to push the hammer forward. This is called "push-off," and if the hammer falls when this is done the gun is unsafe and should be checked by a qualified gunsmith.

AUTOLOADER CHECKOUT

Once the gun is checked and double-checked to be unloaded, lock the slide in the open position and take a look at the outside. Like the revolver, look at the screwheads on the grips; they should be clean and in good condition. Check for any splits or looseness in the grips. Check that the sights, front and rear, are tight on the slide, as it's not uncommon for them to loosen under the forces of the slide's reciprocation.

Like the revolver, check the muzzle's condition. It should be free of nicks, burrs, or any damage. The muzzle is critical to handgun accuracy, so look carefully.

At the breech end of the barrel look at the

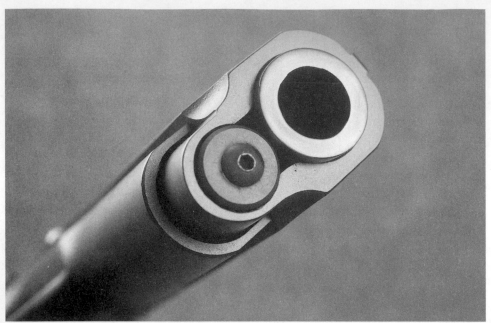

Muzzle should be free of nicks or damage.

The barrel ramp (shown here with slide removed for better clarity) should be relatively smooth, even, and symmetrical. Any damage here can affect feeding reliability.

ramped portion which guides rounds into the chambers; it should be clean and without gouges or scratches, which can affect the feeding reliability of the gun. Check the bore for pitting or rust.

Double check, again, that the gun is unloaded, and gently let the slide down. The gun should now be in battery, striker or hammer cocked, and can be dry fired. Pointing the muzzle in a safe direction, pull the trigger and hold it back. The sear should release, letting the hammer down or the striker to fly forward. Be sure to hold the trigger back - do not let the trigger reset!

As the trigger is being held back, pull the slide all the way to the rear and let it go forward under its own power. If the gun has a visible hammer, it should remain in the cocked position. (If the gun's hammer dropped when the slide ran forward, it is extremely unsafe and needs immediate attention!) Now slowly release the trigger; it should make a discernible "click" as it resets. After it has reset, pull the trigger again; if the sear doesn't release, there is likely a problem with the disconnector mechanism and is unsafe to fire.

Again operate the slide to cock the gun. If the gun has a manual safety, put it into the "on" position and try to pull the trigger; the gun should not fire. Take your finger off the trigger and immediately release the manual safety; if the gun fires without the trigger being touched, the safety is defective.

For autoloaders with a decocking mechanism, operate the slide to cock the gun and then operate the decocker. The hammer or striker should drop with an audible sound; pulling the trigger should result in the hammer or striker being cocked and then released to fire.

For guns with a combined decocker/safety, such as some Beretta, Ruger and Smith & Wesson autos, use the slide to cock the gun and apply the decocker. When the hammer or striker has dropped, leave the safety in the "on" position and pull the trigger - it should move with very little resistance and should not fire the gun. Put the safety/decocker in the off position and pull the trigger again; the gun should now fire.

The failure of any of these tests indicates a gun that is unsafe to use, and should be sent to a gunsmith before using.

Finally, gently let the slide go forward (closed) and put an empty magazine in the gun. Pull the slide all the way to the rear; it should lock in the open position. Remove the magazine with the slide locked back; the slide should stay locked. If either test fails either the magazine or the slide lock mechanism needs attention from the gunsmith.

SINGLE SHOT CHECKOUT

Single shots are simple to check. Start by making sure that the gun is unloaded, then double-check just to make sure.

Once the exterior and muzzle have been checked for obvious signs of abuse or neglect, open the action. Take a look down the bore for any rust or pitting, and the chamber area for any damage. With a break-open action, the extractor/ejector should be in the "out" position (to eject a fired case.) Close the action and open it again, looking for the movement of the extractor.

A bolt-action will normally be cocked at this point; a break action will need to be cocked. If there is a manual safety, apply it and pull the trigger. The gun should not fire. Release the safety; if the gun suddenly fires, the safety mechanism is faulty and needs to be repaired.

For guns with hammers, cock the hammer and push on the hammer tang; the hammer should stay cocked. If it drops under the pressure, it is unsafe to use and must be repaired. On a break-action pistol the hinge point should not feel unduly loose, nor should it wobble when the action is open. While aftermarket oversized pins for Thompson-Center handguns are available to

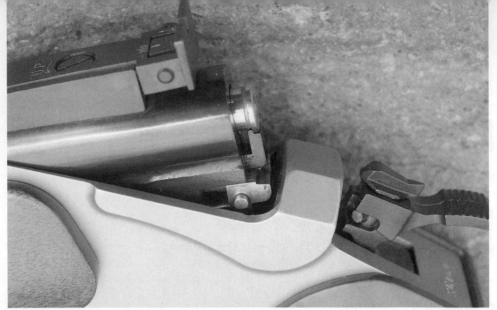

The extractor in a break-action pistol pulls the expended casing free of the chamber, should be in the extended position when the action is opened.

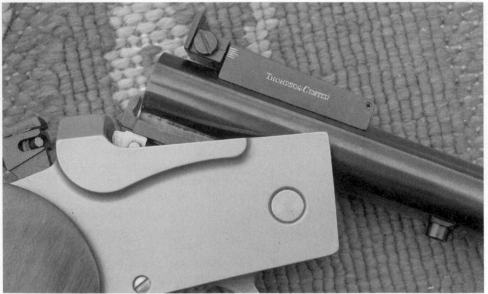

The barrel fit on the hinge pin should be snug but not tight; should open easily, but not exhibit noticeable wobble.

help take up the wear, other brands may not enjoy such support.

The bolt on a bolt action pistol should operate without grittiness and should not be extremely difficult to open. When the bolt is closed it should lock up tightly, but not so much that the handle is hard to move.

If the gun is scoped, check the screws that hold the mount to the barrel. They should be tight. If the gun has iron sights, check front and rear for any looseness. While sight or scope issues are not usually safety issues, they may be an indication of abuse or poor maintenance.

IF YOU LIKE THE BOOK IN YOUR HANDS,
YOU'LL LOVE...

You'll see revolvers in a whole new light even after spending just a few minutes with *Gun Digest Book of the Revolver*.

Written by the same author, Grant Cunningham, as the very book you're holding, *Gun Digest Book of the Revolver* delivers valuable information about the design, operation, and capabilities of revolvers, as well as the accessories associated with them.

❝ Like a Star Wars light saber, the revolver is seen by some as an elegant weapon more suited for another time. They're wrong. It's a very functional one, very serviceable in the here and now, and that's why so many folks still use them. Grant Cunningham has done an excellent job of explaining why. ❞

- Massad Ayoob
renowned shooting instructor and CCW authority

TO ORDER Visit your local firearms shop, national bookseller, or direct from the publisher at **GunDigestStore.com** or call **1-855-840-5120**